There is a Season

An Intentional Approach to Sustenance

A Cookbook
To Foster Health,
Environmental Stewardship
& Community Connections

Editors
Suzanne Keifer & Rita Mathew

RELIABLE TRANSFORMATIVE AUTHENTIC

https://www.rta-cpa.com

2nd Edition ISBN 978-1-7356204-1-1

There is a Season: An Intentional Approach to Sustenance

Editors: Suzanne Keifer & Rita Mathew

Front Cover: "Abundance" by Sally Wyche Coenen
Back Cover: "Honeycomb" by Emma Joanna Traynor
Layout and Design: Emma Joanna Traynor
        The text of this book was set in IM Fell DW Pica Designed by Igino Marini

Photographs by Wingate Downs
Festive Gourd Upkari, Sweet Bell Pepper Stir Fry, Mango Mousse with Jackfruit – Back Cover , Quinoa
Pulao for Mayank - Title Page, Spices - 10, Mango Mousse with Kiwi - 37, Legumes (Pulses, Dal) – 137

Printed in the U.S.A by Greater Georgia Printers, Inc., Crawford, GA

Library of Congress Control Number: 2021911223

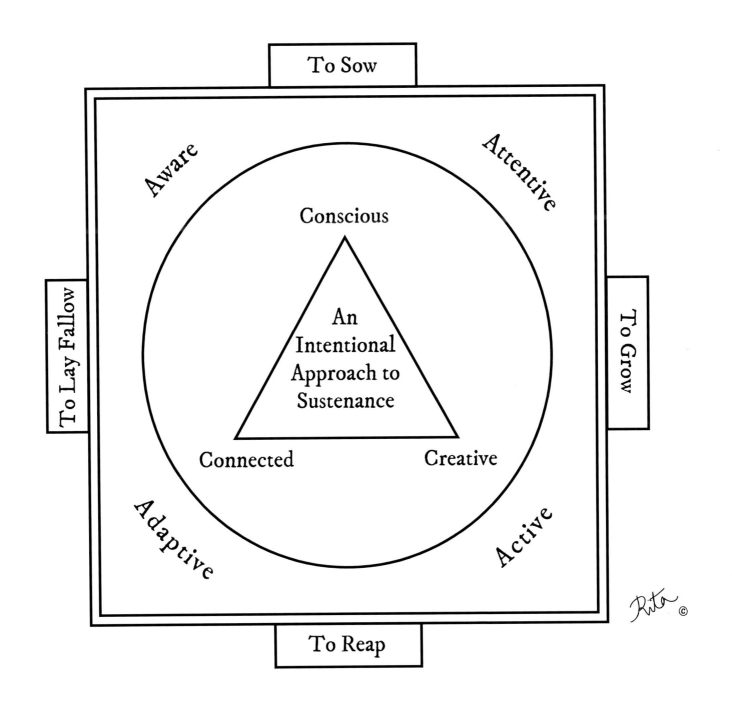

Reviews

The essays are thoughtful, the paintings throughout are lovely, great photos and the recipes look amazing.
- Sally Coenen, Artist, Athens, GA.

I am very excited that this was a collective community project, that the funds will be used locally, and we all got a little peek into our friends' and neighbors' kitchens. A great idea!!!
- Rebecca Lockman, One of four founding members, Mindful Breath Sangha, Athens GA

The method of organizing the recipes and information by season makes the book very special. This methodology - which draws the gardener into cooking and the chef into gardening - is very appealing. I also enjoyed reading about the contributors and the articles were very interesting.
- Mary Ellen Quinn, Ph.D. Associate Professor of Nursing, College of Nursing, Augusta University, Athens GA (Retd.).

This book is more than a cookbook. The text is a guide to help you to learn how to cook with the season, especially using local seasonal vegetables, and to appreciate the taste. This book will simplify your work in the kitchen and it has a lot of easy recipes. Over time you will have your favorite recipes as your palate expands. Changing one's diet, preparing healthy meals and enjoying food make good health. Suzanne Keifer and Rita Mathew have done a great job by creating a book that will enhance your eating pleasure and knowledge of how to eat by season.
- Carolina Dear, RYT-500 & E-RYT-500 & RPYT Ayurvedic Clinical Specialist Practitioner, Jesup, GA.

"There is a Season", edited by Suzanne Keifer and Rita Mathew, is a most unusual cookbook. It contains scrumptious recipes using familiar garden ingredients as well as international recipes that will expand your palate. It includes surprises such as how to sprout beans and grains, and how to make Mozzarella cheese in 30 minutes. Actually, it's more than a cookbook, focusing on individual health, environmental stewardship, and community connection. "There is a Season" is an excellent resource for recipes as well as for browsing.
- Rosemary Stancil, Co-author of Simply Scrumptious Microwaving, Kids' Simply Scrumptious Microwaving, and The Microwave Cooks Complete Companion. Athens, GA

Publisher's Note: Proceeds from sale of this book support environmental education programs in Athens, GA.

Table of Contents

Front Cover "Abundance" by Sally W. Coenen

Mandala by Rita R. Mathew

Spring

Summer

Fall

Winter

Year-Round

Back Cover: "Honeycomb" by Emma J. Traynor

Foreword

There are many dozens of cookbooks available today and most contain delicious sounding recipes, often drawn from various cultures. So, why publish another one? Take a quick look at just the Introduction and the answer is obvious. *There is a Season* is much more than a cookbook, though it certainly contains alluring seasonal recipes. *There is a Season* is really all about food with insightful essays on how to produce it in home gardens; the value of gardens to introduce children (and adults) to nature; and a fundamental connection to food, beyond packages in supermarkets. Practical tips on rainwater harvesting, composting, raised beds, refuge from pesticides for pollinators, growing and using medicinal plants, and evocative poetry "seasons of grief, love, and hope embedded in seeds", are all essential parts of this beautiful work.

We are deluged on an hourly basis with reports of massive wildfires, intense hurricanes, heat waves, droughts, floods and pandemics, all having some links to climate change, and all mostly beyond our control as individuals. A looming catastrophe of global food shortages also seems increasingly real but unlike the previous catastrophes, as individuals and communities we can do something about it. *There is a Season* provides an intellectual and practical foundation for individual and community action. For example, some claim that the high CO_2 levels that drive global warming actually increase food production because plants "feed" on CO_2. However, high night time temperatures increase respiration that depletes some of this photosynthate. Because modern cultivars are selected to maximize yields rather than nutritional quality, it is not surprising that CO_2-driven productivity results in plants containing more sugar and starches than vitamins and essential nutrients.

There is a Season offers an implicit and sometimes explicit antidote to the decreasing nutritional quality of our vegetables, legumes and grains. First, grow traditional varieties and species of plants that have not been selected just for yield, but for taste, nutrition, and local environmental resilience. Then, fertilize them with compost that releases nutrients for plant growth slowly and with more balance. And, finally reap your reward with delicious recipes, and the peaceful feeling that many have when they are one with nature.

Ron Carroll, Ph.D.
Professor of Ecology-Emeritus
Odum School of Ecology

Acknowledgements

A big thank you to all those who shared their recipes, which are both local and exotic. While most of our contributors live in the Athens area, there are those who live outside Georgia and outside the United States, making this a truly internationally collaborative effort.

Heartfelt gratitude to Claire and Bob Clements, Sally and Dan Coenen, Andy Kavoori and Christine Joseph, for their guidance and encouragement not only for this project but also for their support of community collaborations. Thanks also to Gary Wade who leads the Plant-A-Row project, and embodies the spirit of this book. We appreciate Laura Ney's enthusiastic support of bringing science to the community. Suzanne's embrace of diverse ideas, and willingness to consider possibilities for inclusion are to be admired. Without Emma's creative genius and attention to detail, this book would not have been possible. Thanks also to Rita. She has been the lighthouse for this project.

Bon appétit!

ARTICLE AUTHORS:
Anand Chockalingam, M.D.
Anne Shenk
Christine Joseph, Ph.D.
David Berle
Gary Wade, Ph.D.
George Edward Van Giesen III
Ranjit Mathew, M.D., Ph.D.
Rich Panico, M.D.
Rita Mathew, CPA
Robert Westerfield
Sheila Patel, M.D.
Suzanne Keifer
Virginia Nazarea, Ph.D.
Viviane Van Giesen

RECIPE CONTRIBUTORS: UNLESS OTHERWISE INDICATED, ALL CONTRIBUTORS ARE FROM ATHENS GA.
Alice Roshin Jacob, Ernakulum, India
Allan Cobb – MG 2020
Beverly Simpson
Candi Hoard – MG 2020
Caroline D'Souza - Mumbai, India
Christi Heston – Wellington, CO
Claire Clements – Artist
Donna Yates – MG 2005
Eva Stalnaker – MG 2020
Feliciano Bernal – Decatur, Ga
Frank and Cheryl Johnson – MG 2005
Gary Wade – MG 2007
Greg and Laura Killmaster
Isaac Swier – MG 2020

Jackie Zogran – MG 2020
Jean Colquett – MG 2000
Jim Weck – MG 2017
John Aitken – MG 2011
Juanita Broon – MG 2012
Linda Tedrow – MG 2014
Liz Conroy – MG 2010
Luca Huckleberry Mathew – Morristown, NJ
Mariam Jacob – Ernakulam, India
Marilyn Fuller – Woodstock GA
Nancy Welch – MG 2016
Pam Tidwell – MG 2020
Rela Alice Jacob – Chennai, India
Rita Mathew – MG 2020
Rosemary Stancil – MG 2017
Supplemental Nutrition Assistance Program
        Education (SNAP-Ed)
Susie Burch – Artist
Sylvia Dawes – Artist
The Keifer Family (all over the US):
        Angela Hatfield,
        Angela Logan,
        Anna Mae,
        Christine Guilloton,
        Eric, Hannah, Harry,
        Narcie, Rachel,
        Sharon and
        Suzanne – MG 2020
Reverend Manjula Spear – Athens, GA.
Tinu Ann Jacob, Kuala Lumpur, Malaysia
Tracey Massey
Vimal Sinha

Virginia McClelland – MG 2016
Viviane Van Giesen – Artist

COVER ARTISTS:
FRONT: Sally Coenen, Athens GA – "Abundance".
BACK: Emma Traynor, Savannah, GA –
        "Honeycomb".

ARTWORK CONTRIBUTORS:
Bob Clements – "Girl Eating Radish".
Emma Traynor, Savannah, GA – "Daylily with Bee",
        "Hydrangeas with Butterfly".
Joanna Wright – Illustrations.
Kie Johnson – "Fragile, Handle with Care".
Laura Ney – Infographics, "Spring", "Summer",
        "Fall", "Winter".
Mary Ann Cox – "Community Connection".
Rich Panico – "Renewal".
Susie Burch – "Farmers' Market", "Side by Side".
Viviane Van Giesen – "Tomatoes".

PHOTOGRAPHY
Wingate Downs, Wingate Downs Photography,
        Athens, GA
Cora Keber, Director of Education, State Botanical
        Garden of Georgia, Athens, GA

REFERENCE FOR NUTRITION CHARTS:
https://nutritiondata.self.com

"Community Connection"
©2021 **Mary Ann Cox**

Introduction

Rita Mathew, Co-Editor

Poires Belle Helene, Aji de Huacatay, Quinoa Pulao, Venison Meatballs with port sauce! Mouth-watering recipes from South Georgia, to Southeast Asia; from Europe: France and England; from South America: Mexico, and Peru; from the Far East: Malaysia, Vietnam and Papua New Guinea, are featured in *"There is a Season"*.

That said, it is much more than just a "cookbook". It is a recipe for intentional living, the three Cs – conscious, creative and connected. Research shows that these qualities and others such as empathy, compassion, and gratitude offer mental and physical resilience at a time of crisis. Thus, an Intentional Approach to Sustenance is a pathway for those in pursuit of well-being. It is a visual treat, a book of wisdom, and a reference guide for years to come!

But what does Sustenance mean? Soil, water, climate, seeds, plants and pollinators all play a part. Arranged in seasons, the themes - Individual Health, Environmental Stewardship, and Community Connections - remind us that there is a time to sow, a time to grow, a time to reap, and a time to lay fallow.

Spring (Individual Health)

Dr. Sheila Patel, Chief Medical Officer, Chopra, NY, combines evidence, based on scientific research, with knowledge of traditional healing systems to present the benefits of seasonal living. She makes a case for "a framework that teaches that our bodies are not separate from the natural world but intimately connected to it"!

Dr. Anand Chockalingam, whose interests are stress cardiomyopathy, and reversing heart failure through both conventional medicine and mind-body interventions, shares insights on cultivating healthy eating habits through a method of self-enquiry. He concludes, "Let hunger guide your inner journey."

Dr. Rich Panico, a medical practitioner, who has a deep and multi-faceted understanding of the human condition, with experience spanning several decades, provides pointers in ecotherapy.

Based on the science of happiness, in "Naming Rites" Rita Mathew shares insights in how active listening, and positive thinking can transform mere consumption of food to health and abundance.

SUMMER (ENVIRONMENTAL STEWARDSHIP)

ANNE SHENK's essay, "Helping Children Blossom in the Garden", is so vivid, it's almost possible to hear the excitement in the children's voices as they sow seeds and eat radishes.

Colony Collapse Disorder is only one of the factors of concern when studying pollinators. To gain a broader perspective, "On Being Intentional: The three Cs of Bees" looks at the role of bees in an ancient society. RITA MATHEW poses questions such as "When were bees domesticated? What were the conditions under which they thrived? What lessons do they offer?"

GEORGE EDWARD VAN GIESEN III, discusses the merits of water conservation and offers practical advice in "Harvesting Rainwater is more fun than a barrel of Monkeys".

FALL (ENVIRONMENTAL STEWARDSHIP)

PROF. VIRGINIA NAZAREA's poems were penned during the process of grieving for the loss of her friend, life partner, and fellow scholar, distinguished professor of Agriculture and Anthropology, Prof. Robert Rhoades. "Seeding Place" is a Cognitive Map of the interactions between displaced people, their memories, and the associated affect.

What's fantastic about Fall? Vegetable Gardening, according to PROF. GARY WADE, who has guidelines for growing asparagus, beets, carrots, and much more!

Master Gardener Suzanne Keifer's "Composting: Life (Re)cycle" has data to show that an environmental steward is someone who is serious about composting.

WINTER (COMMUNITY CONNECTION)

An anthropologist dreams of going to Papua New Guinea! PROF. CHRISTINE JOSEPH transports the reader, first, to the Trobriand Archipelago, to New Delhi, India.

If living in an apartment, or restricted space poses a challenge to growing vegetables, then "Raised Garden Beds" by PROF. DAVID BERLE and "Grow your own Transplants" by PROF. ROBERT WESTERFIELD offer useful, and practical information for novices in gardening.

YEAR-ROUND (COMMUNITY CONNECTION)

In every ending, there is a new beginning. Prof. Westerfield looks forward to spring: "Warm Season Vegetable Cheat Sheet" prepares the master gardener for planting tomatoes, peppers, cucumbers and green beans! Prof. David Berle offers wonderful tips on growing medicinal plants. In this section are also real life stories from PROF. GARY WADE and VIVIANE VAN GIESEN on the importance of sharing the fruit of labor with those in need, and how seasonal living is all about "Dancing to the Music".

Spring

"Renewal"
©2021 Rich Panico

Traditional Wisdom and Seasonal Eating

Sheila Patel, MD. Chief Medical Officer, Chopra, New York

Dr. Patel is a board-certified family physician who enjoys bringing the knowledge of traditional healing systems into her practice to help people create healthy lifestyles. As part of her role at Chopra, she creates content on natural healing practices and shares it with others through various online and social platforms. She is a lead educator for Chopra certifications and has lectured at various wellness and integrative medical conferences. Her passion is to make the knowledge of natural healing accessible to all to help individuals heal and thrive.

It has been known for thousands of years that food has medicinal benefits. Various foods have unique effects on our bodies and minds, and we can use specific foods at particular times to balance and heal ourselves. One of the main observations made regarding food and nutrition was that our bodies have biological cycles that are synchronized to the cycles of nature. Seasonal foods correspond to what our bodies need at certain time of the year. Our bodies have evolved with, and adapted to, our local seasonal changes. Traditional healing systems were built on a framework that teaches that our bodies are not separate from the natural world, but are intimately connected to it and dependent on nature for our health and well-being. By understanding that we are part of the larger ecosystem of nature, traditional systems teach us how to recognize the effects the seasons and climate may be having on us, allowing us to adjust our food accordingly in order to stay healthy.

There is much written in the textbooks of traditional healing systems regarding proper nutrition. Following these principles keeps us healthy year-round. However, modern society has taken us far away from these natural eating principles. Never in the history of the world have there been the assortment of "manufactured" foods, foods grown in nutrient-poor soils, and foods grown with additives, chemicals and hormones that humans routinely consume today. In addition, we have increased access to foods from around the world at all times. Yet despite having access to an abundance and variety of foods, chronic disease is on the rise worldwide, and we have moved farther and farther away from natural eating principles.

As we are beginning to learn, we must go back to a more natural way of eating in order to heal and thrive as a species. Our ancestors were more in touch with nature and used nature's cycles in traditional agricultural practices. The solstices were times to plant certain crops, and plants were harvested according to the weather, which could change from year to year. In many ancient cultures certain foods were harvested only during specific phases of the moon. These principles are seen today in the biodynamics approach to food and nutrition, a holistic, ecological, and ethical approach to agriculture. According to these philosophies, the spirit, or intelligence, of nature is integrated into what we eat, and we do well to take into consideration our connection to nature as we choose the foods we consume. This mindset calls on us to understand that how we treat the environment affects us in profound ways, because the environment is simply an extension of our own physical bodies.

Many of the principles of healthy eating that were known for millennia are now being backed by science. Science tells us that eating a whole-food, plant-based diet that is grown in rich soil, free of chemicals and additives, provides the best way to ward off chronic disease and to keep us healthy. When foods are grown and harvested according to nature, phytonutrients, such as anti-inflammatories and anti-oxidants, are in rich abundance and can play a key role in keeping us healthy. Food forced to grow out of season often contains fewer nutrients. Plant-based foods from nature are also rich in fiber. They aid in removing waste from the body and encourage the growth of healthy bacteria in the gut, as well as having other benefits.

One principle appreciated long ago, and now being validated by modern medicine, is the importance of gut health for overall health. Ancient physicians said that, "most disease begins in the gut." When our gut is not functioning properly, we cannot digest or metabolize food into nourishment for our bodies. In addition, when we do not have the right amount or diversity of healthy bacteria and other microbes in our gut, we cannot digest and metabolize many foods, and we may even have issues with the integrity of the intestinal wall. Much research is being done on the gut microbiome, the millions of genes from the microbes in our gut, and how to keep these microbes healthy. Interestingly, research shows that the population of bacteria in our gut changes depending on the season. In hunter-gatherer tribes of today, the microbiome changes as the tribe's diet changes from the wet to the dry season. The local, seasonal foods that we eat affect our own microbiomes, and changes in the outside temperature also causes shifts in gut bacteria to accommodate to the new foods being harvested.[1] Studies in other animal species reveal shifts in the gut microbiome that occur along with many other seasonal physiological changes. It appears that changes in weather often trigger a shift toward microbes that are ready to digest the foods of the season.[2] There is also evidence that this same process occurs in humans. Our bodies appear to have evolved to adapt to seasonal changes. Research shows that people who live in colder climates have different microbial compositions than those who live in warmer climates.[3] Therefore, eating local and seasonal foods can contribute to improved digestion and metabolism.

An approach related to eating seasonally, which is not followed in Western nutrition, is the classification by Eastern medical systems of foods by their qualities. Qualities such as "heating" or "cooling," "heavy" or "light," are applied to foods based on how they affect us physiologically. The underlying point is that different categories of foods affect our metabolism and digestion in different ways. We can see these effects in our lives, as we recognize the difference in how we feel after eating "cooling" foods such as cucumber and watermelon compared to how we feel after eating "heating" foods such as ginger and garlic. Indeed, a growing body of research focuses on the positive role of "thermogenic" foods, which parallel in many regards the "heating" foods long recognized in the East. Taking these ideas into account, the traditional healing systems teach us that we can counter the accumulation of heat from the environment, particularly in the hottest months of the year, by eating cooling foods. Conversely, during the cold months, we do well to eat more heating foods and spices to stimulate digestion and metabolism, and modify blood flow to guard against the loss of body temperature.

1 Smits, S.A., Leach, J.L., Sonnenburg, E.D., Gonzalez, C.G.,Sonnenburg, J.L. (2017). Seasonal cycling in the gut microbiome of the Hadza hunter-gatherers of Tanzania. Science, 357(6353), 802-806, doi: 10.1126/science.aan4834

2 Ferguson, Laura V., Dhakal, Pranav, Lebenzon, Jacqueline E., Heinrichs, David E., Bucking, Carol, and Sinclair, Brent (2018) Seasonal shifts in the insect gut microbiome are concurrent with changes in cold tolerance and immunity. Biology Publications, 98, https://ir.lib.uwo.ca/biologypub/98

3 Suzuki, T.A., Worobey, M. (2014) Geographical Variation of Human Gut Microbial Composition. Biology Letters, 10(2), doi: 10.1098/rsbl.2013.1037

There are also foods that are considered "light" or "heavy". The types of foods nature produces are in line with what can keep us balanced during a particular season. For example, many of the light foods such as leafy greens, vegetables, and fresh fruits are abundant in the spring and summer to lighten the body in anticipation of increased activity during these months. In contrast, "heavy', or "grounding", foods such as squashes and root vegetables ripen as the weather transitions to the dry, windy autumn and the cold winter.

Thoughtful nutritionists have increasingly urged us to take account of these lessons of nature as we shape our diets. As we examine these recommendations, we find that they are being validated by microbiome research. As we are exposed to cold weather in the late fall and winter, traditional eating tells us to eat more cooked foods to stay grounded while adding invigorating spices to warm ourselves up. Exposure to cold can lead to shifts in metabolism; the body tends to absorb calories faster, and the gut composition trends towards microbes that digest heavier, starchier foods better. While research is still ongoing, it looks like our bodies are meant to slow down and nourish ourselves in response to the cold so we can survive the winter.[4] In the spring, traditional recommendations are to eat dry and light foods after a winter of heavier foods. It feels natural to switch to foods that nature gives us in the spring and early summer, such as greens and vegetables. When summer comes, nature gives us fresh fruits and more fresh greens and vegetables that can cool us down. These recommendations may be most easily understood in the context of a typical four-season climate, but these same underlying principles operate everywhere on the planet, based on local climate and seasons.

In light of this traditional knowledge, here are some tips for eating in alignment with nature and its seasons:

- Eat local and seasonal foods as much as possible.
- Eat organic, non-GMO foods that are ethically treated.
- Eat more plants that contain healing phytochemicals.
- In the summer, eat light, cooling foods such as salads, greens, and fresh fruit.
- In the fall and early winter, eat more cooked, moist, and heavy foods with plenty of warming spices.
- In the late winter and early spring, lighten the diet with vegetables and greens that are raw or lightly cooked.

When we look to the wisdom of ancient healing systems, we understand the intimate connection between our bodies, the environment, and the microbes within us that function as one ecosystem. We understand that food is our medicine and that plants from nature help us heal. We also honor the fact that we evolve with nature, and that nature's cycles are our cycles, too. When we reconnect with this ancient wisdom, eating in alignment with nature becomes a sacred act, rather than one that destroys our health and the health of the planet. If we eat in keeping with this wisdom, we can heal both ourselves and our world.

---

4. Chevalier, C., Stojanovic, O. Colin, D.J., Zamboni, N. Hapfelmeier, S., Trajkovski, M. (2015) Gut Microbiota Orchestrates Energy Homeostasis During Cold. Cell, 163, 1360–1374, doi: 10.1016/j.cell.2015.11.004.

Celebrating Food and Better Health

Anand Chockalingam, MD

Anand Chockalingam is a Cardiologist based in Columbia, MO. His major interests are stress cardiomyopathy, reversing heart failure and mind-body interventions. He has over 70 publications. In addition, he has pioneered a novel Heartful Living cardiac wellness method of improving health and resilience through self-inquiry and mindfulness tools.

Our way of life has unrecognizably changed within the last few generations. Exercise and physical activities are increasingly difficult given our busy schedules. Obesity is on the rise world over. Two thirds of the population is dealing with the physical and psychological effects of excess body weight. Major cities across the world find 60-85% of their population are sedentary, causing 2 million deaths globally. Increased frequency of eating, larger portion size and reluctance to prepare fresh meals at home are daily challenges. At the same time, marketing of 'fun' treats, 'party' snacks, 'energy' drinks and sugar added beverages contributes to excess calories. Children have developed a sweet tooth, and crave processed food, while adults often resort to 'comfort' foods to overcome stress and anxiety.

AN INTENTIONAL APPROACH TO HEALTH

Health is the freedom to pursue life passionately. Recognizing that much of our health will always remain our responsibility is the first step. Recognizing and working towards our true passion is vital to optimizing physical health and mental wellbeing. Many may find their work, creativity and interest is intellectual and may be pursued online. However, the needs of our body having evolved over millions of years on the foundation of using physical energy to thrive cannot be neglected. Therefore, we have to find ways to workout, exercise or embrace sports to regularly challenge the body[1]. To avoid chronic diseases like diabetes, heart failure, cancer and dementia there is only one other thing that has been proven to work- and that is diet! Yes, our chance of chronic long-term disease is reduced by 70-90% when we eat healthy.[2]

> Which diet is healthy?
> Can we eat without guilt?
> How do we teach healthy eating habits to future generations?

1   Cosmides L, Tooby J. Evolutionary psychology: new perspectives on cognition and motivation. Annu Rev Psychol. 2013;64:201–29.
2   Chockalingam A, Dorairajan S, Anand K. Higher Consciousness through Self-Inquiry can improve Cardio Metabolic outcomes, Mental Health and Resilience, Mo Med. Mar-Apr 2021;118(2):15-20.

Why is there no consensus on what to eat and which diet to follow? Self-inquiry, or Siddha Consciousness, which explores several mind-body methods, has been documented in Tamil texts dating back over 5000 years.[3] These tools were taken to various parts of the world in ancient times and are popular even now as Kung-Fu in China, Zen in Japan, Soen in Korea, and Yoga in India.[4] The central theme is training the body and calming the logical mind towards ogam (union of mind and body) and realizing uvagai (extreme joy) in daily life. These principles of introspection and intentional living have withstood the test of time, and shown to lead to healthy, integrated lifestyles.

CONNECTING HUNGER WITH GRATITUDE

One of the recommendations of Siddha philosophy focuses on Gratitude. Emotional eating to overcome anxiety, or for social reasons, often adds calories and leaves us feeling guilty. Next obstacle to healthy eating is habitual eating by the clock, to minimize hunger during our daily work demands. The best time to eat is when you are truly physically hungry because you need the energy contained in food after fasting several hours.

Eating with a deep sense of gratitude is never guilt-inducing! For people needing to lose weight, connecting within and experiencing this gratitude is encouraged. It may be for daily events, friends, family or life circumstances. By developing a new relationship with food, not only does eating become a celebration but it also leads to optimism and emotional strength to cope with challenging stressful situations.

Mahatma Gandhi employed fasting as a meditative practice to gain spiritual strength needed to unite a vast country. The self-inquiry mindful eating practice for heart health documents how connecting hunger with gratitude has benefits for physical, emotional, and spiritual wellbeing.

WHERE IS THE SCIENCE?

Science is continuously figuring out what is healthy for us. Not surprising, that the ideal diet for the heart includes some of the oldest foods which naturally suit our biology - plant based foods like vegetables, fruits, nuts, multigrain bread, brown rice and pulses. Reducing meat, oil, snacks, and carbonated drinks with refined sugar reduces risk of heart disease.

Our intuition has known all along what makes us energetic and alert. Let us listen to our bodies and eat right. Numerous heart patients are rediscovering themselves and their new taste for healthy foods. Feasting and celebrating life through food is vital. This may well be the highest achievement of the logical mind! Food is our pride and privilege. It is the reward for our labor. Let us celebrate eating as a meditation, every day mindfully! The path forward, to ideal weight and a lifetime of health, is through celebrating food and life. Let hunger guide your inner journey.[5]

3   Weiss R. Recipes for Immortality : Healing, Religion, and Community in South India: Healing, Religion, and Community in South India. Oxford University Press; 2009. p. 80.
4   Powell W. Martial Arts MacMillan Encyclopedia of Buddhism. MacMillan Reference; USA: 2004. pp. 214–218.
5   Seeking Hunger. by Anand Chockalingam, MD, Mo Med. 2021;118(2):167.

"Daylily with Bee"
©2021 **Emma Traynor**

Nature and Healing

Rich Panico, MD

Dr. Panico, a graduate of the Emory School of Medicine, is a board-certified psychiatrist. He was the founder and former director of the Mind-Body Institute at Athens Regional Medical Center, former medical director of Advantage Behavioral Health Systems and was division chief of psychiatry at Athens Regional Medical Center for many years. In addition to being an esteemed physician, he is also a yogi and an artist. He is a long-time student and practitioner of classical yoga and its therapeutic applications and has taught this older interior form of yoga and meditation for three decades. His painting, "Renewal" is featured in the Spring section of this book.

Healing is a fuzzy term as opposed to the statistical, goal-oriented world of contemporary bio-medicine which is concerned with concepts more amenable to measurement like cure, mortality, remission, and outcomes.

Healing is about a sense, a perception of wholeness, integration, engagement, or flourishing and can even be independent of symptoms or clinical course as in someone with terminal cancer who comes to a place of wholeness and peace even in the face of death.

Most people can create a significant positive response to being in nature. Some individuals seek experiences in the landscape or seascape, or in the garden, or drawing or writing in and about nature, to address feelings of tension, fragmentation, disconnection, anxiety, stress and so on. This response to nature is not magic. It is based in profound changes in endocrine signature and attendant changes in various biological domains. The understanding of these positive changes is captured within the study of allostasis and allostatic load, concepts which are now accepted scientific ways to understand the stress response and how to mitigate its disease producing phenomena.

In short, regular engagement of significant duration with the landscape or nature helps us "remember" who we are at a fundamental level that is: part of nature itself and in so doing an attunement or resonance with the landscape occurs and edifying biological phenomena are elicited.

The scientific study of nature-based interventions (for example ecotherapy)[1] are just beginning and difficult because of the multiple active variables introduced by say gardening or walking in nature. I would not recommend waiting for "evidence" to demonstrate efficacy or convince you intellectually but instead discover for yourself with a regular dose of "nature" taken daily over time. Do it long enough to discover your therapeutic dose and favorite form of engaging with nature. Decide for yourself if this is worthwhile.

---

1 Summers, James K., Vivian Deborah N. (2018) Ecotherapy – A Forgotten Ecosystem Service: A Review. Frontiers in Psychology, 9 (1389), doi: 10.3389/fpsyg.2018.01389.

From center, clockwise: Black pepper, cumin seeds, coriander seeds, cinnamon pieces, green cardamom, mustard seeds, fenugreek seeds, cloves, turmeric powder and root.

Naming Rites

Rita Mathew, CPA

An accountant by vocation, Rita has served in various professional capacities throughout her career of 30 years. To be an accountant is to know what counts: this has been the driving force for her activities in sustainable development, education, and health. She is passionate about serving and caring for people and amongst her many endeavors, one was to lead a relief effort for a fishing village struck by the 2005 Tsunami in South India. She has been invited twice to the Rashtrapati Bhavan, New Delhi: in 1971, to meet President V.V. Giri, and in 2006, to meet President A.P.J. Kalaam.

What's in a name? Some may say that a curry will be just as spicy if called something else. Lakoff and Johnson find that in the western tradition, meaning has very little to do with what people find meaningful in their lives.[1] But delving into naming rituals for a curry, or broadly contemplating their metaphorical connections with our experience of food may be just what is needed to add a little spice to life. Will the connections between names, forms, and functions of exotic sounding dishes provide food for the soul? That remains to be discovered.

IS IT A CURRY OR A MASALA?

Commercially available "curry" powder, and garam "masala", embody a blend of spices. But these same terms also refer to the cooked dish to which these spices lend a flavor. The spice powders are marketed with an underlying promise that a teaspoon of the product's contents can transport a dish to a faraway, eastern land. If it were only true!

"Curry", *kari* in Sanskrit, actually means "to make", "to put together" or "to synthesize" almost in a transformational sense. Author, and chef, Shanti Rangarao (1968),[2] explains that the word "curry" refers to the process of grinding numerous ingredients to a paste, which is called masala or maasol.

The first step in understanding the process of making a masala is to start with the main ingredient, the coconut, *Cocos nucifera*. The Southwestern coastline of India, home to the displaced Saraswat community, has an abundance of fresh coconut. One hundred percent of this fruit is useful. The husk is used for coir ropes and mats, and the hard shell can serve as a dipper. It is, though, the fruit's pure, white, pulp that is of interest here. This fleshy pulp is grated or ground to a fine paste, which is then strained through a muslin to get coconut milk. In an undiluted form, this milk is thick and used in

---

1 Lakoff, George and Johnson, Mark (2003) Metaphors We Live By. p ix. Chicago: The University of Chicago Press.
2 Rangarao, Shanti (1968) Good Food from India. p 132. Mumbai India: Jaico Publishing House.

special preparations. Another form of the milk is watered down and useful for daily consumption. A dish prepared with coconut, a staple of a Saraswat diet, is neither a complicated curry, nor is it a spicy masala. Not only is the coconut masala simple and healthy, but its preparation also reflects the effort required in abstracting the essence from a region's living ecosystem.

Another important use of the word Kari is in reference to the Karivepalla plant, whose aromatic leaves, kari patta (leaves), are widely used in cooking. A common technique in naming, using a part to refer to the whole, is possibly the reason why European traders began to call dishes garnished with kari leaves as a "curry".

The Karivepalla plant bears the scientific designation Murraya Koenigii, having been named after Swedish botanist Johann Andreas Murray. To a master gardener, this scientific name refers to a tropical to sub-tropical tree, in the family Rutaceae. It typically grows anywhere from 13 to 30 feet tall in the moist forests of India, where it is also known the Kurbev plant. Its pungent and aromatic leaves, called *kari* leaves, are widely used both as a medicinal herb and as seasoning in South Indian cuisine. Especially to the Saraswat community, kari leaf seasoning is an authenticating stamp for a dish; it is symbolic of health, community, and abundance.

Unfortunately, growers also sell *Helichrysum italicum* as a curry plant, even though it is unrelated to the true curry plant, and its leaves are inedible. The *H. italicum* is an ornamental, annual flowering plant of the Asteracea family, valued for its silvery foliage, warm fragrance and bright yellow blooms. Its leaves are not recommended as a substitute for the Murraya koenigii leaf in cooking. Fortunately, the scientific method encourages master gardeners to investigate and discover the true nature of things. And in this case, it turns out that eating curries, if done properly, involves knowing scientific names of ingredients, as well as the underlying processes.

So how do we name foods and food-generating plants? Does taste, whether sweet or spicy, dictate the name? Does it matter whether what we eat is dry or moist? Does seasonality matter? Does the name have a cultural role? And what does the name mean?

3 Chilli hot, or 5 Chilli hot?

Culinary writers have perpetuated the myth that "curry" is a complex blend of hot spices. The term "masala," particularly "*garam masala*," has likewise been used to conjure up images of fiery heat with graphics of three, four, or five hot, red chillis. Although the word "garam" does mean hot, the reference is rooted in traditional wisdom which classifies foods based on their cooling or warming effect on the body.

Additionally, spices like cinnamon, cloves, black pepper, tephal, nutmeg, and cardamom (see picture on page 10) are grown in the hot, southern states of Karnataka, Kerala, Andhra Pradhesh, Telengana, and Tamil Nadu. These spices are famous in part because of the important role they once played, and still play, in international trade. They are now, however, grown in many home gardens. And by fine chefs, they are used judiciously, individually or in various creative combinations, to add a sophisticated touch of delicate flavor to both vegetarian and non-vegetarian dishes.

Metaphorical references to spices are common in literature. Indeed, author James Scott Bell, compares good writers to good chefs, "Good chefs have their secret spices, ingredients they use to give their creations something extra and unique. For writers, the spices you add to make your plot your own include: characters, setting and dialogue."[3] A good chef does not throw ingredients haphazardly into a dish, and neither should a good writer; so, it is important to understand the rites and rituals associated with local cuisines.

How dry is it?

Depending on how moist or dry the dish is determines whether the prepared item is called *upakari* [*oo puh kuh ree*], *sukké*, *saglé*, or *kalvan*.

A simple upkari is the driest; vegetables are stir-fried and grated coconut is sprinkled as a garnish on top after the dish is cooked. Sukké, a moderately dry vegetable, has coconut masala front and centre. Unlike an upakari which has only one vegetable, sukké has two or more ingredients, and is thus a step-up from an upakari. Rather than chopping, dicing, or grating, sometimes the vegetable is used in toto, meaning whole or sagle. Finally, a dish with the consistency of a thick pea soup, is categorized as kalvan. One well-known kalvan is dal, which is made from protein-rich and high-fiber-content lentils.[4]

Kalvan, far from eliciting heart burn, is only lightly spiced. With the addition of jaggery (brown sugar) and tamarind, it can also have a sweet and sour tang, which gives it the name *ambat*; if it has a coarse texture, it is called a *ghushi*.

Many of these dishes are made with sprouted beans and combined with a vegetable, such as the ivy gourd or bitter gourd, resulting in a protein rich, balanced meal. Vegans, and those with allergies to wheat products find that the coconut-based sauces provide a nourishing alternative to the buttery, rich, gravy made with enriched flour.

Seasons and Festivals

In India, food is associated with festivals, *Utsava*, celebrations of life and community. There are over 30 festivals, several in each season, and cuisines to match. A harvest feast, for example, would not be complete without a sukké, in which fresh fruit such as grapes, pomegranate seeds, pineapple, and cut mangoes keep company with vegetables – the very blend of ingredients depicted in the cover art of this book, which is titled "Abundance." Sukké, in the context of a side dish, actually means dry. Dry might

---

3 Bell, James Scott (2004) Write Great Fiction: Plot & Structure. p 16 Cincinnati, Ohio: Writer's Digest Books.
4 See Legumes (Pulses) on page 36

be a good thing, especially during the months of monsoon. Thus, Sukké is closely related to the Sanskrit word *sukha*, which means happy. Another meaning that crops up is *upakaar*, a favor received. Harvest festivals in particular, celebrate the favor received from nature. Thus, we see that naming attempts to capture points of essence in the rich and differing seasons and deep connections in life.

SOUND WAVES AS LIFE

Upa in Sanskrit means to sit near. More specifically *upasana*, means to approach closely in meditation in the hope of lifting the veil of ignorance. Might this possibly be the reason why some dishes came to be grouped as upakari? Their role, after all, is to sit near and attend to the main dish, which in South India is rice. Names, in this instance, as in many others, give depth to what might otherwise seem mundane and lacking in significance.

When names, forms, and functions come together, the meaning they convey as a whole, is more than the sum of their individual parts. They transport from the concrete to the abstract, and even mystical; from the realm of ordinary, to that which is vibrant, alive, and intentional.

Poets and writers use the 'lyrical voice' to their advantage to convey meaning through the sound of the words. An example is the famous Sanskrit composition, "*Soundarya Lahiri*," or Waves of Beauty, by 8th century philosopher, Adi Shankara. Unique to the Sanskrit language is the theory that each sound of the alphabet is a wave, *lahiri*, from which originates the word, lyrical. The waves, have a beat and a rhythm; the word rhythm, in fact, has its root in *Rta*, or order. Thus, words are not only metaphoric expressions, but they also have creative power to make deep
impressions. Sounds play an important role in how we interpret the content of what we read and hear.

Seasoned with kari leaves and coconut milk as mother sauce, upakari, sukké, sagle, and kalvan invite us to partake in and to savor the abundance of an intentional life. Or, as the point might be put in poetry:

> Imagine,
> Mindfully eating,
> Upakari.
> Aware
> of the abundance received
> as a favor.
> Approach,
> In loving-kindness.
> Become
> Transformed.
> To your authentic self.
>   - Rita

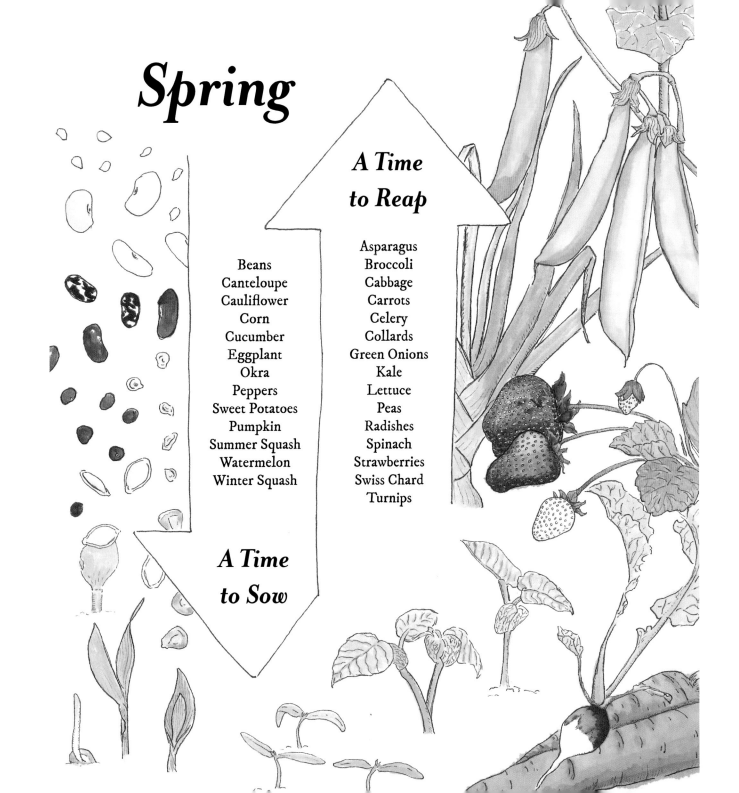

Spring

A Time to Reap

Beans
Canteloupe
Cauliflower
Corn
Cucumber
Eggplant
Okra
Peppers
Sweet Potatoes
Pumpkin
Summer Squash
Watermelon
Winter Squash

Asparagus
Broccoli
Cabbage
Carrots
Celery
Collards
Green Onions
Kale
Lettuce
Peas
Radishes
Spinach
Strawberries
Swiss Chard
Turnips

A Time to Sow

			Produce (1 Cup, raw. Unless otherwise stated)										Spices (1 Tbsp)									
			Asparagus	Broccoli (1 cup chopped)	Lettuce (1 cup shredded)	Peas	Radishes (1 cup sliced)	Spinach	Mangos (1 ripe whole, 336 gm)	Peaches (1 ripe whole, 175 gm)	Pomegranate (1 ripe 282 gm)	Strawberries (1 cup, halves, 152 gm)	Black Pepper	Cardamom	Chilli Powder	Cinnamon	Cloves	Coriander Seeds	Cumin Seeds	Garlic (3 cloves)	Ginger (1 tsp)	Turmeric
Nutrition	Calories	**Grams**	27	30.9	5.4	117	18.6	6.9	201	68.3	234	48.6	15.9	18	23.6	19	21	14.9	22	13.4	1.6	23.9
	Carbohydrates		5.3	6	1	21	4	1.1	50	17.3	52.7	11.7	4.1	3.9	4.1	6.2	4	2.7	2.7	3	0.4	4.4
	Protein		2.9	2.6	0.5	7.9	0.8	0.9	2.8	1.6	4.7	1	0.7	0.6	0.9	0.3	0.4	0.6	1.1	0.6	0	0.5
	Fat		0.2	0.3	0.1	0.6	0.1	1	1.3	0.4	27.6	0.5	0.2	0.4	1.3	0.1	1.3	0.9	1.3	0	0	0.7
	Fiber		2.8	2.4	0.5	7.4	1.9	0.7	6	2.6	11.3	3	1.7	1.6	2.6	4.1	2.2	2.1	0.6	0.2	0	1.4
Vitamins	Vitamin A	**% DV**	20	11	53	22	0	56	50	11	0	0	0	0	44	0	1	0	2	0	0	0
	Vitamin C		13	135	11	97	29	14	152	19	48	149	2	2	8	0	9	2	1	5	0	3
	Vitamin K		70	116	78	45	2	181	18	6	58	4	13	-	10	3	12	-	0	0	0	1
	Folate		17	14	3	24	7	15	12	2	27	9	0	-	2	0	2	0	0	0	0	1
Minerals	Iron		16	4	2	12	2	5	2	2	5	3	10	4	6	4	3	5	22	1	0	16
	Calcium		3	4	1	4	3	3	4	1	3	2	3	2	2	8	4	4	6	2	0	1
	Potassium		8	8	2	10	8	5	14	10	19	7	2	2	4	1	2	2	3	1	0	5
	Sodium		0	1	0	0	2	1	0	0	0	0	0	0	0	0	1	0	0	0	0	0

Ammai's Green Papaya Thoran

Rita Mathew

Ingredients

- 3 cups green Papaya (prepare as directed and grate)
- Coconut masala
  - ¾ cup fresh coconut (grated)
  - 3 shallots or pearl onions (finely sliced)
  - 1 small Thai green chilli (thinly sliced)
  - ½ tsp garlic minced
- 1 Tbsp water
- Kari Leaf Seasoning (Recipe on page 36)

1. To prepare the Papaya - Cut off the stem and root end. Peel at least ⅛th of the skin otherwise the vegetable will taste bitter. Cut in half, length wise and scoop out the seeds along with the inner fibrous part. Grate the papaya and set aside.

2. Prepare the Kari Leaf Seasoning in a medium heavy pan. When ready, add the coconut mixture to the hot pan. Sauté for 1 – 2 minutes.

3. Add the grated papaya to the pan and stir. Sprinkle water, cover and cook on a low flame for 10 minutes. Serve hot as a side dish along with rice and yogurt.

VARIATIONS OF THORAN

Examples of other vegetables which may be substituted for the papaya are provided below along with the equivalent weight for 3 cups. Care must be taken to prepare the vegetables appropriately by grating, cutting into a specific length, cubing, or slivering.

- ½ lb Broccoli (chopped)
- ½ lb Brussel sprouts (chopped)
- 1 lb Carrot (grated)
- 1 large Plantain raw (trim ends, lightly peel skin, cut in 1-inch by ¼ inch pieces.)
- ½ lb (1 cup) dried Black-Eyed Beans (soak in cold water for 6 hours, drain and cook; or use 2 15 oz cans)
- ¾ lb Butternut or Acorn Squash (trim ends, peel, scoop out seeds just like we did for the papaya. The difference is that instead of grating, the Squash is cubed into 1-inch pieces)

A simple Upkari (see next page, page 19) to which has been added onions and fresh garlic is a Thoran. It may be prepared with a variety of vegetables, roots and gourds, on condition they stay firm when cooked.

Dr. Cherian Joseph, Ranjit's maternal uncle, was the first Director of Health Services in the state of Kerala, India. He had distinguished himself by eradicating Malaria for the first time in India. Naturally, he was very conscious of health and nutrition. It made sense that his wife, Ranjit's aunt, who was called Ammai (variation of mother) served Green Pappaya Thoran very often, not only because it grew in abundance in her garden, but also for its nutritional value.

Anna Mae's Sauerkraut

Suzanne Keifer

Ingredients

- 5 pounds cabbage
- 3-4 tablespoons either canning or sea salt
- 3-5 gallon crock, a plate that fits inside the crock, and something to weight the plate down

This recipe was given to me verbally by my sister-in-law as how she remembered her mom made it.

1. Core the cabbage, slice very thinly (if you have a Mandoline, that would be perfect). I've heard some folks use a food processor with flat blade.

2. Layer the cabbage alternately with the salt. Work it up with your hands to get the salt thoroughly incorporated into the cabbage. Tamp the cabbage down tightly, finally pressing down with the plate and holding it down with whatever weight you decide to use. The object is to get the cabbage to "stew" in its own juices. Place in a cool and dry location for 3-6 weeks and cover it with a kitchen towel (you need to check it daily, removing any bloom. Gas bubbles are okay as that indicates fermentation.

3. At the end of the fermentation period, skim off any bloom or stuff that looks spoiled. Place finished sauerkraut in canning jars. Anna Mae completed the process by canning them so they'd last for a while. If you plan to use it immediately, you're able to skip that part. Canning will kill of any bacteria but allow you to keep it much longer.

Asparagus Upkari *(Dry vegetable side dish)*

Rita Mathew

1. Prepare the Kari Leaf Seasoning in a heavy bottom pan. When done, stir fry the pieces of asparagus for 2 minutes.

2. Add salt and water to the pan, cover and cook on low for 10 minutes. Sprinkle fresh grated coconut as garnish. Serve hot.

VARIATIONS OF UPKARI
Equivalent substitute for 3 cups of Asparagus
- 1 lb Bottle Gourd [Calabash]
(trim ends, peel, remove seeds and fibrous pulp, cube into 1-inch pieces)
- 1 lb Carrots (trim ends, peel and grate)
- 1 lb cut Green Beans (cut in ½ inch pieces)
- 1 lb Okra (trim ends, cut in ½ inch pieces)
- 1 large Plantain (Raw) (trim ends, lightly peel skin, cut into 1-inch by ¼ inch pieces)
- 1 lb Sweet Potato (peel and cut into ½ inch cubes), pictured here.
- 1 lb Turnip (trim ends, peel and grate)
- 1 lb Zucchini (julienne into 1-inch long pieces)

Upkari is the simplest side dish in the line-up of possible partners to rice, which is the main dish in the South Indian cuisine. The starting point for its preparation is the Kari Leaf seasoning. To this is added a vegetable, which may be cut, julienne, or cubed.

Ingredients

- 3 cups Asparagus (1 lb. wash, trim ends and cut in ½ inch pieces)
- 1 tsp salt
- 2 Tbsp fresh grated coconut for garnish
- 1 Tbsp water
- Kari Leaf Seasoning (see recipe on page 36)

NUTRITIONAL PROPERTIES
High in fiber, turnips may help to reduce inflammation of the colon as well as the risk of diverticulosis. Research has shown that, thanks to the compound sulforaphane, those who consume high amounts of cruciferous vegetables have a lowered risk of developing cancer.

Avocado and Guava salad à la Rémy

Rita Mathew

Ingredients

- 1 firm California Avocado
- 1 ripe Guava
- 1 ripe Mango
- 1 stick celery (chopped)
- 1 tomato cut into wedges
- ½ cup cooked garbanzo beans
- 1 tsp lemon juice
- 1 tsp chopped cilantro
- ½ tsp black pepper (optional)
- 1 tsp chaat masala (available in Asian food market)

1. Peel and slice the avocado and mango.

2. Slice the Guava.

3. Place the sliced fruits and vegetables in a bowl.

4. Add the remaining ingredients and toss gently before serving.

Bacon, Egg, and Cheddar Bites

Pam Tidwell

Ingredients

- 1 tsp olive oil
- 2 cups coarsely chopped fresh spinach
- 2 slices cooked bacon, chopped (can use turkey bacon for less calories)
- 3 large eggs
- 3 Tbsp low-fat milk
- Dash salt
- Dash ground black pepper
- 6 Tbsp shredded white or sharp cheddar cheese

1. Heat oven to 350°F. Thoroughly grease (or use cupcake liners) 6 regular-size muffin cups.

2. Heat oil in 8-inch non-stick skillet over medium heat, add spinach. Cook and stir about 1 minute, or until spinach is wilted. Remove from heat and add the chopped bacon.

3. In a small bowl, whisk together eggs, milk, salt, and pepper. Stir in the spinach and cheese. Divide the mixture among the muffin cups.

4. Bake 18-22 minutes or until the egg bites are puffed and the tops and centers are set. Let cool 5 minutes, then loosen and remove from cups. Serve warm.

Baked Spinach

Rosemary Stancil

Ingredients

- 2 (10 ounce) boxes frozen chopped spinach
- 2 large eggs
- ⅔ cup whole milk
- 1 (15 ounce can) sliced mushrooms, drained
- 2 cups grated sharp Cheddar cheese, divided
- Salt, pepper, nutmeg, and hot sauce to taste

1. Preheat oven to 350°F.

2. Thaw spinach. Place spinach in a colander and press out liquid. Beat eggs and milk together.

3. Combine spinach, egg/milk mixture, mushrooms, 1 ½ cup cheese, salt, pepper, nutmeg and hot sauce to taste. Spread mixture in a greased 2-quart casserole dish, and sprinkle reserved ½ cup cheese on top. Bake uncovered 30-35 minutes.

Banana Pudding

Linda Tedrow

Ingredients

- ¾ cup sugar
- 2 Tbsp flour
- ¼ tsp salt
- 2 cups milk
- 3 eggs, separated
- 1 tsp vanilla
- 6 ripe bananas, sliced
- Vanilla wafers

1. Combine sugar, flour, and salt in top of a double boiler, stir in milk. Cook over boiling water, stirring until thick.

2. Beat egg yolks and gradually stir into hot mixture. Return to boiler, cook 5 minutes stirring constantly. Remove from heat, add vanilla.

3. Line a 1-quart casserole with wafer, bananas, and the custard mixture, ending with custard.

4. Beat egg whites stiff, but not dry. Add ¼ cup sugar and beat until forms stiff peaks. Pile on top of the pudding.

5. Bake at 425°F for 5 minutes.

Broccoli Salad

Christi Heston

Ingredients

- 1 bunch broccoli, chopped
- ⅓ cup sunflower seeds
- 1 cup mayonnaise
- ¼ cup sugar or honey
- ⅓ cup golden raisins
- 1 small red onion, finely chopped
- 2 Tbsp red wine vinegar
- ½ lb. bacon, crisp and crumbled

1. Mix all the ingredients together in a large bowl. Let stand in the fridge 1 – 2 hours before serving.

Cajun Cabbage

Pam Tidwell

Ingredients

- 1 ½ - 2 pounds ground beef
- 1 large onion, chopped
- 1 bell pepper, chopped
- ½ - 1 Tbsp hot sauce, depending on taste
- 1 15 oz can whole kernel corn
- 2 14.5 oz cans diced tomatoes
- 1 pound smoked sausage, cut into pieces
- 1 medium head cabbage, roughly cut up.

1. In a large sautée pan, brown ground beef. You can drain or leave drippings. Add everything else and cook until cabbage is done.

Chicken Stew

Suzanne Keifer

Ingredients

- 2 cups baby carrots
- 1 8-ounce package sliced mushrooms
- 1 small onion, chopped
- 8 chicken thighs
- 1 cup chicken broth/stock
- 3 Tbsp cornstarch
- 1 tsp dried tarragon
- ½ cup heavy cream
- 1 tsp salt
- ½ tsp pepper

1. In a slow cooker, place vegetables on the bottom. Then chicken. Mix broth/stock, cornstarch, tarragon, salt and pepper and pour over the chicken. Cover and cook on low 8-10 hours or 4-5 hours on high.

2. With a slotted spoon, remove the chicken and veggies, skim off fat. Stir in cream and serve. This goes really well over boiled Yukon Gold or Red Creamer potatoes.

Serves 4.

Notes

Claire Clements' Quick Black Bean Soup

Claire Clements

This is one of those recipes that you can put together in 5 minutes. Yet it always is a favorite with everyone. Even kids like it- and vegetable haters too; although you may want to use a bit less hot sauce for those people.

Preparation time: 5 minutes
Cooking Time 10 minutes
Servings 2-4

1. Reserve 1 cup of the beans in a separate bowl, place the remaining beans, the vegetable broth and the salsa in a blender jar. Process until fairly smooth, then pour into a saucepan.

2. Mash the reserved beans slightly with a fork or bean/potato masher. Add to the saucepan with the remaining ingredients. Cook over-medium heat for 10 minutes to blend flavors. Adjust seasonings to taste before serving.

Hints: This is great to make ahead of time and then heat just before serving.

Add: green onions, vegan sour cream, croutons. Your choices. I double and triple this recipe and have it for a couple of days.

Ingredients

- 3 15-ounce cans black beans drained and rinsed
- 1 ¾ cups vegetable broth
- 1 cup fresh salsa
- ¼ teaspoon ground oregano
- ¼ teaspoon chilli powder
- ⅛ teaspoon smoked chipotle chilli powder (optional).
- Several dashes hot sauce (optional)

Dumpling Soup

Rosemary Stancil

Ingredients

- 2 (32-oz) containers chicken broth
- 1 Tbsp grated fresh ginger
- 2 (10-oz) packages frozen pot stickers, including sauce packet, if one
- 1 carrot, coarsely grated
- 6 green onions including the white part and about 3" of the green part, diagonally sliced
- ½ tsp (or more, according to taste) soy sauce

1. Bring broth, ginger, and pot sticker sauce packet(s) to boil. Add pot stickers, carrot, green onions, additional vegetables, if using, and soy sauce and simmer 8-10 minutes.

• For a starter soup, use fewer vegetables. For a heartier soup, add more vegetables.

Variation: Italian Tortellini Soup:
Make the dumpling soup, substituting tortellini for pot stickers, and Italian seasonings (oregano, basil, garlic) for the ginger. Add 1 (15-oz) can diced tomatoes with liquid.
Substitute additional vegetables of choice such as baby spinach, kale, chard, or zucchini. To serve, sprinkle with grated Parmesan cheese.

• Additional vegetables if desired: finely shredded cabbage, slivered red peppers, sliced mushrooms

Easy Potato Salad

Suzanne Keifer

Ingredients

- 14 small red potatoes (about 2 ½ lbs), scrubbed well
- 6 slices crumbled, crisp bacon (can omit if desired)
- 6 hard-boiled eggs, roughly chopped
- ⅓ cup finely chopped red onion
- ⅓ cup finely chopped celery (about 1 rib)
- 1 cup ranch dressing
- 2 Tbsp chopped Italian parsley
- 1 tsp salt
- ½ tsp freshly ground black pepper

1. Place the potatoes in a saucepan and add enough water to cover them by about 1". Bring to a boil over high heat and cook until they are just tender (about 15-20 minutes). Drain and let them cool. Cut the potatoes into ½ or ¼, depending on their size. (Should be bite-sized).

2. Combine the potatoes with the remaining ingredients and toss gently to combine. Refrigerate until ready to serve.

Festive Ivy Gourd (Tindori) Upkari

Rita Mathew

1. Wash and trim the Tindori. Cut length-wise in quarters and put the pieces in a bowl of cold water for 10 minutes. Drain the water, and steam cook with the turmeric, salt and water for 10 minutes.

2. Prepare the Kari Leaf Seasoning in a medium pan. If using urid dal, add it to the Kari Leaf Seasoning and stir for a minute. When done, put the cooked tindori and cashew nuts in the pan. Stir well, cover and cook on low heat for 5 minutes.

3. Mix in the fresh coconut before serving.

Ingredients

- 3 cups Tindori (1 lb.) Wash, trim ends and cut in ½ inch pieces.
- ½ tsp turmeric
- 1 tsp salt
- 3 Tbsp water
- 1 cup raw cashew nuts
- 1 tsp roasted urid dal (optional)
- Kari Leaf Seasoning (see recipe on page 36)
- 2 Tbsp fresh grated coconut

Coccinia grandis, the ivy gourd, belongs to the family Cucurbitaceae, its common names are Tindori, Kovakka, and Gourde Écarlate De L´Inde Tindola in French. The leaves of the plant are edible, and have medicinal value in reducing diabetes and obesity. Cashew nuts being expensive are used in a dish which is prepared for the annual Harvest Festival, New Year's festival, and even for the marriage feast.

Fruit Pizza Pie

Pam Tidwell

Ingredients

- 1 (8-oz) package cream cheese
- ½ tsp vanilla
- ½ cup sugar
- 1 small can mandarin oranges
- 2 kiwi fruit
- 2 bananas
- 1 (8-10 oz) package fresh strawberries
- 2-3 Tbsp peach preserves
- 1 package sugar cookies, from grocer dairy case

1. Slice and pat cookie dough to fit your pan and bake at 300°F until golden brown. Let cool. Mix cream cheese, sugar, and vanilla, spread evenly over the cooled crust.

2. Slice strawberries (reserving 1 whole one), bananas, and kiwi. Arrange strawberries, bananas, and then kiwi on mixture. Place a strawberry in the center and the mandarin oranges around it. Mix peach preserves with small amount of water and make a glaze. Spread on top of the fruit.

3. Keep as cool as possible and eat as soon as possible so the crust does not get soggy from the fruit.

Garlic Shrimp Asparagus Over Rice

Jackie Zogran

Ingredients

- 1 lb. uncooked extra-large shrimp – peeled and deveined
- Salt and Pepper to taste
- ¼ tsp. red pepper flakes
- 1 tsp onion powder
- 3 Tbsp ghee butter or olive oil
- 2 cups mushrooms sliced
- 1 bunch of asparagus – ends trimmed and cut in half
- 1 Tbsp fresh parsley chopped (optional)
- White or Brown Rice (follow cooking instructions for the rice)

1. In a bowl, add the shrimp, salt, pepper, red pepper flakes, and onion powder. Mix everything well.

2. In a skillet add 1 Tbsp ghee or olive oil over medium heat. Add the garlic and sauté for 30 seconds. Add the shrimp and sauté for about 4 minutes or until the shrimp are cooked through. Be careful not to overcook them. Set aside.

3. In the same skillet, add 1 Tbsp olive oil or ghee and the mushrooms. Sauté for 5 minutes. Then add the asparagus and cook until it is tender. Stir occasionally.

4. Return the shrimp to the skillet and mix everything well to combine. Garnish with fresh parsley and serve over rice. Enjoy!

Goat Cheese Quiche

Suzanne Keifer

1. Lightly grease an 8" loose-bottom tart pan (I used a 9" pie pan and it worked fine). Roll the pastry out to about 1/8" thick and large enough to fit the pie or tart pan and enough left to crimp. Prick the bottom with a fork and chill for 30 minutes to prevent the pastry from shrinking during baking.

2. Meanwhile, make the filling. Pour the cream into a saucepan, add 2/3 of the goat cheese and all the thyme and warm over a low heat for 3-5 minutes, whisking until smooth and silky. Remove from the heat and leave to cool while you make the rest of the filling.

3. Heat a fry pan over medium heat. Add the butter, oil and onion and fry for 5 minutes, stirring occasionally, until softened but not brown. Add the artichokes and carrot, mix well, and cook for 5 minutes until softened, then add the spinach and cook for another 2 minutes until wilted. Tip out onto paper towels and press dry.

4. Add the eggs and nutmeg to the cooled cream mixture, season with salt and pepper, then whisk to combine.

5. Heat the oven to 325°F. Line the pastry bottom with parchment paper and cover with baking beads. (If you don't have these, you can use a small oven-proof plate, ramekin, etc). Bake the pastry for 12 minutes and then remove.

6. Turn the oven up to 350°. Brush the bottom of the pastry with the balsamic reduction. Spoon the vegetable mixture over the bottom of the pastry and put small dollops of the remaining goat cheese over the vegetables. Pour in the egg mixture and bake for 35 minutes, or until firm to the touch.

Pictured on Back Cover

Ingredients

- ½ oz unsalted butter
- 9 oz. Savory Short Pastry (recipe to follow or you can use a 9" pre-made pie crust)
- 7 oz. heavy cream
- 3 ½ oz soft goat cheese
- 2 long thyme sprigs
- 2 Tbsp good olive oil
- 1 medium onion, finely chopped
- 2 ½ oz drained bottle artichokes, thinly sliced
- 2 ½ oz carrot, peeled and finely diced
- 3 oz baby spinach, stems removed and coarsely torn or chopped
- 2 eggs, lightly beaten
- ¼ tsp freshly grated nutmeg
- 1 Tbsp reduced balsamic vinegar (recipe to follow)
- Sea salt and freshly ground black pepper

Suzanne Keifer

Balsamic Reduction

1. Put ¾ - 1 cup of good balsamic vinegar in a small pan and bring to a boil. Immediately reduce heat to simmer and allow to cook 10-12 minutes. Remove from heat. It will continue to thicken as it cools

Savory Pastry

- 4 ½ oz butter, diced (approximately 9 tbsp)
- 2 cups plain flour
- Pinch of salt if you used unsalted butter
- 1 egg yolk
- 3 Tbsp milk or water (You can use the last oz of the heavy cream and add 1 tbsp water)

1. Put butter, flour and salt in a bowl and mix with hands until crumbly. Add egg yolk and milk and continue to work the dough until the texture is smooth. On a lightly floured surface, knead for 1-2 minutes until texture is silky smooth. Wrap in a clean cotton towel and refrigerate 2 hours prior to use.

Granny's 7 Up Cake

Donna Yates

Ingredients

For the cake:
- 1 box lemon cake mix
- 1 4-serving size box of instant lemon pudding mix
- 1 bottle (10 oz) 7 Up soda
- ¾ cup cooking oil
- 4 eggs separated

For the Filling/Icing:
- 1 cup evaporated milk
- 1 cup granulated sugar
- 3 egg yolks
- 1 stick butter
- 1 tsp vanilla
- 1 small can crushed pineapple drained
- 1 ½-2 cups shredded coconut

1. Preheat the oven to 350 degrees. Grease and flour 3- 8" round cake pans set aside.

2. Combine the cake mix , instant lemon pudding mix, 7 up, cooking oil, and egg yolks in a medium mixing bowl. Beat the mixture for 2 minutes.

3. In a separate bowl beat the egg whites until stiff and gently fold into cake mixture.

4. Pour into the prepared cake pans and bake 30 to 35 min until a wooden toothpick inserted in the center comes out clean. Cool in the pan for a couple of minutes. Remove from the pan and cool completely on wire racks.

Filling/Icing:

1. In a medium saucepan combine the butter, evaporated milk, granulated sugar, and egg yolks.
2. Cook over medium heat stirring frequently for 10 to 12 minutes until thickened. Remove from the heat and add the vanilla, crushed pineapple, and coconut.

3. Place one cooled layer cake layer on serving plate and top with one-third of the filling. Top filling with the second cake layer. Add the last layer to the top and top it with the last third of the filling.

Greek Pasta Salad

Rosemary Stancil

Ingredients

- 1-pound orzo
- ⅓ cup olive oil
- 3 tablespoons lemon juice
- 2 tablespoons Cavender's Greek Seasoning
- ⅓ cup sliced kalamata olives or 1 (4 ½ ounce) can sliced black olives, drained
- 1 (4 ½ ounce) jar diced pimentos, drained
- 5 green onions including the bottom half of the green tops, sliced
- Salt and black pepper to taste

For a light meal, add one pound of cooked shrimp or cooked chicken pieces before refrigerating overnight. Serve on a bed of lettuce.

Yield: 4-6 servings

1. Cook pasta according to package directions. Drain.

2. Add to the pasta olive oil, lemon juice, Greek seasoning, olives, pimentos, and green onions. Stir together. Season with salt and pepper.

3. Refrigerate overnight. The flavor is better after the next day.

Harry's Southern Style Collards

Harry Keifer with special help from our good friend Stella Sykes

Ingredients

- 2 sweet onions, finely chopped
- 2 smoked ham hocks
- 1 small head cabbage, coarsely chopped
- 4 cloves garlic, finely chopped
- 3 – 32-ounce chicken stock or broth
- 3 lbs collards, trimmed and chopped
- ⅓ cup apple cider vinegar
- 2 Tbsp white sugar
- 1 ½ tsp salt
- ¾ tsp freshly ground black pepper

1. Combine the onions, ham hocks and garlic in a stockpot; add the chicken stock/broth. Cook this mixture over medium heat until the meat falls off the bone. (About 2 hours).

2. Remove the bones from the stock mixture. Stir in collards, cabbage, vinegar, salt, sugar, and pepper and cook another 2 hours. All done!

Hearty Vegetable Lasagna

Linda Tedrow

Ingredients

- 1 – 16oz package lasagna noodles
- 1-pound fresh sliced baby bella (or cremini) mushrooms
- ¾ cup chopped green bell pepper
- ¾ cup chopped onion
- 3 cloves garlic, minced
- 2 Tbsp vegetable oil
- 2 (26-oz) jars pasta sauce
- 1 tsp dried basil
- 1 (15-oz) container part-skim ricotta cheese
- 4 cups shredded Mozzarella cheese
- 2 eggs
- ½ - ¾ cup Parmesan cheese

1. Cook the lasagna according to package directions, until al dente (about 10 minutes). Rinse with cold water and drain well. To preserve the shape of the noodle, lay them on a piece of parchment paper.

2. In a large saucepan, cook and stir mushrooms, green peppers, onion, and garlic in the oil. Stir in the pasta sauce and basil, bring to a boil. Reduce heat and simmer about 15 minutes.

3. Mix the ricotta, 2 cups of the mozzarella, and the eggs.

4. Preheat the oven to 350°F. Spread 1 cup of the pasta sauce in the bottom of a 9x13" baking dish. Layer ½ each the lasagna noodles, ricotta mixture, sauce, and Parmesan cheese. Repeat layering and top with the remaining 2 cups of mozzarella cheese.

5. Bake, uncovered, for 40 minutes and let stand 15 minutes before serving. This can also be layered in a slow cooker and cook on low for 4-5 hours.

Herbed Spinach and Rice

Virginia McClelland's friend Shelly

Ingredients

- 1 10-oz package frozen spinach, thawed
- 1 cup cooked brown rice
- 1 cup shredded sharp cheddar cheese
- 2 slightly beaten eggs
- 2 Tbsp margarine
- ⅓ cup milk
- 2 Tbsp chopped onion
- ½ tsp Worcestershire sauce
- 1 tsp salt
- ¼ tsp rosemary

1. Pour the above mixture into a large casserole or baking dish.

2. Bake at 350°F for 20-25 minutes or until a knife inserted in the center comes out clean. This can be mixed ahead of time and baked later.

Hot Chili Crackers

Candi Hoard

Ingredients

- 12 to 14 oz of peanut oil
- 1 Tbsp garlic powder
- 1 Tbsp onion powder
- 1 Tbsp Cayenne
- 3 Tbsp crushed red pepper flakes

These crackers are amazing with a big bowl of chili, pimento cheese, or plain.

1. Put 4 to 6 sleeves saltine crackers in a large container or a large zip-loc bag.

2. Mix the oil and spices together in a small mixing bowl.

3. Pour this mixture over the crackers. Turn the container over every 30 minutes for 2 to 3 hours.

Huancaina Sauce

Allan Cobb

Ingredients

- ½ cup vegetable oil
- 9 oz yellow chilis -- seeded, white insides removed, cut into halves
- ¼ red onion -- chopped
- 2 cloves garlic
- 1 ¾ cups(14 fl oz) evaporated milk
- 4 ½ oz queso fresco
- 4 saltine crackers

Classic Peruvian sauce for pastas and appetizers.

1. Heat the oil in a skillet over high heat, add the chili halves, onion, garlic and cook, stirring for 7 minutes, until softened. Place in a blender and add the evaporated milk, queso fresco, and crackers. Salt to taste and blend until smooth. Refrigerate.

Kari Leaf Seasoning

Rita Mathew

Ingredients

- 1 sprig of Kari leaf (10-12 leaves)
- 3 Tbsp oil
- 1 tsp mustard seed
- 1 dry red chilli (broken into quarters)
- ⅛ tsp asafoetida (available in Asian fresh vegetable markets)

1. Add the oil to a moderately hot, medium heavy-bottom pan.

2. When the oil has heated sufficiently, put the mustard seeds in the pan, and cover with a transparent lid. When the seeds begin to pop, add the red chilli pieces and stir briskly for a minute.

3. Add asafoetida and Kari leaves only after the chilli is cooked, making sure the ingredients don't burn.

Use as directed in the recipes for Upkari, Sukké, Saglé and Kalvan.

Kari Leaf Chutney (Dry)

Rita Mathew

Ingredients

- 4 oz Kari leaves (remove from stems)
- 3 Tbsp oil
- 1 cup roasted ground peanuts
- 2 tsp red chilli powder
- 1 tsp turmeric
- 1 Tbsp salt

1. Add the oil to a moderately hot, large heavy bottom pan.

2. Add the ground peanuts, chilli powder and turmeric. Stir for 5 minutes. Remove from fire and blend in a food process.

3. Cool completely and store in air tight containers.

Mango Mousse

Rita Mathew

Ingredients

- 1 cup Mango pulp
- 1 cup Cool Whip
- 3 Tbsp Pineapple Walnut cream cheese (softened)
- 3 Tbsp sugar (optional)
- 1 envelope unflavored gelatin (optional)
- 6 Shortcake shells

Toppings:
- 3 Tbsp Strawberries
- 2 Tbsp Blueberries,
- Sliced Kiwi
- 3 pieces halved Jackfruit (optional)

1. Mix gelatin in 1 cup boiling water until dissolved (optional for vegetarians).

2. Whisk to a smooth consistency all the ingredients, either by hand or in a blender. Pour in a bowl and chill for a few hours in a refrigerator.

Optional: Scoop 1 Tbsp into Shortcake shell. Decorate with fruit toppings.

Pictured on Back Cover with Jackfruit Topping.

Onion Pie

Allan Cobb

Ingredients

- 6-8 medium onions
- 2 tablespoons vegetable oil
- 6 large eggs
- 1 cup soft breadcrumbs
- ½ cup grated parmesan cheese
- ½ cup minced fresh parsley

This is a great way to use your abundant onion harvest!

1. Preheat oven to 350. In a large skillet, sauté the onions until soft, but not brown. Drain well.

2. In a large bowl, beat eggs, stir in the breadcrumbs, cheese, parsley and sautéed onions. Pour in a greased 10 in pie plate.

3. Bake for 30 - 45 minutes. Test with a knife, comes out clean when done.

Pasta Primavera

Compliments of Feliciano Bernal, Executive Chef Sprig Restaurant, Decatur, Ga

Ingredients

- 1 cup basil pesto (Chef makes his from scratch; I use an 8 oz jar of Classico Pesto)
- 8 oz. cherry tomatoes, cut in ½
- 8 oz. sliced mushrooms
- 1 cup spring peas
- Shredded Parmesan to garnish
- 2 lbs spinach fettucine
- 2 grilled chicken breasts (optional)

1. Prepare fettucine according to package directions. While the pasta is cooking, sauté mushrooms 2-3 minutes in a small amount of good olive oil in a large frying pan, add peas and tomatoes and sauté another couple of minutes.

2. Once pasta is cooked, drain, and add to the vegetables. Pour the pesto on top, toss gently to mix. Serve in pasta bowls and garnish with the shredded Parmesan. If desired, you can cut the chicken breast in strips and place on top.

This recipe is a great way to use up vegetable you have in the fridge and you can add just about any vegetable – broccoli, squash, bell peppers, onions, etc. Be creative!

Pasta Salad

Pam Tidwell

Ingredients

- 16 – oz box tri-color corkscrew or bowtie pasta
- 1 – 2 packets dry ranch-style dressing
- Assorted veggies – squash, broccoli, carrots, peppers, mushrooms, olives, tomatoes to equal about 4 cups of vegetables.
- 1 Tbsp mayonnaise
- Parmesan cheese to taste
- 1 – 2 dashes Hot sauce
- ¾ cup Italian dressing, or enough to marinate all ingredients until well coated.

1. Microwave squash, broccoli, carrots, peppers, and mushrooms for 30 – 60 seconds. Cook pasta according to package directions until al dente and drain. Add the mayonnaise and dry ranch dressing to the pasta and mix well.

2. Add the assorted vegetable and stir to combine. Sprinkle with Parmesan cheese and a couple of dashes of hot sauce. Add the Italian dressing and stir until well-blended. Add the tomatoes and toss at the last minute.

Note: The amount of vegetables will dictate how much Italian dressing is used.

Pickled Eggs

Sylvia Dawes

Ingredients

- Eggs 1 or 2 dozen
- 14.5 oz. can Beets, undrained
- 1 to 2 cups White Vinegar
- Large Onion thinly sliced
- 1 Tbsp Whole Cloves
- 1 Tbsp Salt and ½ Tbsp Pepper (Optional)

1. Place eggs in a pot with cold tap water. Add about 1/2 cup salt to the pot and bring to a full boil for 5 minutes. Remove from heat and let eggs sit for 20 to 30 minutes. Drain water, peel eggs and let them sit in the pot filled with cold water.

2. Mix: Beets, onion, cloves, vinegar, salt and pepper, peeled eggs.

3. Let sit in the liquid overnight or up to 3 days.

Serving idea: Lay fresh lettuce leaves on a platter. Slice pickled eggs and onion slices on top of green leaves. You may dress the platter with thinly sliced carrots and pickles. Voilà!

Quick Pea and Kale Pesto

Greg and Laura Killmaster

1. Rinse and cut both sides off stem of kale. Stack kale and roll up into a log shape. Cut fine slices starting at one end of the roll so it looks like cut tobacco. Cut remaining strips in half or thirds.

2. Cut onion in paper thin rings, then cut the rings in half (if they are thin enough, the taste isn't overwhelming when raw). Another option is to lightly sauté the onion in olive oil.

3. Cook pasta according to package directions and set colander in sink ready to drain. Spread Kale around evenly in bottom of colander. Once pasta is cooked, pour over kale in colander to drain pasta and wilt kale. Once steam has left the pasta and it is drained fully, put content of colander in large mixing bowl.

4. Mix in pesto and stir to evenly distribute kale and sauce.

5. Put pasta on a plate and generously grate parmesan over the pasta. Layer remainder of ingredients on top for each serving - onions, then sprouts, then olives and peas on top. Freshly squeeze 1/4 lemon on top evenly.

6. Salt and pepper to taste.

Ingredients

- 1 lb. shell pasta (or any pasta for that matter)
- ½-1 cup pesto depending on what you prefer (we use a cashew pesto but any good quality version will be fine)
- 1 thin sliced medium onion
- ⅓ jar pitted Castelvetrano (or other green olives)
- 3 large leaves kale with stems removed (collards can be used in place of the kale)
- Half bag frozen organic peas thawed
- Olive oil
- Parmesan cheese
- 1 lemon cut into quarters
- Broccoli sprouts
- Salt and pepper

Rémy La Madeleine

Rita Mathew

Rita Mathew

Ingredients

- 1 cup Strawberries
- 1 cup Blueberries
- 1 cup Raspberries
- 1 bright orange, ripe Persimmon
- ½ cup roasted Pistachio
- ½ cup heavy cream
- 1 Tbsp sugar
- 4 Cinnamon Graham crackers (each 2in)
- 4 Dessert Bowls (4 oz)
- Fresh mint and Hershey's kisses for garnish

Makes 4 Servings

1. Rinse all the fruits. Peel the Persimmons. The inside of a ripe persimmon will be bright orange/red in color. Hull and cut into 1/8 th inch pieces both the strawberries and persimmon. Mix all the fruit and chill. Coarsely chop the pistachios. Whip the heavy cream until it starts to thicken and add sugar.

2. Place the crackers in each desert bowl. Spoon the cream mixture over the crackers, saving 4 tsps for topping. Spoon the fruit mixture and nuts. Garnish with cream, mint and Hershey's kiss.

"Hydrangeas with Butterfly"
©2021 **Emma Traynor**

Rustic Caramelized Beets

Isaac Swier

Prep time 15-20 min – Cook time 30 – 45 minutes

1. Scrub and peel beets. Remove greens and chop coarsely, set aside. Slice beets into ¼ inch rounds.

2. In a large sauté pan, melt butter and sauté dice shallots.

3. Add beet rounds to shallot/butter mixture. Crack pepper over beets and toss in a pinch of salt, to taste (as well as other herbs as preferred).

4. Turn beets to ensure even cooking, ensure caramelization and golden-brown edges.

5. As beets begin to glaze and become tender, reduce heat add chopped greens. Sauté for about 5 minutes, or until greens begin to wilt.

6. Add wine and allow simmering and reducing until most liquid has cooked off.

Ingredients

- 4-6 beets red and/or golden with greens (or substitute Swiss chard)
- 1 large shallot, diced
- 3 tablespoons butter
- Salt and pepper to taste – and other herbs to pair if used as a side
- ¼ to ½ cup sweet white wine
- Optional : preferred soft cheese, Bucheron, feta, etc.
- Optional: warm, crusty French style bread

I've found this recipe can often turn beet haters into – if not lovers – appreciators. Your choice of a sweet white wine will help bring out the delicious fruity notes often overlooked in fresh beets. If you're looking for a heavier, more robust flavor, feel free to substitute the white wine for a red, and deglaze with balsamic vinegar, and add some fresh parsley to your greens to really make them pop with flavor. While my preferred course includes a warm bread spread with a soft cheese, this recipe can also be adapted in so many ways: substituting olive oil for butter, with walnuts, orange zest, and a splash of cider vinegar – the beets become an amazing centerpiece on top of an arugula salad. With mustard seed (or Dijon), garlic, horseradish, coriander, parsley, and vinegar, it becomes a wonderful and pungent side for many Slavic dishes. The list is a long as your imagination is broad.

Salami Mixed Vegetables

Rela Alice Jacob

Ingredients

- 1 cup broccoli florets
- ½ cup torn lettuce pieces
- 1 zucchini
- 1 large capsicum (green pepper)
- 8-10 salami slices
- 3 Tbsp fresh cream
- 1 ½ Tbsp soy sauce
- ½ Tbsp butter
- 1 tsp Chili flakes
- Salt and Pepper to taste

This is an easy to cook salad/side dish which can be quickly made with whatever is available in the kitchen.

1. Heat the butter in a pan and add the capsicum and heat for 5 minutes. To this add zucchini and the broccoli. Sauté the mixture until semi done and add the fresh cream. Heat the mixture until the cream thickens and gets bound to the veggies. Add salt and pepper to taste. To this add the fresh lettuce leaves and salami and sauté the mixture until almost cooked. Then add the soy sauce and mix again on low flame. Take the pan off the flame and add the chili flakes on top for flavor and enjoy the dish!

Salsa

Eva Stalnaker

Ingredients

- 32 oz. Canned Petite Diced tomatoes
- 1/2 c diced onion, red or sweet
- 1 bunch chopped cilantro
- 2 Poblano chilies, roasted and peeled
- 2 Anaheim chilis, roasted and peeled
- 1 Jalapeño chili, roasted and peeled
- 5 Tomatillos, roasted
- 5 Cloves garlic, roasted
- 1 or 2 limes (use your preferred amount)
- Salt to taste

1. Roast the chilies and tomatillos until dark all over. Place the peppers in a plastic bag for 15 minutes to steam. Peel and remove seeds. Wrap unpeeled garlic cloves in foil and roast along with peppers and tomatillos.

2. Put tomatillos, tomatoes, peppers, cilantro and the garlic in a blender and puree. Finely dice the onions and stir in. Squeeze in the lime juice and salt to taste.

Salsa Verde

Allan Cobb

Ingredients

- 2 pounds green tomatillos - peeled, washed and quartered
- 1 whole head of garlic
- 1 large bunch of cilantro
- 2 oz olive oil
- The juice of 1 small lime
- Salt
- Ground Black pepper

A great use for wilting cilantro and a reason to grow tomatillos!

1. Preheat oven to 375. Roast tomatillos and entire head of garlic for 25 - 30 minutes.

2. Next, combine all ingredients in a blender, cutting the top off the garlic, you can squeeze out the roasted insides. Blend until desired consistency.

Snake Gourd Upkari

Rita Mathew

Ingredients

- 3 cups cubed Snake Gourd
- ½ cup cooked whole black Chana dal, or sprouted Mung bean, or black-eyed beans
- ½ tsp turmeric
- ¼ tsp jaggery (unrefined brown sugar)
- 1 tsp salt
- 3 Tbsp water
- 2 Tbsp fresh grated coconut
- Kari Leaf Seasoning (see recipe on page 36)

1. Trim ends, and lightly scrape the skin. Scoop out the seeds and fibrous pulp, if any, before cutting in 1-inch cubes. It does not have to be pre-cooked like the Ivy Gourd.

2. See page 137 for a description on how to sprout mung beans and cook black Chana.

3. In a medium pan, prepare the Kari Leaf Seasoning. Add the cut gourd, beans, and remaining ingredients to the seasoning. Stir well and add the water. Cover and cook for 10 minutes on low heat.

4. Serve with rice and dal.

According to seed morphologist Wolfgang Stuppy of Kew's Millenium Seed Bank, *Tricosanthes cucumerina*, or Snake Gourd, is far more curious than its seeds. Part of the Cucurbitaceae family, snake gourd must be picked when it is firm, dark green with white stripes - that is before it ripens. It can be stuffed, baked, pickled or stir-fried.

Spicy Okra

Ingredients

- 1 pound fresh okra
- 1 Tbsp vegetable oil
- 1 medium onion, coarsely chopped
- 1 pound tomatoes, chopped (about 3 medium tomatoes)
- 1 jalapeño pepper (or habanero chile), pierced 3 times with a fork
- ½ tsp salt
- ¼ tsp black pepper

1. Slice rinsed okra crosswise, cut into ½" to 1" slices.

2. Heat oil in a heavy skillet, over moderately high heat. Sauté onion for about 3 minutes. Add tomatoes (including juice) and chile and bring to a boil. Stir the mixture for 8 minutes. Add okra and cook, gently stirring until okra is tender, about 5 minutes.

3. Stir in salt and pepper, discard the chile.

Spinach Salad

Suzanne Keifer

Ingredients

- 3 Tbsp diced red onion
- ½ cup white sugar
- ¾ tsp ground black pepper
- ¼ tsp celery salt
- 2 ¼ tsp ground mustard
- ¾ cup vegetable oil
- ¼ cup white wine vinegar
- 3 eggs
- 10 oz. fresh spinach, coarsely chopped
- ¾ head lettuce
- 6 oz crumbled cooked bacon
- 1 ¼ cup croutons
½ cup of red onion, cut into rings

1. Boil eggs. Once hard, peel and chop.

2. In a saucepan, combine the diced onion, sugar, black pepper, celery salt, mustard, oil, and vinegar.

3. Whisk over high heat until the onions are translucent. Remove from heat and refrigerate until cool.

4. In a large bowl, combine the spinach, lettuce, eggs, bacon, croutons, and onion rings. Toss gently.

5. Pour the dressing over the top of the salad and toss to coat evenly.

Spinach Quiche

Pam Tidwell

Crust

- 2 cups flour
- 2 cups shredded sharp cheddar cheese
- 1 ½ cup finely chopped pecans
- 1 tsp salt
- ½ tsp paprika
- ⅔ cup oil

1. Mix all ingredients and set aside ¼ of it. Press the remainder in the bottom of a 13x9" baking dish and prick with a fork. Bake 10 minutes at 350°F. Cool slightly.

1. Heat oven to 375°F.

2. Mix filling ingredients and pour into the baking dish. Sprinkle reserved crust mixture on top and top that with the pecans.

3. Bake for 1 hour and 10 minutes. Make sure filling is not gooey. If you halve the recipe, you can make it in a deep-dish pie pan or a square baking dish.

Ingredients

For the Filling:
- 20 oz. frozen chopped spinach, cooked and well drained
- 1 tsp salt
- 4 Tbsp butter
- ½ cup chopped onion
- Dash of pepper and nutmeg
- 2 cups cottage cheese
- 6 eggs
- 1 cup whipping cream
- ½ cup shredded sharp cheddar cheese

Espinacas con Garbanzos
(Spinach with Chickpeas)

Rosemary Stancil

Ingredients

- 1 medium yellow onion, diced
- 2 tablespoons olive oil
- 3 garlic cloves, minced
- 1 tablespoon grated fresh ginger
- 2 teaspoons ground coriander
- 2 teaspoons smoked sweet paprika
- 1 teaspoon ground cumin
- 1 (15-ounce) can chickpeas, drained
- 1 (28-ounce) can diced tomatoes, with juice
- ½ cup water
- 1 teaspoon Kosher salt or to taste
- Freshly ground black pepper to taste
- 2 (10-ounce) packages frozen spinach *

1. Sauté onion in the oil until tender, about 5 minutes. Add the garlic and ginger and cook until fragrant, about 2 minutes. Add the coriander, paprika, and cumin and cook until fragrant, about 1 minute.

2. Add the chickpeas, tomatoes and water and stir to combine. Cover, reduce heat to low, and simmer for 20 to 30 minutes. Season with salt and black pepper.

2. Add the spinach and stir to combine. Simmer 10 – 15 minutes. Taste and season with additional salt and pepper if needed.

*To substitute fresh washed garden spinach for frozen, use an 8- quart or larger pot and 3 pounds of fresh washed spinach. Place 2/3 cup water in the pot along with 1 ½ pound fresh spinach. Cover and simmer 2 minutes or until the spinach has wilted enough that the remaining spinach can be added. Stir and add remaining 1 ½ pound spinach. Cover again and simmer another 2-4 minutes until all the spinach has thoroughly wilted. Drain and continue with the first step.

Spinach with Mung Dal

Caroline D'Souza

1. Soak the dal in water for an hour, or until it swells.

2. Boil the dal in a little water, with a little salt and a pinch of turmeric until it is almost cooked. it should feel soft. Keep aside.

3. Wash spinach leaves very well under running water. Cut off the stalks. Cut the spinach leaves fine, put in a colander and wash again under running water. Leave aside to drain.

4. Finely chop 2 medium-sized onions.

5. Heat a little oil in a skillet. Keep flame on low heat. Add half a teaspoon of mustard seeds. When they start spluttering, quickly add half a teaspoon of cumin seeds. Add in chopped onions and fry till pink.

6. Add a pinch of turmeric powder and stir.

7. Now add the almost- cooked mung dal and stir for a while, till well-mixed with onions.

8. Add the finely cut spinach and a little salt and half a Maggi cube to enhance taste. Mix well.

9. Cook for 10 minutes on slow heat, until the water from the spinach evaporates.

10. Garnish with fresh or dried coconut or grated cheese, before serving.

Nutritional benefits: Iron-rich; helps digestion.

Ingredients

- ½ cup mung dal (Split mung beans/lentils - see page 137)
- 1 bundle spinach
- ½ a Maggi© cube
- 2 medium onions, finely chopped
- ½ tsp mustard seed
- ½ tsp cumin seeds
- Pinch turmeric

Squash Pie

Pam Tidwell

Ingredients

- 2 cups cooked squash, well drained
- 1 cup milk
- 1 cup sugar
- 2 eggs
- ¼ stick butter
- 4 Tbsp self-rising flour
- 1 Tbsp lemon extract
- 1 tsp vanilla

1. Mix all ingredients together in a food processor or blender. Pour into an unbaked 9" pie shell.

2. Bake at 375°F for 40 minutes.

Stir-Fry Cabbage

SNAP Ed

Ingredients

- 1 small head cabbage
- 1 bell pepper, if desired
- 1 onion
- 1 tablespoon oil
- ½ tsp garlic powder
- ⅓ cup water
- ½ tsp salt
- ¼ tsp black pepper

1. Cut up cabbage, pepper, and onion. Mix in a bowl.

2. Heat oil in a frying pan. Add cabbage mixture and stir fry for 1-2 minutes.

3. Immediately add garlic powder and water. Cover pan.

4. When water comes to a boil, turn down heat and simmer for 5 minutes. Add salt and black pepper. Stir and enjoy!

Strawberry Cream Cheese Pound Cake

Linda Tedrow

Ingredients

- 8 ounces nonfat cream cheese, softened
- 1 cup butter, softened
- 2 tsp butter, softened
- 2 cups white sugar
- 1 tsp salt
- 2 tsp vanilla
- 6 eggs, room temperature
- 3 cups all-purpose flour, sifted
- 2 cups strawberries, muddled

1. Preheat oven to 350°F. Grease a Bundt pan. Cream the cream cheese, all the butter, and sugar together in a bowl until light and fluffy, about 3 minutes. Add salt and vanilla extract and beat well.

2. Add eggs, one at a time, beating completely after each addition. Slowly add the flour, about 1 cup at a time, beating until just incorporated into the batter. Add the strawberries after the last cup of flour and mix slowly for a few seconds.

2. Pour the batter into the prepared Bundt pan. Bake for 1 hour, or until a toothpick inserted in the center comes out clean. Let cool in the pan about 5-10 minutes. Invert and place carefully on a cooling rack and let cool completely.

Strawberry Jalapeño Jam

Allan Cobb

Ingredients

- 2 pounds fresh strawberries, leaves removed
- 4 cups white sugar
- 2 oz lemon juice
- 1 jalapeno, seeded, white inside removed, and finely minced

A great way to keep fresh fruit longer!

1. In a large saucepan, smash strawberries, then mix with sugar, jalapeno, and lemon juice.

2. Stir over low heat until sugar dissolves, then increase heat and bring to a rolling boil. Stir often and boil until mixture reaches 220 degrees F. Transfer to hot, sterile jars, leaving ½ - ¼ inch air space at the top. Process in a water bath to make shelf stable or refrigerate.

Strawberry Smoothie

Jackie Zogran

Ingredients

- ½ cup of fresh strawberries
- 1 cup of unsweetened Almond Milk
- 2 Tbsp Almonds
- 1 Tbsp Chia seeds
- ½ tsp cinnamon

1. Blend all ingredients together in a blender until smooth.

Surprise Salad

Virginia McClelland

Ingredients

- 1 large head cauliflower, broken into florets
- 1 large head lettuce, cut up fine
- 1 medium onion, finely chopped
- 1 ½ cups mayonnaise
- ½ cup Parmesan cheese, grated
- ¼ to ½ cup bacon bits

1. Mix cauliflower, lettuce and onion together in a large bowl. Spread mayonnaise on top.

2. Sprinkle Parmesan cheese and bacon on top of the mayonnaise.

3. Let stand in refrigerator 12 hours or overnight.

4. Mix before serving.

Tortellini or Ravioli

Beverly Simpson

Ingredients

- 1 16 ounce pkg cheese (or other) tortellini or ravioli
- 1 14.5 ounce can diced tomatoes with jalapeño
- 1 cup chopped fresh spinach (optional)
- ½ teaspoon salt
- ¼ teaspoon pepper
- 1 ½ teaspoons dried basil
- 1 teaspoon minced garlic
- 2 Tablespoons flour
- ¾ cup milk
- ¾ cup heavy cream
- ¼ cup grated Parmesan

1. Cook tortellini by package directions.

2. While tortellini cooks, combine tomatoes, spinach, salt, pepper, basil, and garlic in a large saucepan over medium heat. Cook and stir until mixture bubbles.

3. In medium bowl whisk together flour, milk, and cream. Stir into saucepan mixture along with Parmesan.

4. Heat through, then reduce to low and simmer about two minutes or until thick.

5. Drain the tortellini, but do not rinse, then put it into sauce. Stir to coat. Serve.

Tuna Cottage Cheese Sandwich

Virginia McClelland

Ingredients

- 1 cup creamed cottage cheese
- 1 large can tuna, drained
- ½ cup mayonnaise
- ¼ cup chopped celery
- ¼ cup minced green onion
- 5 radishes, diced
- Salt and pepper to taste
- 6 English muffins, split and toasted

1. Combine salad ingredients and spread on muffin halves.

Vidalia Onion Casserole

Pam Tidwell

Ingredients

- 1 stick margarine
- 4 or 5 Vidalia onions, sliced and pulled apart
- Cheddar cheese (or whichever you prefer)
- Ritz crackers

1. Melt margarine in a large skillet. Add onions and sauté about 15 minutes. Put a layer of onions in a baking dish.

2. Cover with cheese and then a layer of Ritz crackers. Repeat layers. Add a small amount of water and drizzle over the casserole.

3. Bake at 350°F for 30 minutes.

Notes

53

Vilasini's Royal Pulao

Rita Mathew

1. Rinse basmati rice in water 2-3 times and then soak in water for 15 minutes. Drain water and keep the rice aside.

2. Heat 1 Tbsp butter and shallow fry the dried fruits and nuts. Transfer to a bowl and set aside. Heat remaining butter in the same pan and saute spices for 1 minute.

3. Add grated ginger and saute for another 30 seconds. Add soaked and drained rice and saute till the grains are translucent.

4. Add 2 cups hot water and salt, bringing to a boil over a medium flame. When it starts to boil, reduce flame and cook covered for 8-10 minutes or until rice is fully cooked. Do not open the lid or stir in between. Turn off flame and let it stand for 10 minutes.

5. Gently stir in the dried fruits, nuts, and garbanzo beans, cover and let it cook for a few minutes. Turn off the heat and transfer to a serving platter.

6. Separately, heat 3-4 Tbsp oil in another pan and shallow fry the onions till they turn brown and crisp. Sprinkle onions and pomegranate seeds over the rice.

7. Garnish with a sprig of cilantro or mint.

Variations:
Dried fruits like raisins, cranberries, cashew nuts and walnuts may be used.

Ingredients

- 1 cup Basmati Rice
- ½ onion thinly sliced
- 3 Tbsp unsalted butter
- ¼ cup dried apricots chopped
- ¼ cup green shelled pistachios
- ½ cup canned garbanzo beans (drained)
- 1 bay leaf
- 2 cloves
- 1 green cardamom
- 1-inch cinnamon stick
- ½ tsp grated ginger
- 3 – 4 Tbsp Oil for frying the onion
- 2 cups water
- Salt to taste
- ¼ cup fresh pomegranate seeds

In Hindi, Vilasini means one who delights in the good and beautiful. Vilasini, my mother, always had delicious, nourishing dishes made from fresh, seasonal ingredients at our dinner table. She could blend the color of the ingredients with an artist's eye for beauty - ruby red pomegranate seeds, orange apricots, green pistachios, and golden roasted cashew nuts transformed a mere Rice dish into a Royal Pulao.

"Fragile Handle with Care"
©2021 **Kie Johnson**

On Being Intentional: 3 Cs of Bees

Rita Mathew, CPA

An accountant by vocation, Rita has served in various professional capacities throughout her career of 30 years. To be an accountant is to know what counts: this has been the driving force for her activities in sustainable development, education, and health. She is passionate about serving and caring for people. Amongst her many endeavors, one was to lead a relief effort for a fishing village struck by the 2005 Tsunami in South India. She has been invited twice to the Rashtrapati Bhavan, New Delhi: in 1971, to meet President V.V. Giri, and in 2006, to meet President A.P.J. Kalaam.

"Wee haue by this Shipp and the Discouerie sent you diurs [divers] sortes of seedes, and fruit trees, as also Pidgeons, Connies, Peacockes Maistiues [Mastiffs], and Beehives, as you shall by the invoice pceiue [perceive]; the preservation and encrease whereof we respond vnto you..." states the letter written by the Virginia Company in London.[1]

This letter, dated December 5, 1621, is evidence of the initial importation of honeybees from Europe to North America. The history of domestication of honeybees, however, can be traced to earlier civilizations. For example, bees and honey are referenced in the Vedas, key philosophical texts of the Indus Saraswati Civilization, which date back to 4000 BCE, making the Vedas more ancient than European history. Indeed, metaphoric use of bees and honey in Vedic poetry, figurines, and geometric designs, helped to illustrate and convey some of the core cosmological theories and practices of *Saraswats* - the fundamental unity of the sentient and insentient universe manifested as a vibration.

With its interdisciplinary approach of integrating records and artifacts, historical archaeology is the preferred method to study long term processes that produce changes both in the environment and in culture. How do bees and honey serve as a bridge to understanding Vedic environmental knowledge? How did this civilization manage environmental resources in a way that allowed it to prosper for over 3000 years? From the perspective of Saraswat theory, representation of bees in Vedic texts can be compared with current knowledge of bee behavior allowing master gardeners to extract lessons about being conscious, creative, and connected, the three Cs, from bees.

BACKGROUND

Not only are there archaeological findings[2] that give support to the Indus Saraswati civilization beginning in 4000 B.C., if not earlier, but there is now also available geo-sensing data revealing the existence of the Saraswati River having been

1 Kellar, Brenda. (2020). Honey Bees Across America. Los Angeles County Bee Keepers Association Newsletter. August.
2 Rao, S. R. (1997) From the Indian Civilization to a Golden Age. Ananya: A Portrait of India. p 38. Queens, NY: The Association of Indians in America.

the source of fertile, nutrient-rich, and abundant loamy soil. It has also been determined that the Vedas were produced by Saraswati rishis (male seers) and rishikas (female seers), initially through oral records, then written, first in the alphabet of *Bhrami*, and later, with a more developed script called *Sarada*.

The Vedic texts which posit a tripartite and recursive universe, present the three regions of earth, space, and sky as reflections in the physical body, the breath, and the mind of human beings.[3] Seers developed a theory of the mind to explain how processes on earth, in space, and within the mind are connected. According to this theory, regularities experienced in sound, light, heat, and other wave transmissions; patterns observed in icicles, leaves, flowers, and honeycombs; cyclical movement of planets, and subsequent effects on tides and seasons are all a consequence of *Rta*, the laws underlying the universe.[4] Since the universe is mirrored in the cognitive system, introspection of concept maps can yield knowledge of *rta* and the corresponding relationships become available to logical analysis. Technological advances are making reliable data from ancient texts available, and those texts have become a rich source for understanding changes in insect and plant species, populations, and their cultural impact on Saraswat civilization.

CONSCIOUS BEE

The predominant approach towards bees, starting with early civilizations such as those in the Nile Valley and Greece, has involved a focus on the economic value of honey. By contrast, in ancient India, Chandogya Upanishad, part of the Vedas, presents "*Madhu Vidya*", Honey-Knowledge, or Bliss of Self.

The Upanishads taught that just as honey "the supreme nectar of plants" was extracted by bees, so also, the Vedas are flowers full of "rasa" nectar; its verses are like bees, extracting the nectar, or knowledge which leads to realization of self as eternal.

> *"As the bees make honey by gathering juices from many flowering plants and trees, and as these juices reduced to one honey do not know from what flowers they severally come, similarly, my son, all creatures when they are merged in that one Existence, whether in dreamless sleep or in death, know nothing of their past or present state, because of the ignorance enveloping them — know not that they are merged in Him and that from Him they came."*[5]

In another image, the heaven is the trestle supporting the honeycombs above; the rays of the sun are the tubular honey-cells of this honeycomb, through which honey streams and forms the body of the sun. The Sun represents Supreme Consciousness; the flowers from which the honey of the sun is obtained are the Vedas, the maxims and songs are like the bees, vehicles through which contents are transmitted to us. Just as bees hover over flowers extracting pollen, self-effort is a prerequisite to obtain immortal sap from the Vedas. Effort leads to splendor, renown, strength and food.[6] Lack of effort results in a state of ignorance and confusion. To be knowledgeable is likened to being fully aware or awake; to partake of

3 Kak, S. (1999) Concepts of space, time, and consciousness in ancient India. ArXiv: physics/9903010v2.
4 Rig Veda 4.23; 10.85; 10.190
5 Swami Prabhavananda and Manchester, Frederick "Chandogya Upanishad" page 69. "The Upanishads – Breath of the Eternal" The Vedanta Society of Southern California (1948).
6 Deussen, Paul. (1980) Sixty Upanishads of the Veda (Volume 1) New Delhi: Motilal Banarsidass. pp. 101-106.

honey, is akin to experiencing a permanent state of daytime that knows no night or darkness. The Upanishads imply the human ability to be aware, to know, and to be transformed. Might this also be the message that Kie Johnson communicates with a golden honeycomb in her painting, "Fragile Handle with Care" at the start of the Summer Section?

Modern scientific evidence of bee behavior verifies that the bee is an apt metaphor for intelligent transformation. Bees keep the same schedule as that of flowering plants which bloom and produce most of their nectar during the daylight hours. Bees are aware of the cyclical nature of day and night. In the tropics there are even strictly nocturnal bees that navigate by moonlight (Moisset, 2011). There are also bee species that become active foragers only at dawn or dusk. This means that those bees are pollinating plants that bloom at those very times.

Foraging bees are aware of the position of the sun in the sky; in addition, they rely on olfactory and visual information to compensate for the presence of complicating factors, such as clouds, that hinder their ability to assess the precise distance of the hive to the sources of pollen. Likewise, the purpose of Vedic compositions is to effect a change in individual consciousness by preparing the five senses and the mind for experiential learning and self-discovery of *dharma*, one's behavior that is in accordance with order that makes life and universe possible, even in the face of the never-ending complications that human existence presents.

CREATIVE BEE

Scientific findings confirm that the world as we know it would not exist if there were no bees to pollinate the earth's 250,000 flowering plants.[7] About 125 million years ago, carnivorous wasps made an adaptive switch to become vegetarian bees. This happened about the time that the first flowering plants evolved.

It is for the creative power and ability to adapt, not prowess for mating, that earns the bee recognition from Saraswats. The virtues of the bee are extolled in the Devi Mahatmyam, when the Creatrix appears in the form of a bee to save the world from life-threatening forces. For this reason, the Creatrix, Devi, has earned the name Bhramari which means bee. [8]

"Having taken a collective bee-form, consisting of innumerable bees, I shall slay the great asura for the good of the world. And then people shall laud me everywhere as Bhramari."

The purposeful creativity of bees is displayed in their waggle dance as they signal the location of valuable resources to their nestmates. The waggle portion of the dance involves the bee moving in a certain direction while waggling her body from side to side and vibrating her wings to produce a buzzing sound. At the end of each waggle run, the bee circles back to her starting point, alternating between clockwise and counter clockwise turns, creating successive rounds of figure-eight patterns. The angle of the pattern, relative to the upward direction, indicates the angle of the flower patch relative to the sun's position in the sky, and the duration of the waggle correlates with the distance from the hive to the flowers. Finally, the overall number of waggle runs signals the quality of the food supply. According to Dukas[9], bees provide a model for intentional, social learning. First, the model bee incurs a cost by spending time and energy learning about the environment.

7 Moisset, B. and Buchmann, S. (2011) Bee Basics: An Introduction to our Native Bees. A USDA Forest Service and Pollinator Partnership Publication.
8 Swami Jagdishwarananda (translator). Devi Mahatmyam. Markandeya Purana, (11:54-55).
9 Dukas, R. (2010) Learning About Distant Food. Insect Social Learning. Encyclopedia of Animal Behavior. 176-179 https://doi.org/10.1016/B978-0-08-045337-8.00058-9.

Second, the returning forager dances selectively to recruit more bees to visit the newly discovered flower patch. Third, after attending an orientation dance session, not only are the recruits able to find the sources of pollen much faster, but they are also able to learn the dance moves that enable them to become recruiters of fellow bees, too!

Brahmari has also been depicted with seven little mothers or Matrikas who assist with learning by presiding over the seven major categories of the Sanskrit alphabet. The Rigveda (IX:102.4) speaks of a group of seven Mothers who control the preparation of Soma, nectar, which is understood to mean communication skills. Atharva-Veda, speaks at length about the Bee and the twin horsemen, lords of light known as the Asvins:

"O Asvins, lords of Brightness, anoint me with honey of the bee, that I may speak forceful speech among men."

Such an association of bees with communication is not farfetched. The Hebrew word for bee, *dbure* (pronounced "Deborah") comes from the root *dbr*, which in turn means "word." The prophetess, Deborah, is described in the Old Testament as being wise. She is named for honey bees and embodies all that the honey bee represents: most fundamentally, wisdom and eloquence.

CONNECTED BEE

Bees live in a community sharing tasks, such as cleaning the hive, keeping predators at bay, and protecting the queen. They are benevolent and share information about the source of nectar. The interconnected state of existence is beautifully described in the Brhadharanyaka Upanishad:

"This earth is honey for all beings, and all beings are honey for this earth. The intelligent, immortal being, the soul of this earth, and the intelligent, immortal being, the soul in the individual being – each is honey to the other. Brahman is the soul in each; he indeed is the Self in all. He is all.......

The race of men is honey for all beings, and all beings are honey for this race of men. The intelligent, immortal being, the soul of this race of men, and the intelligent, immortal being, the soul in the individual being – each is honey to the other. Brahman is the soul in each; he indeed is the Self in all. He is all."[10]

Lothal and other towns of the Saraswati civilization were first rediscovered in 1954.[11] Carbon dating techniques suggest that these communities took root as long ago as 4000 B.C., came to maturity in about 2800 B.C. and began their decline near 1600 B.C. At the height of their maturation, these communities were so advanced that they engaged in town planning, addressed soil erosion and other environmental issues, and emphasized public hygiene to promote overall community well-being. The result was a period of prolonged and widely shared prosperity.

CONCLUSION

How the bee is depicted reflects what society values. Science has made it clear that a narrow-minded focus on economic profit has a detrimental effect on both nature and society. Since consciousness and existence are interconnected, an intentional pursuit of sustenance leads to individual, social, and environmental well-being.

10 Swami Prabhavananda and Manchester, Frederick. (1948) Brhadharanyaka Upanishad. The Upanishads: Breath of the Eternal. pp 89-91 Los Angeles: The Vedanta Society of Southern California.

11 Rao, S. R. (1997) From the Indian Civilization to a Golden Age. Ananya: A Portrait of India. p 36. Queens, NY: The Association of Indians in America.

Toward a Generation of Nature Lovers: Helping Children Blossom in the Garden!

Anne Shenk, Director of Education, The State Botanical Garden of Georgia (retired)

Anne is an environmental educator, and curricula designer who completed her career at the State Botanical Garden of Georgia. In this capacity, she developed, taught and directed a wide variety of programs for the general public, teachers, and young children. Prior to coming to the Garden, she worked with environmental programs in New York, Rhode Island, Colorado, and with Peace Corps in the Fiji Islands. She has been the recipient of numerous grants and awards and served on a number of Boards both in the U.S. and internationally. Connecting people to nature and affecting positive environmental change is the intent at the heart of her work.

"Mmmm, this tastes good!" A young gardener exclaims! "Hey, your radish is a different color than mine!" states another. "What are these red-green leaves called? I feel like a rabbit eating it!" "Can I take some of these home for my Mom? She would like these."

Children, who just four weeks earlier were convinced they didn't like radishes, and couldn't pronounce the word, 'arugala', were now eating these veggies right from the garden, without hesitation. Not just plants, but children too, blossom in the garden. It's a magical moment when they discover that a plant grows from a seed; insects hide under leaves; a wasp prepares a nursery for its larvae in the stem of a plant; and small flowers lose their petals and turn into huge squash.

Having worked at nature centers, schools, and the State Botanical Garden of Georgia for many years, I have, on numerous occasions, witnessed those "ahha" moments experienced by children of varied ages, and backgrounds, as well as their teachers. Through these experiences, I have learned that by expecting 'unexpected' lessons from nature, and granting children's curiosity free reign, a garden becomes a place of unlimited possibilities as a potential place to fall in love with nature.

Never before has it been so critical that our children learn to respect and care for the earth. Nurturing a generation of nature lovers means helping children develop an appreciation for the complex web of life in the garden; providing them with tools to develop empathy for, and a deep concern for earth and its creatures. An added benefit, is that kids develop healthy eating habits with an appreciation for eating local, in-season food.

For many years, I conducted hands-on gardening programs with young girls. Each team of girls had their own garden bed. Giant sunflowers, bean-covered teepees, whimsical scarecrows, a story-telling fence covered with sweet peas, and lots of delicious heathy vegetables graced the garden site. Asked what vegetables they would like to grow, they often responded with plants they were familiar with, '*lettuce, turnips, radishes, tomatoes, and onions.*' While certain plants were not on their list, such as nasturtiums and arugala, the girls planted them and were eager to try them. Herbs, strawberries and flowers also brightened

the flower beds. Whereas previously, tomatoes were from 'row 3 in the grocery store', now the young gardeners knew their true source, what was involved in producing them, and getting a crop of tomatoes to 'row 3'! In the past, they may have opted a burger but now a fresh salad or smoothie was included on their list of delicious options. The outcomes of gardening with children can be rich and important!

Just Getting Started? For parents, grandparents, and educators struggling to find ways to encourage kids to get outside and eat a healthy diet, gardening can be an important tool. It doesn't need to overwhelm you! Gardening doesn't require a perfectly level, large or full-sun backyard. Try planting in a small raised bed or growing a few edibles in the existing landscaping. I recently turned an old swing set into a trellis for beans, cucumbers, and gourds. You might lean a trellis against an outside wall to grow beans or other edible vines. If you don't have a lot of outdoor space, a few containers, and soil in a sunny spot, can be an easy way to grow some sweet cherry tomatoes that kids won't be able to resist.

A modified version of 'square-foot' gardening works great with children. Garden beds can be marked with string to define a series of square-foot areas, where children can, for example, plant one square with nine onions, and another with three rows of radishes; hence, introducing a math activity, while having fun, and not worrying if the seeds are planted in perfectly straight rows. If they seed an area too heavily, the seedlings can always be thinned out once they sprout. Observing what works and what doesn't work is a great way for kids to learn. To maintain children's enthusiasm and sense of discovery, create opportunities for them to make decisions about the garden and welcome their input. Do what you can to make it an exciting, fun experience that they will want to do repeatedly from year to year. Neatness can come later as the next growing season is always just around the corner!

When children participate in gardening, the fruits and vegetables they are inspired to eat will no doubt have a positive effect on their body, which is so important in this time when obesity and other food related disorders affect many of our youth. Activities like shoveling soil, using a heavy watering can, digging in the dirt, and pushing a wheelbarrow, promote gross motor skills and overall strength for a more fit body. More strenuous outdoor activities have been shown to help kids stay calm and focused. Anyway, most kids LOVE to get dirty, so no need to invest in any new clothing for this activity!

Garden maintenance provides additional hours in the sun and fresh air. Kids love to water their gardens! It is helpful to remind them that rain usually falls gently and so they should imitate gentle rain when watering their plants. In the heat of the summer, gardening in swimsuits can be great fun! Of course, weeding, mulching and composting are other great activities that could be educational and fun at the same time.

'Theme' gardens such as a circular 'Pizza Garden' can include onions, peppers, tomatoes, basil and oregano. Another popular theme is a 'Three Sisters Native American Garden' planted with corn, beans and squash. Crops that have cultural relevance to your children are great to include. Stories related to certain vegetables can be researched and narrated to enhance the cultural relevance of certain plants. Interviewing grandparents about vegetables they planted when younger; locating and propagating heirloom seeds; finding places of migration on the map; these are some ways that might lead to investigative skills and discovery.

Looking for ideas to turn your garden into a site for exciting interdisciplinary learning? There are myriad of scientific concepts to be discovered when planting and tending a garden. The wonder of seeing plants grow may spark your kids to ask questions like: Why are worms good for the soil? Why do the plants need sun? How does the plant 'drink' water? Soon you will be talking about decomposition, soils, photosynthesis, pollination and more! Of course, language arts, math, music and history are other topics to consider. While there are numerous books to guide your learning activities, here are a few activities to get your ideas flowing!

Consider starting your gardening day by encouraging a sense of wonder. When your children first arrive at the garden, ask them to investigate the garden and report on what changed since last time they were there. Even if it was just the night before, several changes may have taken place and this really helps sharpen observation skills. Make sure you remind your children to use all their senses. To help children practice scientific skills, encourage them to develop a list of 'I wonder' questions as they check out the garden. Such as 'I wonder' who left those footprints? 'I wonder' how these holes got on the bean leaves? 'I wonder' why these leaves are turning a yellowish-brown? Then ask children if they can come up with a plan to investigate their question. In effect, plans to answer many 'I wonder' questions can lead to mini (or full blown) science experiments. There are numerous books available online to guide science explorations with your children.

Hunts are also great learning activities. For example, an 'Alphabet Hunt' would be to name plants, other garden organisms, and their features starting with nearly every letter of the alphabet. After completing the hunt, another activity might be to discuss the discoveries. A 'Color Hunt' might include cutting small squares of colored paper and hunting for flowers, leaves and insects that are the same color as their paper squares. This activity easily leads to drawing projects as children are encouraged to go back to one of the colored objects and creating art from it. Or, a quick Google search can help you prepare a list of eight to ten plant adaptations that your child can find in the yard and garden.

An 'Insect Visitor Count' offers opportunities to explore multiple science concepts and skills. Children (or you and your child) sit by a cluster of flowers, and count the number of insects that visit the plant in 5-10 minutes. Next, visit other clusters, do the same insect count, and compare findings. Learn together as you pose questions such as, 'what are the insects doing at the flowers? Do they prefer one color of flower over another?' You will discover that they can easily come up with a list of 'I wonder' questions. Our gardener is now an inquiring scientist and the garden is the lab! Prompt them to set up a plan (an experiment) to discover answers to their questions. Add a little math by measuring plant growth from week to week, or counting the flowers on each plant. The list of gardening skills, inquiry activities, theme gardens and general fun can go on and on.

In conclusion, kids can benefit both from more physical activity, and the sunshine they'll get while gardening. Furthermore, time in the garden allows for family connection, team building and promotes communication skills. Planning a garden, planting the seeds and watching them grow gives kids a sense of purpose and responsibility. Let's never underestimate the extent of a young gardener's harvest! Making sure that the plants get enough fertilizer, water and sun fosters mindfulness. The concepts learned while gardening, like composting food scraps for fertilizer or using rainwater, show kids respect and responsibility for our planet. Finally, the self-esteem a child gets from eating a delicious radish or other veggie that he/she has grown is priceless.

Remember, while much of the harvest is tangible and real, much more is intangible. Young gardeners learn about the consequences of their actions; a carefully tended, watered, mulched, weeded and fertilized garden produces good crops. Likewise, an untended garden may wilt and be eaten by insects. However, they also learn that some things, such as a storm uprooting a fence, may be the result of an unplanned event. The joys and hardships in the garden carry over to daily life as children learn the importance of caring for their seedlings and plants. There is so much to gain by designating a garden plot as children do truly blossom in the garden! So please join me in nurturing a generation of nature lovers by connecting them with the garden. And, above all, experience the great joy of gardening with your young person or persons!

Harvesting Rainwater is More Fun than a Barrel of Monkeys!

George Edward Van Giesen III

Edward Van Giesen resides in Watkinsville Ga with his wife Viviane. They have three adult children, Cedric, Ian and Isabella. Edward is passionate about conservation, native plants and harvesting rain. He hopes to help many people around the world realize the benefits of using the water that falls from the skies for the betterment of the environment, animals and all mere mortals.

What happens to the water that runs off your roof after a rain? We know where it comes from, but where does it go? What happens to it along the way? In Georgia, when it rains, it can be a downpour, with a lot of water rushing off the roof. Did you know that you can capture, store, and use this rainwater for a number of end-uses including outdoor irrigation? You can catch as much as 78,000 gallons of water annually from a 2500 square foot single-family home in Athens, Georgia. That's enough to flush the toilets of a family of four for eleven years!

The truth is that we as a society don't think about water until we don't have enough of it. In our current water supply paradigm, we pay to bring water in: often from far away, or deep places; then pay to get rid of it through the sanitary sewer; and, finally, pay to send the rainwater that falls free from the skies to the storm water system; all in a one-way system.

This is the paradox of our complex, but unsustainable urban environment. Too often, water supply strategies are based on an outdated mindset:

> * water is cheap and infinite, and
> * water must be supplied to users through a one-way system.

Both principles represent a misguided vision that must change to meet the realities of the modern world. Since the planet's supply of fresh water is FINITE, and as the earth's population grows, demand for water is only likely to increase. Why waste precious drinking water irrigating the lawn, or washing the car, when we can use rainwater? All water on our planet at some point or another comes from rain:

Athens Co-Op Rainwater System

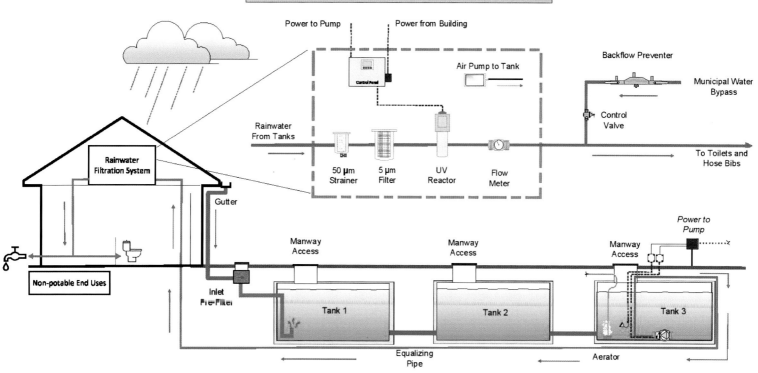

using it straight from the source is an important and viable option to consider.

You may remember that in the summer of 2007 we faced a drought severe enough to ban all outdoor watering in Georgia, and we were dangerously close to water rationing at the community level right here in Clarke County. We were days from the point of no water for the intake pipes in our local reservoir. Even though we were in a drought, we still received approximately thirty inches of rain for the year, a record amount for Southern California where a mere twelve inches falls annually in some areas. Sadly, we had an outdated plumbing code that did not allow for the capture and use of rainwater from rooftops. The plumbing code has since been changed, and now it is perfectly legal to harvest rainwater.

Harvesting rainwater may not solve all the world's water problems, but what it can do is to provide an alternative source of freshwater while reducing demand pressure on municipal water supplies. Harvesting rainwater preserves valuable groundwater and mitigates the impacts of the storm water flows that plague our cities.

It seems like an easily accomplished task: catch and use the rainwater from the roof. However, it is critical to note that rain does not equal rainwater. Rain, before it hits a surface, is just that, rain. But the instant it strikes a surface, it becomes rainwater, and, depending on where it falls, it may not be as clean as you think. Also, don't confuse rainwater with graywater, which is wastewater derived from sinks and showers. Graywater requires much higher levels of treatment than rainwater.

If you have a roof over your head, you can capture rainwater.

Follow these basic principles and guidelines.

1. Install an inlet pre-filter to prevent leaves and other coarse roof debris from entering the cistern.
2. Screen openings to keep mosquitoes and any other animals out. Don't let the tank become a "West Nile breeding ground."
3. Install an overflow pipe equal to the inlet pipe.
4. Place the tank out of direct sun whenever possible. Hot water is conducive to the proliferation of harmful bacteria.
5. Don't use clear or translucent tanks; you'll have pea soup in no time.
6. Protect tank and pipes from freezing (not a problem with an underground tank).
7. Treat/filter the water according to the end use.
8. Inspect your system regularly.
9. Last but not least, do not save your rainwater "FOR A RAINY DAY;" use it so your tank will be empty for the next rain event.

If you want to do this at your home, consider starting small. Just as with a home garden, you will be better off with three tomato plants in pots well taken care of than a garden full of row crops that you may be unable to handle!

A rain barrel scale system can be fun, simple and effective. It will usually hold about fifty gallons of water. Follow the applicable guidelines mentioned above. At a minimum, you will need an inlet pre-filter, a hose bib (spigot) and the barrel itself. Place the barrel on a stable foundation and completely drain it once a year. Don't allow the barrel to accumulate a bunch of organic material. If your water smells bad, you are letting it sit for too long!

More sophisticated systems can range from a series of rain barrels in parallel, holding a few hundred gallons, to larger (above and below ground) cisterns holding tens of thousands of gallons. In addition to an inlet pre-filter, these systems typically require pumps, controllers, filtration in stages and possibly disinfection. Consult a professional with experience in rainwater harvesting when considering taking on a project such as this.

Direct the overflow water to a safe location. Don't send it to the neighbor-that's not nice! Rain gardens are a great way to manage rainwater by allowing the overflow to percolate into the ground. This technique maintains moisture in the soil and decreases stormwater out-flows, reducing the impact on the local environment.

The most common errors in rainwater harvesting that people make are as follows:

- Allowing tanks/barrels/pipes to freeze,
- Omitting the inlet pre-filter,
- Allowing mosquitoes to proliferate in and around the tank, and
- Selecting the wrong kind of pumps and controls.

All of these mistakes are 100% avoidable with the right know-how. Many homeowners are challenged to find the best location for the storage vessel, not realizing that an underground tank offers a lot more flexibility in placement.

Rainwater harvesting is a really good thing. It saves water, takes no energy to capture, and reduces the potential for downstream flooding. Anyone I have ever known who had a rainwater system really enjoyed watching the barrel fill up and an even greater sense of satisfaction when they used it for the first time! Go forth and harvest!

Summer

A Time to Reap

Beets
Bell Peppers
Blackberries
Blueberries
Canteloupe
Corn
Eggplant
Green Beans
Lima Beans
Okra
Raspberries
Strawberries
Summer Squash
Tomatoes
Watermelon
Zucchini

Beans
Cucumber
Eggplant
Okra
Tomatoes
Summer Squash

A Time to Sow

			Produce (1 Cup, raw. Unless otherwise stated)												Meat				Dairy			
			Corn	Cucumber (peeled, sliced)	Eggplant (1 eggplant unpeeled, 1 1/4 lb)	Okra (cubed, 100gm)	Summer Squash	Tomatoes (1 medium whole, 123 gm)	Zucchini (1 medium, unpeeled, 196 gm)	Blackberries	Blueberries	Cantaloupe (1 cup, balls 177 gm)	Raspberries	Watermelon	Chicken (1 lb broiler)	Salmon (Atlantic, farmed fillet 198 gm)	Shrimp (85 gm)	Tuna (Yellowfin, fresh, 85 gm)	Cottage Cheese (1 Cup 2% lowfat)	Egg (1 large)	Milk (1 Cup whole)	Yogurt (1 Cup whole milk)
Nutrition	Calories	Grams	132	14.3	132	31	18.1	22	31.4	61.9	84	60	64	46	234	412	90.1	91.8	194	71.5	146	149
	Carbohydrates		29	2.6	31.5	7	3.8	4.8	6.6	14.7	21.4	15.6	14.7	11.6	0	0	0.8	0	8.3	0.4	12.8	11.4
	Protein		5	0.7	5.5	2	1.4	1.1	2.4	2	1.1	1.5	1.5	0.9	42.1	40.4	17.3	19.9	26.7	6.3	7.9	8.5
	Fat		1.8	0.2	1	0.1	0.2	0.2	0.4	0.7	0.5	0.3	0.8	0.2	6.1	26.6	1.5	0.8	5.5	5	7.9	8
	Fiber		4.2	0.8	18	3.2	1.2	1.5	2.2	7.6	3.6	1.6	8	0.6	0	0	0	0	0	0	0	0
Vitamins	Vitamin A	% DV	6	2	3	7	5	20	8	6	2	120	1	18	2	2	3	1	3	5	5	5
	Vitamin C		17	6	20	35	32	26	56	50	24	108	54	21	8	13	3	1	0	0	0	2
	Vitamin K		1	11	24	66	4	12	11	36	36	6	12	0	4	1	0	0	0	0	1	1
	Folate		18	4	30	22	8	5	14	9	2	9	6	1	3	13	1	0	6	6	3	4
Minerals	Iron		4	1	7	4	2	2	4	5	2	2	5	2	10	4	11	3	2	5	0	1
	Calcium		0	2	5	8	2	1	3	4	1	2	3	1	2	2	4	1	21	3	28	30
	Potassium		12	5	36	9	8	8	15	7	3	14	5	5	13	21	4	11	5	2	10	11
	Sodium		1	0	0	0	0	0	1	0	0	1	0	0	6	5	5	1	31	3	4	5

Artist Salad

Viviane Van Giesen

1. Mix all the salad ingredients in a large bowl.

2. Mix all the dressing ingredients in a jar and shake well.

3. Just before serving, toss the salad with dressing. Amount of dressing is to cooks taste.

4. Sprinkle generously with crumbled feta cheese.

"Bom apetite!" (Portuguese for "Enjoy it!")

(All amounts are adjustable to the cook's taste)

Dressing

- 1/4 cup olive oil
- 2 Tbsp wine vinegar
- 1 Lg garlic clove very thinly cut
- 1 tsp sugar
- A squirt of mustard
- Freshly ground black pepper (optional)

Ingredients

- Romaine lettuce shredded in pieces
- 1/2 purple onion finely sliced (soak it in water until ready to mix in the salad to reduce acidity and bitterness)
- 2 carrots peeled and shredded
- One yellow bell-pepper diced
- About 1/2 cup or more of small broccoli flowerets
- 2 or 3 celery stalks thinly sliced
- 1 large apple cut in small cubes
- 1 can of garbanzo beans (chick peas)
- Finely cut parsley
- About 1/2 cup of nuts (pepitas is the best! but you can use slivered almonds or walnuts or sunflower seeds)
- About 1/2 cup of raisins

Asian Chicken Wraps

Jackie Zogran

- Butter Lettuce
- 1 lb. Chicken (ground or cubed)
- 12 oz. broccoli slaw
- 1 cup chopped onion
- ½ cup teriyaki sauce
- Salt, pepper, garlic powder to taste
- 1 tsp. sesame seeds
- Olive oil

1. Heat olive oil in pan and add onions, cook 5 minutes. Then add chicken and cook until done.

2. Add the rest of the ingredients and cook for another 10-15 minutes.

3. Wash and tear apart lettuce. Spoon mixture into lettuce leaves, roll up and enjoy.

Notes

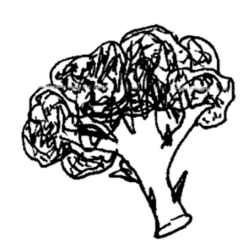

Baby Eggplant Saglé

Rita Mathew

1. Wash and slit in quarters keeping the stem on. Apply salt inside the vegetable and set aside for 15 minutes. Squeeze out the water from each eggplant. Prepare the coconut masala separately. Stuff each eggplant with a spoonful of masala.

2. Prepare the Onion seasoning as follows: Heat the oil in a medium heavy bottom pan. When it has heated, add the diced onions. Fry stirring frequently until they are brown.

3. To the hot pan add the stuffed eggplant and salt. Cover and cook with ½ cup of water on low heat for 15 minutes.

Ingredients

• 8 – 10 small baby eggplants

For the masala:
• 1 cup fresh grated coconut, blended to a fine consistency
• 1 tsp red chilli power
• 1 Tbsp coriander powder
• ¼ tsp fenugreek powder
• ½ tsp tamarind paste
• ¼ cup water
• 1 tsp salt
• ½ cup water

For the Onion Seasoning:
• 1 medium onion diced
• 3 Tbsp oil

Okra Saglé

• Use 16 – 20 tender okra instead of eggplants.

1. Wash, pat dry, and trim ends. Slightly slit in quarters the top of each okra. Prepare the masala separately. Mix in the okra.

2. In the hot pan with Onion seasoning, put the okra and masala mixture. For crisp okra, cover and cook without any water and salt, on low heat for 15 minutes.

Thalli 1: Clockwise from top – Dal, Amrut, Okra upkari, Orange, Chana upkari, Eggplant Sagle, Laddu, Sweet Mung bean khichdi, Sweet Potato fritters. Rice in center.

Blueberry Skillet Pie

Suzanne Keifer

- Basic pie dough (recipe to follow)
- 5 cups (about 1 ½ pound) fresh blueberries
- 1 tsp grated lemon zest
- 1 Tbsp fresh lemon juice
- ¾ cup granulated sugar
- 3 Tbsp cornstarch
- ¼ tsp kosher salt
- ¼ tsp ground cinnamon
- 1 egg beaten with tsp water
- Superfine sugar for sprinkling
- Vanilla ice cream for serving

For the Pie Dough:
- 2 ¼ cups all-purpose flour
- ¾ tsp salt
- ¾ cup vegetable shortening
- 6 – 7 Tbsp cold water

Pictured on Back Cover

1. Combine the flour and salt in a mixing bowl. Add the shortening and blend together with a pastry blender (or your fingers). Work this until the mixture looks like coarse breadcrumbs. Sprinkle on water, 1 tbsp at a time, stirring gently with a fork after each addition. Add just enough water for the dough to form a rough mass. With floured hands, pat the dough into 2 disks and it's ready to use.

For the Pie:

1. On a lightly floured surface, roll out each disk into roughly 15" round about 1/8" thick. Fold one of the disks in half and carefully place in a 10" iron skillet. Unfold and carefully ease the crust around the edges, patting firmly on the bottom and up along the sides. Leave about a 1" overhang around the edge.

2. Fold the excess dough in on itself and press lightly to seal. Using a fork, gently poke holes in several places on the bottom. Wrap the remaining disk in plastic wrap and refrigerate for the decorations.

3. In a large bowl, combine the blueberries, lemon zest and juice and toss to coat. In a small bowl, stir together the granulated sugar, cornstarch, salt, and cinnamon. Sprinkle this mixture over the blueberries and toss to distribute evenly. Transfer this to the skillet. Refrigerate the pie for about 20 minutes. Position a rack in the lower third of the oven and preheat to 375°F.

4. Brush the edges of the crust with the egg wash and sprinkle with the superfine sugar. Bake the pie until crust is golden and filling is thick and bubbly – about 50-60 minutes. If crust becoming too dark, cover with aluminum foil. Transfer the pie to a wire rack and let cool for 1 – 2 hours.

5. Line a baking sheet with parchment paper. Transfer the second dough disk to a lightly floured work surface. Using a 1" and 2" star-shaped cookie cutter (or any shape desired), cut about 17 of each size.

6. Place the larger size stars on the parchment paper, brush with egg wash, then place the smaller star on top, aligning the points of the stars. Brush with egg wash and sprinkle with superfine sugar. Refrigerate 20-30 minutes. Bake in a 375° oven for 10-12 minutes, checking periodically so they don't burn.

7. Transfer to a wire rack to cool. Arrange stars on the pie serve with vanilla ice cream.

Charlie's Salsa

Virginia McClelland

Ingredients

- 1 ½ pecks plum tomatoes (chopped)
- 18 or more mild banana peppers (chopped)
- 4 large onions (chopped)
- 1 24-oz can tomato paste
- 8 tablespoons garlic powder
- 1 cup apple cider vinegar
- 2 tsp. seasoning salt
- 1 small jar (.25 oz) parsley
- 2 to 3 tsp salt

1. Cook the plum tomatoes, banana peppers, and onions over low to medium heat for 1 ½ hours.

2. Cook for ½ hour, place in canning jars and seal.

For water bath:

1. Place sealed jars on rack in large pot. Cover with boiling water to at least 1 ½ inches over the jar tops.

2. Don't pour boiling water directly on to jars. Bring to a new boil and boil jars for 25 minutes. Remove from pot with tongs and let cool.

Notes

Cool Cucumber Kochumbir *(Vegan side dish)*

Rita Mathew

1. Trim the top of the chilli and slice in half. Remove the seeds, and then finely dice the pepper. Mix the grated cucumber with the rest of the ingredients.

2. See page 137 for directions on how to sprout Mung beans.

3. Garnish with cilantro. Serve cold as a side dish with Rice or Naan.

Variations:

Tomato Kochumbir

• 2 cups Tomatoes chopped

1. Use 2 cups chopped tomatoes instead of cucumbers. Alternately, combine tomatoes with cucumbers.

Carrot Kochumbir

• ½ lb raw Carrots (2 cups grated or diced)

Radish Kochumbir

• 2 large Daikon (white) Radishes. (2 cups grated).

See Thalli 2 picture on page 222

Ingredients

• 2 Cucumbers (Peeled and diced)
• 1-inch fresh ginger (finely grated)
• ¼ cup diced onion
• ½ cup roasted crushed peanuts
• ½ cup sprouted green mung beans
• 1 small Thai green chilli
• ½ tsp lime juice
• 1 tsp salt
• 1 Tbsp cilantro

Kochumbir is a salad with finely diced raw vegetables. Sprouted pulses, such as green mung, add protein content.

Coriander Mint Dip

Rita Mathew

Ingredients

- 1/3 cup yogurt
- ¾ cup packed fresh coriander leaves
- ¼ cup packed fresh mint leaves
- ¼ cup green pepper, seeded and chopped
- 1 Tbsp chopped onion
- ½ tsp fresh ground ginger
- ¼ tsp salt
- ¼ tsp sugar
- 1 green chilli (optional)
- 1 Tbsp water

1. Puree all ingredients in a blender until smooth. Chill before serving.

> Coriander seeds are used as a spice, but the leaves, also known as Cilantro, are an annual herb.

Corn, Tomato and Zucchini over Pasta

Frank and Cheryl Johnson

Ingredients

- 4 ears of fresh corn, removed from cob
- 1 medium zucchini, diced
- 4 medium tomatoes, diced
- 3 Tbsp diced onion
- 1-2 cloves of garlic, minced
- 2-3 Tbsp olive oil or canola oil
- 2 Tbsp fresh chopped basil or 1 Tbsp of dried basil
- ½ of 16 oz. package of linguine, spaghetti or angel hair pasta, cooked per package instructions
- Grated parmesan or six-cheese Italian grated cheese to sprinkle over vegetables

1. While pasta is cooking, sauté the onion and garlic until onion is clear. Add zucchini and sauté for about 3 minutes; next, add corn and sauté for about 3 minutes; add tomatoes last and sauté until they are warm. Add chopped basil and cook for about a minute or until basil is wilted.

2. Serve over pasta. Sprinkle with cheese.

Cranberry-Walnut Chicken Salad

Suzanne Keifer

Ingredients

- 4 cups canned chicken, drained (approximately 3 big cans)
- 1 cup toasted chopped walnuts (I sauté them in a small pan about 4-5 minutes)
- 2 ribs chopped celery
- 1 finely chopped shallot
- 1 cup Craisins (generous)
- ⅔ to ¾ cup lite mayonnaise
- 3 Tbsp Tarragon vinegar
- 2 tbsp finely chopped fresh tarragon
- ½ tsp salt
- ½ tsp freshly ground black pepper

1. Mix all above ingredients in a large bowl. Chill in fridge 1-2 hours before serving.

Serves 4-6.

Elote *(Mexican Street corn)*

Isaac Swier

Ingredients

- 6 ears corn, husk attached (or use soaked bamboo skewers)
- ½ Cup mayonnaise
- ½ lime, juiced
- 3 Tbsp neutral oil (canola, corn, vegetable, sunflower, etc.)
- Chipotle chili powder (to taste)
- Cotija cheese (to taste)
- Optional: cumin, kosher salt, fresh cilantro, lime wedges

Time – 15-30 minutes

1. Prepare your corn by peeling the husk, one layer at a time, downwards and bundling together to make a 'handle'. You can tie the husk with kitchen twine if you prefer, or shuck the corn all together and insert a bamboo skewer into the cob. Rinse corn and remove any silk.

2. Heat your grill or griddle to medium-high to high depending on your char preferences. Lightly brush grill surface with oil and space ears out evenly, rotating often, until a speckled or even char is obtained on the kernels.

3. While your corn is cooking, whisk together mayonnaise and lime juice.

4. When the corn has reached a char level that you prefer, carefully remove from heat and spoon the lime mayonnaise over each ear, smoothing into the crevices between kernels.

5. Top with a hearty sprinkle of cotija and chili powder as well as cumin, salt, cilantro, and more lime juice as preferred – and serve.

Filipino Lumpia (Spring Roll) *Narcie Corpus Keifer*

1. Combine all ingredients except for the eggs in a bowl and mix with your hands. Cover this filling and let it sit in the fridge for an hour (or up to 24 hours) before wrapping.

2. Open the lumpia wrappers and cut in half to form rectangular strips or in quarters to make bite size rolls. If you are using spring roll wrappers, you can cut them in half or leave them the bigger size.

3. Carefully peel the wrappers apart and place about a tablespoon of filling on each one. Roll them according to your preference and then dip your finger in the beaten egg and seal the edges. Set the rolls aside until ready to cook.

4. In a small saucepan, heat about 2 inches of oil over medium high. Once the oil is hot, use tongs to place a few rolls in the oil at a time. Let cook for about a minute on one side and then turn to cook the other.

5. When they are lightly golden brown, remove from the oil and place on a paper towel covered plate.

6. Serve with dipping sauces of your choice; preferably sweet and sour sauce.

Ingredients

- 1 pound ground pork
- 1 can water chestnuts chopped
- ½ cup green onion chopped
- 1 cup carrots chopped
- 1 stick celery chopped
- ½ cup sweet yellow onion chopped
- 2 garlic cloves chopped
- 2 tsp sage
- ½ tsp Salt (to your taste)
- ½ tsp pepper
- 1 Tbsp soy sauce
- 2 beaten eggs
- Lumpia wrappers or spring roll wrappers
- 2 cups oil for frying

Fresh Corn Salad

SNAP Ed

Ingredients

- 5 tsp olive oil, divided
- 1 Tbsp lime juice
- ¼ tsp salt
- ¼ tsp hot sauce
- 1 ½ cups fresh corn, cut from cob (about 2 ears)
- 1 ½ cups cherry tomatoes, halved
- ½ cup chopped cucumber
- ¼ cup chopped red onion
- 2 Tbsp minced fresh basil (or 2 tsp dried)
- ¼ cup crumbled feta cheese

1. In a small bowl, whisk 4 teaspoons oil, lime juice, salt, and hot sauce. Set aside.

2. In a large skillet, cook and stir corn in remaining oil over medium-high heat until tender. Transfer to a salad bowl, cool slightly.

3. Add the tomatoes, cucumber, onion, and basil.

4. Drizzle with dressing and toss to coat. Let stand 10 minutes before serving or
refrigerate until chilled.

5. Sprinkle with feta cheese just before serving.

Fruit Salsa

Pam Tidwell

Ingredients

- 2 Granny Smith Apples, finely chopped, not peeled
- 1 cup sliced strawberries
- 1 kiwi, finely chopped, not peeled
- 2 Tbsp apple jelly
- 2 Tbsp brown sugar
- Zest and juice of 1 orange

1. Mix all ingredients together and store in airtight container.

2. This can be served on cinnamon sticks or Wheat Thins. It also can be served on flour tortillas. Slightly dampen the top of the tortilla and sprinkle liberally with a cinnamon/sugar mixture.

3. Bake at 350°F, until crisp. Cut into wedges with a pizza cutter.

Goat Cheese Crusted Chicken with Roasted Green Beans

Juanita Broom

Ingredients

- Chicken breast (if thick, pound so they are even)
- Green beans, ends trimmed
- Mayonnaise
- Crumbled goat cheese
- Salt
- Olive oil
- Sliced almonds
- French's fried onion topping

1. Place chicken breast in oven proof dish. Spread 1 teaspoon of mayonnaise on each breast.

2. Crumble goat cheese on top.

3. Place trimmed beans beside chicken in the same dish. Drizzle olive oil and salt over the beans.

5. Bake at 400 degrees for 30-35 minutes, or until chicken reaches 165 degrees.

6. Remove from the oven and sprinkle fried onions on top of the chicken and sliced almonds on the beans.

Choose amounts based on how many servings you want.

Great Cashew Sauce

Greg and Laura Killmaster

Ingredients

- ¼ cup Cashew butter
- 1 cup olive oil
- 2 Tbsp. Tamari, soy sauce or Shoyu
- Juice of 1 lime
- 2 inches fresh grated ginger
- 1-1.5 inches fresh grated turmeric
- 2 fat cloves garlic
- ⅛ tsp. black pepper
- ½ teaspoon honey

1. Mince garlic and set aside for about 10 minutes. This allows it to develop the most allicin.*

2. Combine all ingredients into a 16 oz. ball jar and whisk to combine.

*https://en.wikipedia.org/wiki/Allicin

Green (or Red) Pepper Chicken

Susie Burch

1. Prepare rice according to package directions.

2. Combine soy sauce, garlic and ginger in a loaf pan.

3. Add cut up chicken to soy sauce mixture and stir gently to combine. Marinate while you prepare the vegetables. Heat oil in a large skillet, add chicken mixture and toss to cook over high heat until browned, well. Taste meat for tenderness. Turn heat to medium low and continue to cook about 10 to 15 minutes until tender.

4. Turn heat back to high and add the vegetables. Toss, cover, reduce heat and cook until crisp tender, about 10 minutes.

5. Mix corn starch into 1 cup of water until well blended. Add to pan, continuing to cook until thickened.

6. Add tomatoes, with juices, heat through.

7. Serve over rice and enjoy. In fact, I'm sure it could be made vegetarian by adding another vegetable like artichoke hearts, or water chestnuts. Any way you prepare this dish is delicious.

Ingredients

- 1 cup of uncooked rice prepared according to package directions
- 1 lb chicken tenders sliced into bite sized pieces (beef can be substituted)
- ¼ cup low salt soy sauce
- 1 clove garlic, minced
- 1 ½ tsp. grated fresh ginger (or ½ tsp ground ginger)
- ¼ cup olive oil
- 1 cup thinly sliced green onion
- 1 cup green (or red) bell pepper cut into strips 1" long
- 3 stalks of celery, cut into bite sized pieces
- 6 mushrooms, sliced
- 1 Tbsp cornstarch
- 1 cup water
- 1 14 oz. can of no salt added tomatoes

Also, I was a Master Gardener Volunteer in both Cobb and Fulton Counties for years prior to moving to Athens. This organization is the best!!

Green Tomato Pie

Jim Weck (My Mother's World-Famous Recipe)

Ingredients

- 1 unbaked pie pastry (to fit 10" pie pan)
- 5 cups sliced green tomatoes
- 1 tsp salt
- ¼ tsp pepper
- ¼ - ½ cup mayonnaise
- 1 cup grated sharp cheddar cheese
- 1 – 5 cloves garlic (depends on how much you love garlic)

1. Preheat oven to 350°F. Spray pie pan with canola oil and lay pastry in the pie pan. (It is optional if you want to bake it in a hot oven for 5 minutes, but not necessary).

2. Mix all the ingredients together with rubber spatula. You can add a red tomato for color.

3. Fill the pie shell with the mixture. Bake for 40 minutes and let sit for 10 minutes before serving. Enjoy!

Guacamole

Rosemary Stancil

Ingredients

- 4 ripe Hass avocado
- 3 tablespoons lime juice
- 8 dashes Tabasco Jalapeno Sauce
- ½ cup diced red onion
- 1 large clove garlic, minced
- 1 teaspoon kosher salt
- 1 teaspoon black pepper
- 1 medium tomato, seeded and diced
- Salt and pepper to taste

1. Cut the avocados in half, remove the pits, and scoop the flesh out of their shells into a bowl.

2. Immediately add the lime juice. Using a large fork or pastry blender, mash the avocados until they are the texture you prefer.

3. Stir in Tabasco, onion, garlic, salt, pepper and tomatoes. Mix well; taste and adjust seasonings if needed.

4. Lay plastic wrap directly on top of the guacamole to prevent surface darkening and refrigerate until ready to serve.

Makes 3 cups.

Haji Ali like Mango Cream
Rela Alice Jacob

Ingredients

- 1 cup fresh cream
- ½ cup condensed milk
- ¼ cup Mango pulp
- ¼ cup cut mango pieces
- Chopped Pistachios

1. Whisk the fresh cream in a bowl (I personally like using a simple spoon to do the same to maintain a fairly thick consistency). To this add the condensed milk and mix thoroughly.

2. Add in the mango pulp and mix it well.

3. Transfer the mixture into a serving bowl and add cut mango pieces to it. Garnish the dessert with chopped Pistachios and enjoy your mango cream bowl!

This is my version of the ever famous Mango Cream from the historic Haji Ali juice centre which was built half century ago in the bustling city of Mumbai. Hope you enjoy it!

Hannah's Tomatoes

Hannah Keifer (granddaughter of Suzanne Keifer)

Ingredients

- 2 large ripe tomatoes
- A big handful of ripe cherry tomatoes
- A couple of sprigs of fresh basil
- 4 oz. (grandma's interpretation) goat cheese.

1. Slice the large tomatoes about ¼" thick. Cut the cherry tomatoes in half. Rough chop the basil and put over the tomatoes. Crumble and sprinkle the goat cheese over the tomatoes.

Hannah has always been in the kitchen helping her mom prepare meals and has become quite the chef, in her own right, now at the ripe old age of almost 10. This is purely her recipe, is very tasty, easy to prepare, and healthy.

Huck's Cucumber Raita

Luca Huckleberry Mathew, Morristown, NJ

Ingredients

- 1 cucumber, peeled and diced (or grated)
- 2 cups yogurt (1 lb)
- ¼ tsp pepper
- ¼ tsp toasted ground cumin
- ½ tsp salt
- 1 Tbsp fresh, chopped coriander leaves for garnish
- Optional: ¼ cup diced onion

Served as a refreshing contrast along with rich, and flavorful rice dishes.

1. Mix all ingredients. Serve cold as a side dish with rice or naan.

See Thalli 2 picture on page 222.

Huck is Rita's grandson. At seven years old, he likes nothing better than Rice, Dal and Cucumber Raita. A healthy choice!

Italian Zucchini

SNAP Ed

Ingredients

- 2 Tbsp olive oil
- ½ cup chopped onion
- 4 medium zucchini, trimmed and sliced
- 1 can stewed tomatoes, low sodium
- ¼ tsp dried Italian herbs
- ¼ tsp ground black pepper
- ¼ cup grated Parmesan cheese

1. Heat oil in a skillet.

2. Add onion and zucchini; stir-fry for about 1 minute. Add tomatoes, herbs, salt, and pepper. Bring to a boil. Cover and steam 4 to 5 minutes or until zucchini is still slightly crisp, or to desired tenderness.

3. Sprinkle cheese on top and allow to melt slightly.

Layered Lettuce Salad

Rosemary Stancil

Ingredients

- 1 head iceberg lettuce or 1 large head Romaine lettuce
- 1 cup diced celery
- 4 eggs, cooked, peeled and sliced *
- 1 (10-ounce) package frozen peas, uncooked
- ½ cup diced green bell pepper
- ½ cup diced red bell pepper
- 1 medium purple onion, thinly sliced
- 1 (15-ounce) can sliced mushrooms, drained
- ½ cup bacon crumbles
- 1 cup mayonnaise
- 1 cup reduced fat sour cream
- 2 tablespoons sugar
- 1 tablespoon minced fresh herbs of choice (optional) – dill, basil, tarragon, oregano
- 4 ounces (1 cup) grated Cheddar cheese

1. Wash lettuce and spin it dry. Tear into bite size pieces. Place in a trifle dish or salad bowl.

2. Layer celery, eggs, peas, green and red bell pepper, onion, mushrooms, and bacon crumbles in order.

3. In a one-quart bowl combine mayonnaise, sour cream, sugar, and optional herbs. Spread over top of layered salad. Sprinkle with grated cheese. Cover and refrigerate for 8-12 hours or longer. Toss when ready to serve.

* To make perfect hard-boiled eggs, steam them. Place about 1 inch of water in a pot with a steamer insert and bring it to a simmer. Place a single layer of eggs in the insert over the water and cover. When the simmer returns, cook for 15 minutes. Take one egg out and peel it to check for doneness. When done, place eggs in ice water for 5 minutes. To peel them, tap each egg on the countertop to crack the shell, then roll them around to break the shell all over for easier peeling.

Great for a crowd. Serves 16.

Lemon Blueberry Bars

Eric Keifer

Ingredients

For the Filling:
- 2 lbs blueberries
- 1 cups sugar
- 1 Tbsp flour
- Juice of 1 lemon
- Zest of 1 lemon

For the Crust:
- 9x9" square baking dish
- 8 oz Lemon snaps
- ½ stick melted butter (4 Tbsp)

1. Preheat oven to 350° F. In a food processer grind lemon snaps. Add melted butter to ground lemon snaps. Place into bottom of 9 x 9 pan. Using bottom of measuring cup press crust to make firm. Bake at 350°F for 7-10 minutes.

2. In a large bowl add blueberries, lemon zest, sugar, flour and lemon juice. Stir to coat blueberries. Once crust is cooked, add blueberry mixture to top of crust. Bake for 25 -30 minutes. After cooking, place on wire rack to cool. Once cooled, cut into bars.

Margo's Main Dish

Candi Hoard

Ingredients

- 1 lb. ground beef or ground turkey
- 2 – 3 cloves of garlic (chopped)
- 1 medium onion (chopped)
- 1 14.5 oz can diced tomatoes
- 1 8 oz small can tomato sauce
- 1 6 oz can black olives, drained and sliced in half
- ½ tsp. salt
- ½ lb. cheddar cheese, cubed
- 1 cup uncooked macaroni

1. Brown ground beef and drain well. Add garlic and onion, cooking for a few minutes.

2. Add can of tomatoes, tomato sauce, black olives, salt, cheese, and uncooked macaroni. Stir well and cover.

3. Simmer 20 minutes, then let stand off heat 10 minutes. Enjoy!

Marinated Green Beans

Rosemary Stancil

Ingredients

- 1 ½ pounds haricot vert
- ¼ cup olive oil
- 2 tablespoons rice vinegar
- 1 teaspoon fresh dill
- 1 teaspoon grated lemon rind
- ½ teaspoon salt
- ¼ teaspoon black pepper
- ½ medium onion, finely chopped
- 1 clove garlic, minced

1. Wash beans. Steam until tender and let cool. To prepare a marinade, place oil, vinegar, dill, lemon rind, salt, pepper, onion, and garlic in a skillet. Cover and simmer until the onions are soft.

2. Cool slightly. Place beans and marinade in a plastic bag. Press air from the bag and seal it. Refrigerate overnight, turning several times to coat the beans with the marinade. Serve at room temperature.

Mexican Style Veggies

Rosemary Stancil

Ingredients

- 2 cloves garlic, minced
- 2 cups sliced onions
- 2 tablespoons olive oil
- 3 carrots, coarsely shredded
- 1 medium zucchini, cut in half lengthwise, then sliced in half circles
- 1 medium yellow squash, cut in half lengthwise, then sliced in half circles
- 1 (28-ounce) can tomatoes, undrained
- 1 (4 ounce) can chopped green chillies, undrained
- 1 teaspoon ground cumin
- 2 (15-ounce) cans black beans, drained
- ¼ teaspoon sugar
- ½ teaspoon salt or to taste
- Hot pepper sauce and black pepper to taste
- Shredded Cheddar cheese

1. In a large skillet, sauté garlic and onions in oil for about 5 minutes. Add carrots, zucchini, yellow squash, tomatoes, green chiles and cumin.

2. Cook uncovered for 15 minutes or until vegetables are tender, stirring several times. Stir in black beans, sugar, and salt. Season to taste with hot pepper sauce and pepper.

3. To serve, sprinkle with cheese.

This delicious side dish is also great served over cornbread for a light meal.

Yield: 6-8 servings

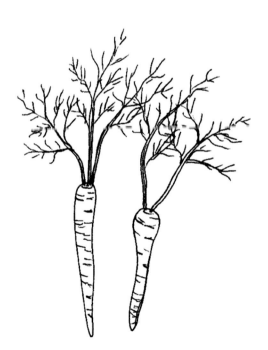

Mom's Zucchini Bread

Jackie Zogran

Ingredients

- 3 cups all-purpose flour
- 1 tsp salt
- 1 tsp. baking soda
- 1 tsp. baking powder
- 3 tsp. ground cinnamon
- 3 eggs
- 1 cup vegetable oil
- 2 ¼ cups white surge
- 3 tsp vanilla extract
- 2 cups grated zucchini
- 1 cup chopped walnuts

1. Grease and flour two 8 x 4-inch pans. Preheat oven to 325 degrees. Sift flour, salt, baking soda, baking powder and cinnamon together in bowl.

2. Beat eggs, oil, vanilla, and sugar together in a large bowl. Add sifted ingredients to the creamed mixture and beat well. Stir in zucchini and nuts until well combined.

3. Pour batter into prepared pans. Bake for 40 to 60 minutes. Cool in pan on rack for 20 minutes. Remove bread from the pans and completely cool.

Oven-Roasted Corn on the Cob with Coconut Ginger Butter

Suzanne Keifer

Ingredients

- 6-8 cleaned ears of sweet corn (I prefer the bicolor)
- 4 Tbsp coconut oil, at room temperature
- 4 Tbsp butter, at room temperature
- 2 Tbsp fresh ginger, grated on a Microplane
- Zest of 1 large orange
- 1 ½ tsp fresh lemon juice
- ½ tsp salt
- ¼ tsp pepper
- A couple of dashes of hot sauce (optional)

1. Pre-heat the oven to 400°F (or you can put them on the grill, wrapped well in aluminum foil). If cooking in the oven, line a rimmed pan with foil.

2. In a small bowl, combine all the ingredients and mix well with a spoon. Rub each ear of corn with the butter mixture.

3. Bake 35-40 minutes, turning halfway through the cooking time.

Peach Seafoam Salad

Jean Colquett

Ingredients

- 1 large can peach slices, drained (save 1 cup juice)
- 1 large box peach gelatin
- 1 8oz cream cheese, softened
- 1 large carton whipped topping

1. Heat 1 cup peach juice to boiling, add gelatin, stir to dissolve. Puree peaches in blender, add softened cream cheese and blend. Add most of dissolved gelatin (whatever it will hold comfortably) and blend.

2. Pour mixture (including remainder of gelatin) in a large bowl. Stir in whipped topping until all is smooth. (I use a small hand mixer on low speed.) Refrigerate until set and serve.

Pickles - Cucumbers, Okra, Peppers

Allan Cobb

Ingredients

- 5 ½ oz pickling salt - about ½ cup
- ½ cup filtered water
- 1 cup white or apple cider vinegar
- 3 pounds pickling cucumbers, peppers, or okra -- 4-6 inches long
- 1 tablespoon black peppercorns
- 1 tablespoon red pepper flakes
- 2 cloves garlic, crushed
- 1 teaspoon dill seed -- not needed for peppers
- 1 large bunch of dill -- not needed for peppers

1. Dissolve the salt in the water in a large pot, add vinegar and bring to a boil. Rinse the cucumbers, okra, or peppers thoroughly. Slice off the blossom end and stem on each cucumber, or cut into ¼ inch slices. Okra is better kept whole.

2. Soak veggies in an ice bath for 10 minutes to crisp. Fill jars with veggies, spices, and dill. Pour cooked liquid until jars are filled, leaving ¼ inch of air space at the top.

Must be refrigerated!

Potato Soup

Beverly Simpson

Ingredients

- 1 cup celery, chopped fine
- 1 cup onion, chopped fine
- 2 1/2 -3 cups potatoes, peeled and chopped
- 1 1/2 cups chicken broth
- 2 Tablespoons butter
- 1 cup of whole milk (You can substitute some half and half or cream for some of the milk if desired.)
- Salt and pepper to taste

Small red potatoes or Yukon Gold make a creamy soup, but any potatoes will do. Use at least whole milk.

1. Sauté celery and onions in large saucepan or stockpot in two Tablespoons butter or olive oil. Use a different stockpot and barely cover potatoes in water and boil softly until tender when forked. Drain most of water. Add chicken broth to potatoes. Mash potatoes with potato masher or similar device.

2. Add onions and celery and milk. Heat to a simmer but do not boil. Season with salt and pepper

Notes

Quinoa Pulao for Mayank

Rita Mathew

Ingredients

- 2 cups Quinoa
- 1 medium onion (thinly sliced)
- 3 Tbsp vegetable oil

Whole Spices:
- 8 peppercorns
- 6 cloves
- 1 cinnamon stick 2inches long (broken to smaller pieces)
- 4 cardamom pods
- 3 cloves garlic (minced)
- 1-inch fresh ginger (finely grated)
- 1 cup fresh or frozen peas and carrots (cooked)
- 2 Tbsps cranberry
- 3 Tbsps roasted cashew nut halves

- ½ tsp salt

1. Soak the Quinoa for at least four hours. Rinse thoroughly until the water is clear. Drain and set aside.

2. In a wide pan, heat the oil. Put the whole spices and stir fry for a couple minutes till they start popping and release an aroma. Put the sliced onion in the pan and fry till it is translucent. Stir in the garlic and ginger paste, cover and cook for a minute. Add the drained quinoa and fry gently for 3 −4 minutes.

3. Add 4 cups hot water and salt to the pan. Cover tightly and cook on medium heat till the water is evaporated and quinoa is cooked. Stir in peas, carrots, cranberries and cashew nuts.

4. Turn off the heat. Cover and let rest for 5 minutes. Serve hot.

Pictured on Inner Title Page.

Rachel's Summer Slushie

Rachel Keifer (granddaughter of Suzanne Keifer)

Ingredients

- 3-4 cups sliced strawberries (you can use frozen if fresh ones are out of season)
- Juice of 2 limes
- 1 -2 cups chilled water
- Honey or stevia to sweeten

1. In a blender, puree the strawberries and lime juice with just enough water to make a slushie.

2. Add honey or stevia to sweeten, if desired.

What better way to get a child to eat (or drink) fruit than to let them make it themselves. This is a healthy, refreshing treat. Rachel loves fruits of any kind; this is her summer favorite.

Ratatouille

Suzanne Keifer

Ingredients

- ¼ cup good olive oil
- 1 medium onion, chopped into 1" pieces
- 1 green bell pepper, seeded and cut into 1" cubes
- 1 small eggplant, peeled and cut into 1" cubes
- 2 zucchini, quartered length-wise and cut into 1" length pieces
- 3 cloves garlic, minced
- ½ red bell pepper, seeded and cut into 1" pieces
- 1 rib celery, cut into 1" pieces
- 1 cup sliced mushrooms
- 1 (28-oz) can and 1 (14-oz) can peeled Roma tomatoes, drained, and coarsely chopped (If using fresh tomatoes, substitute 10-12 for the 28-oz can and 5-6 for the 14-oz can.)
- Salt and pepper to taste
- 2 Tbsp fresh chopped Italian parsley
- Grated Parmesan cheese for serving

1. Heat the oil in a large Dutch oven over medium heat. Add onion, green pepper, eggplant, zucchini, garlic, red pepper and celery. Cook until tender, about 15 minutes, stirring periodically.

2. Stir in the mushrooms and tomatoes, season to taste with the salt and pepper, lower the heat and simmer gently for 30 to 40 minutes. Stir in the parsley and sprinkle the Parmesan on top.

3. This can be served as a side dish or an entrée. I have served it as a savory crepe and paired with a nice Spanish Rioja or Australian Shiraz.

Notes

Red Wine Spaghetti Sauce

Angela R. Keifer

1. In a large pan, sauté the garlic in the olive oil until aromatic. Add the chopped peppers and onions and continue to sauté until soft. Add the tomatoes.

2. Slowly pour the wine into the pan. Simmer for approximately 30 minutes. Add the tomato paste, sugar, and oregano, adjusting for taste.

3. Let it simmer another 10-15 minutes and enjoy.

Ingredients

- 1-2 Tbsp good olive oil
- 1-2 cloves garlic, pressed
- 1 bottle medium-bodied red wine (red Burgundy, Bordeaux, Temperanillo)
- 1 red bell pepper, seeded and chopped
- 1 green bell pepper, seeded and chopped
- 1 yellow bell pepper, seeded and chopped
- ½ - 1 medium onion, chopped
- 2 (14.5 oz) cans diced tomatoes, drained (10-12 fresh Roma tomatoes, diced)
- 6 – 8 Tbsp sugar
- 12 oz tomato paste.
- ¼ tsp fresh oregano

Roasted Red Salsa

Isaac Swier

Ingredients

- 2 pounds Roma tomatoes, halved lengthwise
- 4 cloves of garlic, unpeeled
- 1 large white onion, peeled, sliced ¼ inch thick slices
- 1 large jalapeno, quartered (for a more mild salsa, scrape seeds and membrane out and discard)
- 1 large bunch fresh cilantro, chopped finely
- 1 lime, juiced
- ½ Tbsp kosher salt

Time – 12 minutes

1. Preheat oven broiler to high. Place unpeeled garlic, onion, jalapeno, and tomatoes on a large baking sheet, skin side up. Broil for 5 to 10 minutes, or until tomatoes and jalapeno have blackened thoroughly on top.

2. Remove pan from oven, peel skin from garlic, and transfer other roasted ingredients into a large bowl along with the now peeled cloves of garlic. For a thin or smooth salsa, blend ingredients with a standard or immersion blender, or food processor. For a chunky salsa, dice as finely as desired.

3. Add cilantro, lime juice, and salt to taste.

Rustic Peach Galette

Suzanne Keifer

Ingredients

- 1 refrigerated pie crust
- 6 oz. softened cream cheese
- ⅓ cup sugar
- 1 egg, separated
- 1 tsp almond or vanilla extract
- 3-5 peaches, pitted, peeled, and sliced (depending how big the peaches are)
- 2 Tbsp raw sugar

1. Preheat oven to 375°F. Line a cookie sheet with parchment paper. Allow the pie crust to sit at room temperature for 10 minutes, then unroll it and place on the parchment paper.

2. In a bowl, combine the cream cheese, white sugar, egg yolk, and extract. Mix until well combined and spread it on top of the pie crust, leaving about 1 ½" around the edge without filling. Place the peaches in a swirl direction starting in the center on top of the cream cheese mixture.

3. Fold the crust edge up, crimping slightly on top of the filling all the way around the pie crust. Lightly brush the edges with beaten egg white. Sprinkle entire galette with the raw sugar.

4. Bake 30-35 minutes until the edges are golden brown.

Sautéed Corn and Zucchini   *Rosemary Stancil*

Ingredients

- 4 small zucchini
- 2 to 3 cloves garlic, minced
- 2 cups diced onion
- 2 tablespoons olive oil
- 2 cups fresh whole kernel corn
- ½ cup diced red bell pepper or 2 ounces jarred pimento peppers, drained
- ½ teaspoon sugar
- 1 teaspoon salt or to taste
- ¾ teaspoon lemon pepper
- 2 ounces (1/2 cup) shredded mozzarella cheese (Optional)
- 2 tablespoons chopped fresh basil

1. Cut zucchini lengthwise into quarters.

2. Then, thinly slice crosswise. Sauté zucchini, garlic and onion in oil for several minutes.

3. Add corn, red bell pepper, sugar, salt, and lemon pepper.

4. Cook, stirring frequently, until zucchini is tender.

5. Place in a serving dish and sprinkle with mozzarella cheese (optional) and basil while still warm.

Yield: 6 servings

Notes

Sea Bass with Tomatoes, Olives, and Capers

Marilyn Fuller

Ingredients

- 4 tsp good olive oil
- 4 (5 oz) skinless sea bass fillets (or other white fish)
- 1 cup diced onion
- ½ cup dry white wine
- 1 cup diced tomatoes (if using canned, preserve the juices)
- ½ cup pitted and chopped Kalamata olives
- 2 Tbsp capers, drained
- ¼ tsp red pepper flakes, optional
- 2 oz baby spinach leaves (about 2 lightly packed cups)
- Salt and freshly ground black pepper, to taste

1. In a large non-stick skillet, heat 2 teaspoons of the oil over medium-high heat, add the fish and cook until opaque (about 2-3 minutes per side per ½" of thickness of the fish).

2. Transfer the fish to a serving platter and tent with aluminum foil to keep warm.

3. Heat the remaining 2 teaspoons of olive oil in the same skillet; add the onions and cook for about 2 minutes.

4. Add the wine and cook until reduced by half (about 2 minutes). Add the tomatoes and simmer for 5 minutes. Add the olives, capers and red pepper and cook for 1 minute. Stir in the spinach and cook until it's wilted, about 3 minutes.

5. Season with salt and pepper and spoon this mixture over the fish.

Sharon's Summer Salad

Sharon Keifer (sister-in-law of Suzanne Keifer)

Ingredients

- 2 ½ lb red cherry tomatoes
- 1 ½ lb yellow cherry tomatoes
- 1 (14.5 oz) can of chickpeas, drained and rinsed
- 1 ½ cucumber (preferably English), peeled and sliced
- 2 avocados, peeled, cored, and diced
- ¼ cup chopped fresh parsley
- 3 oz. feta cheese crumbles

For the Dressing:
- ½ cup good olive oil
- ¼ cup fresh lemon juice
- 1 tsp. Dijon mustard
- 2 cloves garlic, minced
- ¼ tsp salt
- 1 Tbsp. fresh basil, chopped
- ¾ tsp dried oregano, or if you have fresh, ½ tsp chopped

1. Cut the tomatoes in half. Mix all ingredients in a large bowl.

2. Put all the dressing ingredients into a blender and pulse until well-mixed.

3. If you do not have a blender, whisk the dressing ingredients until well-mixed. Pour over salad when ready to eat.

Southern Salsa

SNAP Ed

Ingredients

- 1 (15.5 oz) can black-eyed peas
- 1/3 cup green onions, diced
- 1/3 cup green bell pepper, diced
- 1 small tomato, diced
- ½ bunch fresh cilantro
- 3 Tbsp lime juice
- 1 tsp canola or vegetable oil
- ½ tsp salt-free seasoning (like Mrs. Dash)
- ¼ tsp black pepper

1. Drain and rinse the black-eyed peas in a colander and place into a medium bowl. Add diced green onion, bell pepper, and tomatoes to the bowl with the peas.

2. Trim stems and chop cilantro into small pieces. Add to the black-eyed pea mixture.
Combine lime juice, oil, seasoning and black pepper in a jar with tight-fitting lit. Shake well.

3. Pour the lime juice mixture over the pea mixture and stir well. Serve as a salad or with tortilla chips.

Southwestern Squash

Rosemary Stancil

Ingredients

- Non-stick cooking spray
- 1 ½ pounds yellow summer squash, diced
- 1 medium onion, diced
- 3 tablespoons butter
- 1 (4 ounce) can diced green chiles, undrained
- 2 cloves garlic, minced
- 2 tablespoons flour
- 1 ¼ teaspoon kosher salt, divided
- ½ teaspoon plus 2 dashes freshly ground black pepper, divided
- 1 ½ cups shredded Monterey Jack cheese
- 2 eggs
- 2 cups small curd cottage cheese
- 2 tablespoons chopped parsley
- 14 Ritz crackers, finely crushed

1. Preheat oven to 350°F . Spray a 2-quart baking dish with cooking spray.

2. Sauté squash and onion in butter 4 or 5 minutes or until tender.

3. Fold in chiles, garlic, flour, 1 teaspoon salt and ½ teaspoon black pepper. Fold in Monterey Jack cheese, and spread evenly in the prepared baking dish. In a small bowl, combine eggs, cottage cheese, ¼ teaspoon salt, 2 dashes ground black pepper and parsley. Spread over squash mixture.

4. Sprinkle finely crushed crackers over cottage cheese mixture. Spray cracker crumbs with cooking spray. Bake uncovered for 40 minutes or until mixture is hot and crackers are lightly browned.

**Can be assembled and refrigerated a day before baking.

Spaghetti Squash

Viviane Van Giesen

Ingredients

- 1 spaghetti squash
- 4 ripe tomatoes chopped
- 3 Tbsp olive oil chopped
- 2 cloves of garlic
- Salt and pepper
- ½ cup shredded mozzarella
- ¼ cup parmesan
- Scallions or Parsley, finely chopped (optional)

1. Warm oven to 350°F.

2. Prick squash with fork and microwave 9 minutes on each side. While the squash is in the microwave, chop the vegetables.

3. Heat olive oil in a large frying pan, add garlic and sautée them until golden. Add tomatoes, season with salt and pepper. Reserve.

4. When the squash is ready, cut it in half, scrape out the seeds. Scrape the insides and put it in a lightly oiled glass baking dish. Add the tomatoes mixture to the spaghetti squash and toss them well.

5. Top with mozzarella, parmesan and put it in the oven until it is hot and cheese is melted, approximately 15-20 minutes.

6. Top it with fresh chopped scallions or parsley, or both! Enjoy!

This is super simple and so good. You know it's summer if you see a spaghetti squash for sale. You must use fresh tomatoes in this dish.

Spinach & Romaine Salad with Strawberries & Poppyseed Dressing

Ingredients

- 5-6 oz baby spinach
- 1 large head Romaine lettuce, chopped
- ¼ quart fresh strawberries, sliced
- ¼ small sweet onion, sliced thinly

For the Dressing:
- ¼ cup light mayonnaise
- ¼ cup plain nonfat yogurt
- 2 Tbsp balsamic vinegar
- ¼ cup non-fat milk
- 2 Tbsp poppy seeds
- 2 Tbsp honey

1. In a jar with a tight lid, combine all the dressing ingredients and shake well to combine.

2. In a large salad bowl, combine the salad ingredients.

3. Pour dressing over salad and toss to coat evenly.

Spinach Dip

Rosemary Stancil

Ingredients

- 1 (10-ounce) package frozen chopped spinach, thawed
- 2 tablespoons minced green onion
- 1 cup mayonnaise
- 1 ½ tablespoon (½ ounce) dry Ranch seasoning and dressing mix
- 1 teaspoon lemon juice
- 1 (8-ounce) can water chestnuts, drained and minced (Optional)

1. Drain and squeeze excess water from spinach.

2. Combine spinach, onion, mayonnaise, Ranch dressing mix, lemon juice and optional water chestnuts.

3. Serve with crackers and/or vegetable dippers.

Yield: 2 cups

Stuffed Peppers

Pam Tidwell

1. Preheat oven to 375°F.

2. In a medium mixing bowl, combine the rice, chicken, spinach, cheeses, and tomatoes. Add the pesto and mix well. Salt and pepper to taste.

3. Cut the bell peppers in half lengthwise, remove and discard the ribs and seeds.Spoon the rice mixture into the pepper halves. Place them in a 2-quart square baking dish and cover.

4. Bake for 40-45 minutes, or until the peppers are tender and the filling is well heated through.

5. Garnish with fresh basil, if desired.

Ingredients

- 1 cup cooked brown or white rice, cooled
- ½ cup cooked, chopped chicken breast
- ½ cup chopped spinach
- ⅓ cup shredded Italian blend cheese
- ¼ cup chopped tomatoes
- 2 tbsp shredded Parmesan cheese
- ⅓ cup basil pesto
- 2 large bell peppers, any color
- Salt and pepper to taste

Summer Baked Tomatoes

Tracey Massey

Ingredients

- 3 tomatoes
- Salt as needed
- 1 summer squash, finely diced
- ½ cup dry herb stuffing mix
- Several fresh basil leaves (or substitute dry)
- ¼ tsp ground black pepper
- ¼ cup shredded mozzarella cheese

1. Preheat oven to 350F.

2. Slice tomatoes in half horizontally, sprinkle cut side with salt, and place cut sides down on paper towels to absorb excess liquid.

3. Hollow out halves, leaving sides approximately ¼ inch thick. Retain and chop pulp.

4. Place chopped pulp and remaining ingredients into a mixing bowl and combine thoroughly.

5. Stuff mixture into hollowed tomato halves. Bake in preheated oven for approximately 20 minutes, or until squash is soft and cheese is melted.

Summer Pasta Salad

Jackie Zogran

Ingredients

- 1-pound cooked spaghetti
- 1 green pepper, chopped
- 2 tomatoes chopped
- 1 small red onion chopped
- 1 regular size bottle of Italian Dressing
- ½ bottle McCormick or Durkee Salad Seasoning

1. Boil, and when done, drain spaghetti and add all ingredients. Mix together.

Summer Vegetable Salad

1. Preheat oven to 375°F. Cut bread into cubes and place on baking sheet. Drizzle vegetable oil over bread and toss to spread evenly. Bake for about 8 minutes until bread is golden brown.

2. Rinse and dry green beans. Cut in half and place in a microwave safe bowl with ¼ cup water.

3. Microwave for 3 minutes then immediately put green beans in ice water to stop cooking.

4. Set aside while you prepare the other ingredients.

5. Cut zucchini and summer squash in half lengthwise, then slice.

6. Combine squash, zucchini, green beans, tomatoes, and mozzarella cheese. Pour Italian dressing over the vegetables and toss gently to coat evenly. Add toasted bread cubes right before serving.

Ingredients

- 4 slices whole grain bread
- 1 tsp vegetable oil
- 1 cup green beans
- 1 zucchini
- 1 yellow summer squash
- 2 tomatoes, chopped
- 1 cup shredded part-skim mozzarella
- 1 cup lite Italian dressing
- 1 dash black pepper (optional)

Sweet Bell Pepper Stir-Fry

Rita Mathew

Ingredients

- 8 oz assorted mini sweet peppers (yellow, red, orange)
- 1 medium onion finely sliced
- 2 Tbsp Oil
- 2 cloves garlic (minced)
- 1 hot green chilli
- 10 kari leaves
- 1 cup cooked sprouted Mung beans (optional) (directions for sprouting on page 137)
- ½ tsp salt

1. Wash the sweet peppers, trim tops and slice length wise.

2. Heat the oil in a medium sized pan. Stir fry the onion until they are translucent. Stir in the minced garlic, green chili and kari leaves.

3. Cover the dish, and cook on medium heat for 2 minutes. Mix in sliced sweet peppers, add the salt, cover and cook for 5 minutes.

4. Add the sprouted Mung beans, cook for another 15 minutes before serving.

Pictured on Back Cover

Tomato Basil Pie

Allan Cobb

1. Preheat oven to 350 and grease a 9 X 13 baking dish. Spread 2 sleeves of crushed crackers and layer the bottom of the baking dish. Pour half the tomatoes over the crackers.

2. Sauté onions in olive oil, salt, and pepper until tender. Layer half the onions on top of the tomatoes.

3. Layer 1 sleeve of crackers, then pour the rest of the tomatoes over. Now add the rest of the onions.

4. In a separate bowl, add the mayo, cheeses, and chopped basil, mix well, then spread
over the top.

5. Last, add the remaining sleeve of crackers to top it off. Bake for 30 - 40 minutes, until golden brown.

Ingredients

- 2 lbs diced tomatoes
- 1 box Ritz crackers, crushed
- 2 medium onions, chopped
- 1 ½ cups shredded sharp cheddar cheese
- 1 cup grated Parmesan
- 2 cups mayonnaise
- 3 tablespoons chopped fresh basil
- ⅓ cup olive oil
- ¼ teaspoon salt
- ¼ teaspoon ground black pepper

Tricolor Sprouted Mung Bean Breakfast Dish

Rita Mathew

This Sprouted Mung Bean dish makes for a nutritious breakfast or brunch dish.

1. See directions to sprout and cook green mung beans on page 137.

2. Put 1 cup cooked sprouts in a large mixing bowl.

3. Add the remaining ingredients and stir well before serving.

Optional - ½ cup yogurt

Mung Bean Kochumbir

1. If serving as a side dish for lunch, omit fruits, and add diced cucumber, grated carrots, diced bell pepper and tomatoes. Add 1 tsp of roasted cumin and 1 chopped green chilli.

2. Garnish with 1 Tbsp chopped mint or cilantro.

Pictured on Back Cover.

Ingredients

• 1 cup sprouted cooked green Mung bean (see page 137 for directions on sprouting)
• ½ cup apples (peeled and chopped)
• ½ cup blueberries
• ½ cup fresh peach (cut in pieces)
• ½ cup cranberries (chopped)
• ½ cup shelled roasted pecans (chopped in ¼)
• ½ tsp lemon juice
• 2 Tbsp Honey
• ¼ tsp salt

Optional:
• ½ cup diced cucumber
• ¼ cup grated carrots
• ¼ cup diced bell pepper
• ¼ cup tomato pieces
• 1 tsp cumin powder
• 1 tsp chopped Thai green chilli

Turkey and Squash Skillet

SNAP Ed

Ingredients

- 1 pound ground turkey
- 4-5 yellow squash, sliced
- 1 green pepper, chopped
- 1 (14.5 oz) can stewed tomatoes
- ¼ tsp ground pepper

1. In a medium skillet, brown the ground turkey, drain off grease and rinse turkey in a colander.

2. Return turkey to the skillet.

3. Stir in squash, green pepper and tomatoes. Add ground pepper (if desired). Cook over medium heat for 10 minutes or until desired tenderness. Serve hot.

Vegetable Pulao

Caroline D'Souza

Ideal as a stand-alone dish or as the main dish in a course dinner. This easy-to-prepare fragrant, nutritious vegetable pulao is rich in Vitamin A, Folates, and magnesium.

1. Soak the rice in water for an hour; it will swell a bit. Rinse in running water and drain in a strainer.

2. Finely cut the onion and tomato. Keep shelled peas and corn ready.

3. Heat 2 teaspoons of oil, on low heat, in a heavy bottom pan.

4. Add cumin seeds, cloves, pepper corns and cinnamon.

5. Add the finely cut onion and fry till pink. Add tomato and fry again till it forms a paste.

6. Add carrot, green peas and corn and stir.

7. Add the rice and stir lightly. Crumble the Maggi © cube and add along with two cups of hot water.

8. Cover tightly and cook for 15 – 20 minutes on medium heat.

9. Add a dash of lemon juice and mix, to ensure well separated rice grains.

10. Serve piping hot. Garnish with thinly- sliced boiled egg, or finely chopped coriander.

Ingredients

- 1 cup basmati rice
- ½ cup diced carrots
- ¼ cup green peas
- ¼ cup corn
- 1 medium-sized tomato
- 1 medium-sized onion
- 4 to 5 cloves
- few cumin seeds
- 4 to 5 pepper corns
- small piece of cinnamon
- 1 Maggi © cube
- 2 cups hot water
- a pinch of salt
- dash of lemon juice

Wild Blackberry Jam

Allan Cobb

Ingredients

- 2 pounds washed wild blackberries -- about 10% un-ripe to provide more pectin
- 4 cups white sugar
- 2 oz apple cider vinegar
- 1 tablespoon finely chopped mint leaves

1. Mix ingredients together in a large saucepan. Stir over low heat until sugar dissolves, then increase heat and bring to a rolling boil. Stir often and boil until mixture reaches 220 degrees F.

2. Transfer to hot, sterile jars, leaving ½ - ¼ inch air space at the top. Process in a water bath to make shelf stable or refrigerate.

Yogurt Crunch Parfait

SNAP Ed

Ingredients

- 3 Tbsp fresh blueberries
- 4 oz lemon low-fat yogurt
- 1 Tbsp crushed breakfast cereal

1. Spoon blueberries into a cup and top with yogurt.

2. Sprinkle the cereal on top and serve immediately.

112

Zippy Tomato Sauce

Rev. Manjula Spears

- 12 ripe tomatoes
- 2 large onions
- 2 bell peppers (any color)
- 2 cups vinegar
- 2 cups sugar (or your favorite sweetener)
- 2 Tbsp salt
- 1 cup (or to taste) fresh hot peppers

1. Cut tomatoes, onions, and bell peppers into chunky pieces.

2. Mix ingredients in a large pot and bring to a boil for 10 minutes. Lower the heat and simmer for 2 hours.

3. Pour into jars and let it seal.

This recipe was taught to me by my neighbor Runell Thaxton when she was 83 and still growing her own food. It is her creation. I make it every summer fresh from the garden and add it to vegetable dishes and soups throughout winter to add a little warmth and sweetness.

Notes

Zucchini Bread

Allan Cobb

Ingredients

- 3 cups All Purpose Flour
- 1 teaspoon salt
- 1 teaspoon baking soda
- 1 teaspoon baking powder
- 1 tablespoon ground cinnamon
- 3 eggs beaten
- 1 cup vegetable oil
- 2 ¼ cups white sugar
- 3 teaspoons vanilla extract
- 2 cups grated zucchini
- 1 cup chopped walnuts (optional)

A great way to use your abundant zucchini harvest!

1. Preheat oven to 325 and grease and flour two 8 X 4-inch pans.

2. Sift the flour, salt, baking powder, soda, and cinnamon together in a bowl. Beat eggs, oil, vanilla, and sugar together in a large bowl. Add sifted ingredients to the creamed mixture and beat well.

3. Stir in zucchini and nuts until well combined.

4. Pour batter into prepared pans and bake for 45-60 minutes. Stick a knife in the middle to test, it will come out clean when done.

Spicy Zucchini Bread

Suzanne Keifer

Ingredients

- 1 tsp baking soda
- 3 cups all-purpose flour
- 1 tsp baking powder
- 1 tsp each cinnamon, nutmeg
- 1 cup chopped pecans
- ¾ cup vegetable oil
- 3 eggs
- 2 cups sugar
- 2 tsp vanilla extract
- 3 cups shredded zucchini

1. Combine first six ingredients in a large mixing bowl; make a well in the center of the mixture and set aside.

2. In another bowl, combine oil, eggs, sugar, and vanilla. Mix well. Stir in the shredded zucchini. Add this mixture into the dry ingredient mixture, stirring until just moistened.

3. Spoon into 2 greased and floured loaf pans. Bake at 350°F for 1 hour. Cool loaves 10 minutes in pans and then remove to wire racks.

"Tomatoes"
©2021 *Viviane Van Giesen*

Seeding Place

by Virginia D. Nazarea

Dr. Virginia D. Nazarea is Professor of Anthropology and Director of the Ethnoecology/Biodiversity Lab at the University of Georgia. She co-founded the Southern Seed Legacy with her husband, Dr. Robert E. Rhoades. She has published several books on biodiversity conservation including Cultural Memory and Biodiversity, Heirloom Seeds and their Keepers, and Seeds of Resistance, Seeds of Hope. A forthcoming volume, Moveable Gardens: Itineraries and Sanctuaries of Memory, sheds light on the many ways plants and food root us in times of displacement.

A random collection of musings on seasons of grief, love, and hope embedded in seeds

. . .

color my dreams amber
in all the many shades
of undulating grains

seedpods like sanctuaries
glowing hearths and fiery sunsets
summer asters and autumn leaves

spore-dotted ferns in misty glades
dust in the mid-afternoon heat
rocks in the dusky haze

hair growing on a baby's scalp
medals pinned on a child's chest
tears flowing on a grandmother's
cheek

. . .

you brought home a mess of greens
peppered with okra, and tomatoes
bounty of bounties, sometimes
just a wee bit overwhelming
for your wife who didn't know
a thing about "putting up"
having come from a land
of eternal verdant summer

your leavetakings were just about
as original as your homecomings
but i shall always remember
you coming home
farm-steeped at sundown
bearing gifts of freckled eggs
in pretty shades of beige and blue
amid a tumble of beans

. . .

alternating scorching sun, drenching rain
stripping layers of love, security, comfort
empty, angry, pit-of-the stomach churning
until there's nothing left but the germ of life
a paradox, a mystery why it's there at all
and then life stirs as if a rebellious child
unwilling to accept the terms of its banishment
clinging to memories, and then to beauty
not just of what's left, but what's blossoming
unsolicited, incongruous, out-of-place
and yet persistent, tugging, a wily trickster
until it wins, until the churning stops
life, driven underground, seeps out again
cool breeze, dappled light, mist lifting

. . .

pushed on a plane
by her pilot husband
on the "fall of vietnam"
heavy with their first child
spirited off to an alien land
harsh, strange, and cold
she broke the ground
she sprinkled her seeds
lemon grass, bitter melon
chives, mango, papaya, too
flavors and aromas of home
her backyard domesticated
as memories anchored
a new self, emerging

. . .

i garden, therefore i am
i pickle, therefore i am
the trauma of forgetting
the salve of re-membering
what time has rendered asunder
rooted and ripened together again

. . .

google maps show
no school buses
scratching chickens
or barn cats
no mothers rushing
no immigrants lining up
a precise landscape
without emotion
generosity
or sacrifice
a space, not place
wounds without causes
memory obliterated

. . .

love
like rain
falls
like honey
spreads
like a garden
overflows

Fantastic Fall Vegetable Gardening

Gary Wade, Ph.D.

Gary Wade is a retired UGA Professor, Extension Program Coordinator for the Department of Horticulture, and AAMGA member. He was the first statewide coordinator of the Georgia Master Gardener program. He edited the first training manual, developed training resources and helped initiate new Master Gardener training programs in over 50 counties across Georgia. In 1987 he helped form the Georgia Master Gardener Association, one of the first statewide organizations in the U.S.

Because of our relatively mild winter climate, Georgians can grow two major gardens a year: a spring/summer garden and a fall/winter garden. One of the frustrating things about transitioning from the summer to the fall garden is that we sometimes have to sacrifice some of the summer vegetables while they are still producing to make way for the fall crops. Peppers and tomatoes, for instance, will often bear fruit until the first fall frost. However, it is equally disheartening to plant too late in the fall only to have crops like broccoli or cauliflower killed by a hard freeze in January. While most fall vegetables prefer cool weather, many will not tolerate hard freezes below 25oF. The ideal situation would be to have unused space reserved for the fall garden while the summer garden is still producing, so there would be no excuse for not planting on time. But when property size is limited, having separate spaces for summer and fall gardens is not always possible.

FALL GARDENING BASICS

Major cool-season crops that can be planted in fall include beets, broccoli, cabbage, carrots, cauliflower, collards, Brussel sprouts, garlic, kale, kohlrabi, leeks, mustard, onions, parsnips, rutabaga, spinach, Swiss chard, and turnips. Asparagus can also be planted in fall, although it is a perennial and not just a cool-season crop. (Many perennial herbs and specialty crops, like arugula, endive and Bok choi can also be planted in fall).

It's always good to start with a soil test to determine the nutritional needs of the soil. Soil testing is available for a nominal fee through your county extension office. Without the benefit of a soil test, a general recommendation would be to cultivate the area, then broadcast 10-10-10 fertilizer at a rate of 1 lb. (2 cups) per 100 sq. ft. over the area to be planted and work it into the top few inches of soil with a stiff rake.

OTHER CONSIDERATIONS

- To get a 4 to 6 week jump on the planting season, consider planting seedling plants purchased from a garden center. Vegetable plants generally available in the fall include cabbage, broccoli, Brussel sprouts, cauliflower, mustard greens, collards, and lettuce.
- Many fall crops can be direct-seeded, including beets, carrots, kale, lettuce, turnips, parsnips, rutabaga,

spinach, mustard, radishes, Swiss chard, kohlrabi, and leeks.

• Onions planted in fall are best planted from plants or onion sets. Garlic is best planted from cloves instead of seed.

• Most fall crops will benefit from additional fertilizer during the growing season. Side-dress beets, broccoli, cabbage, carrots, cauliflower, Brussel sprouts, kohlrabi, onions, and turnips with additional 10-10-10 fertilizer (1lb. (2 cups) per 100 sq. ft. or approximately 100 linear feet of row) at four-week intervals during the growing season. Leafy greens, including lettuce, collards, mustard, spinach and Swiss chard, will benefit from liquid feed, such as Miracle-Gro, applied every two weeks.

• Consider succession planting of seeded crops; that means planting a few seeds every two to three weeks so the crop does not all mature at once. Repeated plantings of crops like lettuce, kale, mustard, spinach, Swiss chard, radishes and turnips will extend the harvest season.

• Consider designating two months of the year (preferably January and February when we have the greatest likelihood of hard freezes) as soil improvement months, when the garden is fallow and free of all crops. Apply six to eight inches of fall leaves over the surface of the garden along with a light sprinkling of a nitrogen fertilizer such as ammonium nitrate (1/2 cup/100 sq. ft.) or 10-10-10 fertilizer (2 cups/100 sq. ft.) to provide energy for the microbes that will be breaking down the leaves. Then use a tiller to incorporate the leaves into the top twelve inches of soil. Repeat the tilling every two to three weeks until the leaves are well broken down.

NEVER LET YOUR LEAVES LEAVE HOME!

Remember....The average date of the first frost in fall is November 15, give or take two weeks.

General Guidelines for Growing the Major Fall-planted Vegetables

Asparagus is a perennial plant that may grow for 20+ years in the garden, so it's best to establish it in an area to itself where it will not be disturbed, such as a 10 ft. x 10 ft. raised bed separated from the rest of the garden. Asparagus is established from crowns purchased from garden centers or mail-order nurseries. Plant the crowns twelve inches apart in soil enriched with organic matter. Do not harvest the shoots the first year, but let the plant grow vegetatively. Tender new shoots can be harvested the second year and each spring thereafter. Recommended varieties include Jersey Giant, Jersey Prince, Jersey King and Viking KBC.

Beets are planted from seed. Broadcast seed over the soil surface and cover lightly. Once they germinate, thin and transplant individual plants two to four inches apart to give them space to develop their roots. Beet leaves and roots are both edible. Recommended varieties include Detroit Dark Red, Red Ace and Ruby Queen (there are many others).

CABBAGE, BROCCOLI, CAULIFLOWER, COLLARDS AND BRUSSEL SPROUTS can be grown from seed, but most home gardeners purchase transplants that already have a four to six week jump on the growing season. Seeds are typically planted in seeding flats in late July or early August, then transplanted into pots for planting in early September. Space plants twelve to eighteen inches apart, depending on variety. Brussel sprouts and cabbage are the hardiest of all these plants and are capable of surviving temperatures into the low 20's without damage. However, broccoli, cauliflower and collards will take mild freezes, but their leaves and buds will be damaged at temperatures below 25oF.

CARROTS AND PARSNIPS have similar cultural requirements. They need a loose, well-drained soil. Seeds are very small, and it is difficult to obtain a stand if the soil is crusty. Try mixing the seeds with dry sand to get even distribution. Then, instead of covering with soil, cover the seed 1/8-inch deep with sawdust or manufactured potting soil. Seeds need to stay moist during germination, so cover them with a couple of layers of moist newspaper until they germinate. Thin the plants when they are one to two inches tall and plant them ten to inches apart. Recommended varieties of carrots are Apache, Camden, Chantenay, Danvers 126, and Orlando Gold. Parsnip varieties include All American, Hollow Crown, and Harris Model. Most carrots mature in seventy to ninety days from seeding, while parsnips may take more than a hundred days. However, parsnips are very cold hardy and can survive temperatures in the low 20's.

GARLIC is planted in fall and harvested May or June of the following year. First, purchase cloves from a nursery or garden center, and don't use those from the grocery store. Those in the grocery store may not be the type that grows well in your area. They also are treated with a chemical to extend their shelf life and to prevent them from sprouting. Plant individual cloves four inches apart in rows spaced twelve inches apart. Make certain the pointed end (growing point) of each clove is facing upward. In spring, cut off any flower heads that form on the end of the stalk because they rob energy from the developing bulbs. After digging, store bulbs in a cool, dark place. They keep for months. Do not separate the bulb into cloves until you are ready to cook with them. Common varieties are Purple Stripe, Porcelain, Rocambole, Silverskin and Mild French.

LETTUCE seeds require light to germinate, so scatter them over the soil, rake them ever so lightly to disperse them on the soil surface, then use your hand to tamp them down to assure contact with the soil. Be sure to save some seeds back for succession planting at two to four week intervals to extend the harvest season. A variety of leaf lettuces, bibb (romaine-type) lettuces and small heading lettuces can be grown. The large-headed iceberg lettuce found in grocery stores does not grow well in the South. Once lettuce seeds germinate, thin them out by transplanting individual plants six to twelve inches apart, depending on the type of lettuce and mature size. Water with liquid feed each two weeks to boost them along. When harvesting, use a knife to cut the plant off at ground level, leaving the root in the ground. If you pull up roots and all, the soil will be scattered over the plants, and cleaning will be more difficult.

MUSTARD GREENS, KALE AND SPINACH are all planted from seed, and all have basically the same cultural requirements. Thin out the plants when they are two inches tall, and transplant them six to ten inches apart. Like lettuce, they can be boosted along with liquid feed applied each two weeks during the growing season. Harvest the outermost mature leaves, leaving the younger leaves in the center to grow and mature for later harvest.

ONIONS AND LEEKS are planted in fall and harvested in spring. The cool winter months enhance their mild flavor. Onions are planted from starter plants purchased in bundles of fifty to eighty plants, or from onion sets purchased usually in packages. There are two types of onions, those grown for their green stems and those grown for bulbs. Plant onion sets or plants four inches apart. Unlike onions that produce bulbs, leeks produce fleshy stems and fan-shaped leaves. To produce a succulent white stem, leeks must be blanched or hidden from the sun. To do this, plant them in trenches six to eight inches deep, then mound soil around the base of the stem as the seedling emerge. Common varieties are Alaska, Broad London or Titan. Both leaves and stems of onions and leeks are eaten raw or cooked in stews and soups.

RADISHES are among the easiest of all vegetables to grow. Most varieties mature in twenty-five to thirty days from the time they are seeded, so be sure and save some seed for succession planting at two to four-week intervals to extend the harvest. Harvest radishes when they are young and tender. If left in the ground too long, they often split, become woody and develop a strong, bitter and hot taste. Common varieties are Cherry Bell, Scarlet Globe and Champion. Experiment with radishes; some varieties grows long like carrots while others are round. Some are white and some are red. Check out the seed catalogs for the wide variety of radish varieties available.

SWISS CHARD is a member of the beet family. It is planted from seed, thinned out and transplanted about twelve inches apart. It will tolerate only mild freezes, so it's best to plant it by mid-September, so you can harvest before the first hard freezes of winter. Both leaves and stems can be eaten raw or cooked like spinach. Recommended varieties include Bright Lights, Burgundy, Rhubarb, and Winter King. Swiss chard is very ornamental and is sometime used in flower beds or containers. However, deer like to eat it too.

TURNIPS, KOHLRABI, PARSNIPS AND RUTABAGAS all have the same basic cultural requirements. They can be seeded, then thinned out and transplanted far enough apart to allow for root and top development (six to ten inches for turnips and parsnips, and twelve to fourteen inches for kohlrabi and rutabagas. They should be planted by mid-September to get the crop finished before the first heavy frost, and certainly before hard freezes. Roots and tops of all four plants can be harvested and eaten raw or cooked. There are many excellent varieties of each plant. Look for those known to perform well in the South.

REFERENCES

www.caes.uga.edu. Click on "publications" and search for topic of interest.

Composting: Life (Re) Cycle

Suzanne Keifer

Suzanne Keifer is a retired Physical Therapist, having been in practice for over 40 years in New York, Florida, and Georgia. While her career primarily focused on varying aspects of caring for people, she also developed an affinity (some call it passion) for caring for plants, especially roses, thanks in large part to her aunt. In 2020, she successfully completed the Master Gardener Extension Volunteer Program in Athens-Clarke County and now puts the "why, where, and how" of that training to good use. She currently is busy watching her grandchildren and gardens grow and flourish, volunteering in the Master Gardener program, and enjoying the bounties of Mother Nature.

According to the U.S. Environmental Protection Agency (EPA),[1] landfills in the US received more than 140 million tons of waste annually in 2017. This included almost 31 million tons of food and 18.35 million tons of paper products.

One of the most recent EPA studies (2017)[2] showed that, on average, four and a half pounds of waste were generated per person/per day in the U.S, which included bottles, corrugated boxes, food, grass clippings, sofas, computers, tires, and appliances. This study revealed some interesting statistics about where the total 267 million tons of waste was deposited:

- 67.1 million tons went to recycling
- 26.9 million tons went to composting
- 34 million tons went to energy recovery methods
- 139.5 million tons still went to the landfills.

Since the EPA studies started in 1960, there has been an almost tenfold increase in recycling, composting, and energy recovery per person/per day. Whereas 94% of waste was headed to landfills in 1960, only about 53% was sent to landfills in 2017. In terms of energy and greenhouse gas benefits of recycling, composting, and combustion with energy recovery, EPA's WARM (Waste Reduction Model) tool calculated a savings of over 184 million metric tons of carbon dioxide equivalent. This is comparable to removing almost 39 million cars from the road in one year! So why don't more people try to compost? Is it due to a lack of knowledge? Lack of space? Lack of interest? Most folks have tried to compost at some time in their life but were unsuccessful for any number of reasons: too much work, it smelled, it never turned to compost, etc.

There is an art and science to composting. It requires making a commitment to reduce waste, a skill to be learned. However, once the skill is mastered, it's rewarding to know that you have reduced the amount of landfill waste, saved water by helping the soil to retain moisture from the organic material in the compost, saved yourself some money by not having to buy commercial compost and amendments, and, not to mention, having improved the quality of your and your plants' environment by reducing methane and carbon dioxide. Composting promotes higher crop yields for farmers; aids in restoring forests, wetlands, and

---

1 https://www.epa.gov/facts-and-figures-about-materials-waste-and-recycling/food-material-specific-data
2 https://www.epa.gov Advancing Sustainable Materials Management: 2017 Fact Sheet

habitats by improving poor quality soil; and helps soil recover from contamination by hazardous waste.

There are several composting methodologies ranging from simple to complex; you just need to choose what works best for you:

1) Heaps are just that – just pile up your yard waste and let it sit. After a couple of years, you'll have compost.
2) Hoops (typically made from hog or chicken wire) keep the compost heap tidy and organized. You can add sticks and twigs to help aerate the compost pile. You might still have to dig in and tumble or rotate the material.
3) Bins can be purchased or made at home, and, if made rodent-proof, some organic food waste can be added.
4) Tumblers are enclosed and do the mixing for you. Even buckets (with a tight-fitting lid) can be used if space is an issue. Make sure you only fill the bucket half way to make room for tumbling/stirring.

Only a few ingredients are necessary to make compost: green matter (high in nitrogen), brown matter (high in carbon), water, and air. Together, these ingredients allow fungi, bacteria, worms, and other organics to break down the materials you put in your compost. The best way to ensure a good mix is to include 2/3 dry brown material (leaves, sticks, etc.) and 1/3 green material (grass clippings, fruit and vegetable scraps, coffee grounds, eggshells).

Add water as necessary to make sure the organisms are breaking down the organic matter. You want the consistency to feel like a lightly wrung out sponge. Depending on how often you mix up the compost will dictate how quickly you'll have compost. Turning frequently provides oxygen to the organisms and can speed up the composting process. Temperatures in the compost can reach as high as 120-150°F, thus killing any pathogens or weed seeds in the process. It's necessary that the compost maintain this temperature for at least a few days in order to kill weed seeds. The compost is ready when it looks like rich dark humus. If there are some larger pieces that did not completely decompose, you can put them back into the compost pile to start a new batch.

Some uses for compost include a soil amendment to your garden beds or to poorly performing clay soil. This can be done by adding mulch around your trees, shrubs and plants, or even as a component of potting mix. Green practices, recycling, composting, and energy renewing, work to keep our environment cleaner and healthier. By using nature resources that are available in your home and garden, composting renews, recycles, and restarts the cycle of nature.

WHAT CAN AND CANNOT BE PUT IN YOUR COMPOST:

Yes!	No!
Fresh veggies and food scraps	Cooked food/oils/greases
Crushed eggshells	Cheese and dairy
Coffee grounds/filters/tea bags	Meat and bones
Grass clippings and dry leaves	Poisonous/diseased plants
Cut flowers, plant stalks, twigs, etc	Glossy/coated paper
Shredded newspaper	Pet/human waste
Untreated straw	Treated/painted wood
Untreated wood chips/shavings	Aggressive weeds/grasses

Fall

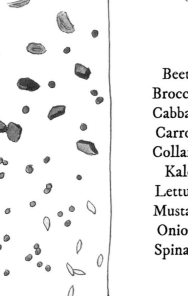

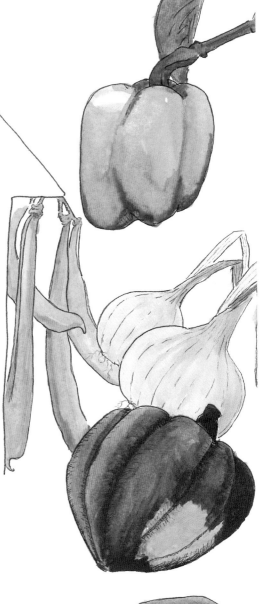

A Time
to Reap

Beets
Broccoli
Cabbage
Carrots
Collards
Kale
Lettuce
Mustard
Onions
Spinach

A Time
to Sow

Beets
Bell Peppers
Broccoli
Brussels Sprouts
Cabbage
Carrots
Cauliflower
Celery
Collards
Green Beans
Kale
Onions
Peas
Potatoes
Spinach
Sweet Potatoes
Swiss Chard
Turnips
Winter Squash

		Produce (1 Cup, raw. Unless otherwise stated)														Legumes (Pulses)					
		1 Avocado (without skin and seed, 136 gm)	Bell Pepper	Carrots (1 cup chopped)	Cauliflower	Celery	Green Beans	Kale	Potatoes (1 large, 369 gm)	Sweet Potatoes	Apples (1 medium, 161 gm)	Bananas (1 medium ripe, 118 gm)	Oranges (1 Florida, 141 gm)	Pears (1 medium, 178 gm)	Plums (1 whole, 66 gm)	Black Chick Peas - Kala Chana (1 Cup cooked 200 gm)	Brown Lentils - Masoor (1 Cup cooked 200 gm)	Green Mung Beans (1 Cup cooked 200 gm)	Orange Masoor Dal (1 Cup cooked)	Pigeon Peas (whole yellow split peas, 1 Cup cooked)	Yellow Split Peas (1 Cup cooked)
Nutrition (Grams)	Calories	227	29.8	52.5	25	16.2	34.1	33.5	284	114	77.3	105	64.9	103	30.4	267	230	212	186	203	231
	Carbohydrates	11.8	6.9	12.3	5.3	3.5	7.8	6.7	68	26.8	20.5	27	16.3	27.5	7.5	44.7	39.9	38.7	23	39.1	41.4
	Protein	2.7	1.3	1.2	2	0.7	2	2.2	7.5	2.1	0.4	1.3	1	0.7	0.5	14.4	17.9	14.2	9	11.4	16.3
	Fat	21	0.3	0.3	0.1	0.2	0.1	0.5	0.3	0.6	0.2	0.4	0.3	0.2	0.2	4.2	0.8	0.8	7	0.6	0.8
	Fiber	9.2	2.5	3.6	2.5	1.6	3.7	1.3	8.1	4	2.1	3.1	3.4	5.5	0.9	12.5	15.6	15.4	8	11.3	16.3
Vitamins (% DV)	Vitamin A	4	11	428	0	9	15	206	0	377	1	2	6	1	5	2	0	1	1	0	0
	Vitamin C	20	200	13	77	5	30	134	121	5	11	17	106	12	10	4	5	3	1	0	1
	Vitamin K	36	14	21	20	37	20	684	9	3	1	1	0	10	5	7	4	7	7	0	12
	Folate	30	4	6	14	9	10	5	15	4	0	6	6	3	1	70	90	80	30	47	32
Minerals	Iron	5	3	2	2	1	6	6	16	5	1	2	1	2	1	24	37	16	20	10	14
	Calcium	2	1	4	2	4	4	9	4	4	1	1	6	2	0	10	4	5	2	7	3
	Potassium	20	7	12	9	8	7	9	44	13	4	12	7	6	3	14	21	15	14	18	20
	Sodium	0	0	4	1	3	0	1	1	3	0	0	0	0	0	1	0	0	0	0	0

Apple Dumplings

Pam Tidwell

Ingredients

- 2 Granny Smith apples
- 1 can crescent rolls
- 1 stick unsalted butter
- 1 cup sugar
- 1 can Sprite
- Cinnamon
- ½ cup chopped pecans
- Vanilla ice cream

1. Preheat oven to 350°F. Core, peel, and quarter the apples. Wrap each quarter in a crescent roll that has been pressed flat and sprinkled with cinnamon and pecans. Melt butter and mix with sugar and Sprite.

2. Place apple bundles in a deep casserole dish. Pour butter mixture over the top. Bake for 45 minutes.

3. Spoon liquid over the apple bundles several times during baking. Serve warm topped with a scoop of vanilla ice cream.

Ash Gourd in Spicy Coconut-Mustard Gravy (*Kuvwale Sassam*)

Rita Mathew

Ingredients

- ½ pound Ash gourd
- 2 roasted red chilis
- ¼ cup grated coconut
- 1 tsp vegetable oil
- 1 tsp mustard seed
- 5 curry leaves
- 1 tsp Tamarind paste
- Salt to taste

1. Peel the skin of the ash gourd and remove seeds. Cut the gourd into 1" cubes and boil in 1 cup of water for 5 minutes. Add salt to taste.

2. Make a coarse masala by grinding the coconut gratings, red chilis, ½ tsp mustard, and tamarind. The texture will be similar to a thick gravy.

3. Add the coconut paste to the cooked ash gourd and bring to a boil. Season with oil, remaining mustard and curry leaves. Serve hot.

Ash Gourd Valval *(Vegetables in Coconut Milk Gravy)*

Rita Mathew

Ingredients

• 1 ½ lb Cauliflower florets
• ¼ lb green beans
• ¼ lb carrots and peas (frozen mix, thawed)
• ½ lb sweet potato
• ½ lb Ash Gourd (peeled and cubed)
• 2 green Thai chillis (sliced lengthwise; remove seeds)
• 1 cup water
• 1 15 oz can of Coconut milk
• 2 oz cashews
• Salt to taste

Garnish
• Kari Leaf Seasoning (see recipe on page 36)

1. Cook all vegetables except Ash Gourd in 1 cup water on medium heat for five minutes. Add Ash Gourd, salt and chillies and cook further till gourd is done. Make sure that the vegetables are not overcooked.

2. Add the Coconut milk and cashews and bring to a boil.

3. Remove from heat.

4. Garnish with Kari Leaf Seasoning.

Coconut Milk

You can purchase full-fat or light coconut milk in cans. Look for it in the Ethnic foods section of your grocery store. You can also buy it in most Asian markets. Coconut milk is not the water found inside the coconut, which is also sold as Coconut Water; and, it is not to be confused with coconut cream.

When preparing coconut milk from fresh coconut, here are some equivalent measures:
1 lb coconut meat yields approximately 5 ½ cups of grated coconut, or 3 cups of coconut milk.

BBQ Meatballs

Candi Hoard

Ingredients

- 5 lbs ground beef
- 2 ½ to 3 lbs sausage (mild)
- Salt and pepper to taste
- 2 eggs
- ¼ can (15 oz) of plain bread crumbs
- Large BBQ Sauce (Williamson Brothers works well)

1. Mix ½ of the jar of BBQ sauce with the meat and other ingredients.

2. Form meatballs and place in a greased pan with sides or several glass baking dishes.

3. Pour the remaining BBQ sauce over the meatballs.

4. Bake for 70 minutes at 325°F. (If not cooked through – bake a little longer).

5. Bake ahead and warm in a 425°F oven. They FREEZE really well!

Brown Chickpeas in Coconut Milk Gravy (Chana Ghashi)

Rita Mathew

Ingredients

- ½ cup Brown Chana
- ½ pound yams
- ½ cup grated coconut
- ½ tsp tamarind paste
- 1 ½ cup water
- Salt to taste

Garnish:
- 2 tsp vegetable oil
- 1 tsp mustard seeds
- 4 whole red chillis
- 10 Kari leaves

1. Soak Chana in water for 8-10 hours overnight, or boil in a pressure cooker until tender.

2. Peel skin of yam and cut into 1" cubes. Boil 1 cup water and drop yam pieces into water, add salt if desired. After 5 minutes, add the cooked Chana.

3. Sauté red chilis in a small amount of oil.

4. Grind to a fine paste with remaining water the grated coconut, roasted chilis, and tamarind. Add the ground mixture to the Chana, mix well, and boil for 2-3 minutes.

5. Season with oil, mustard seeds, cumin, and Kari leaves (see page 36). Serve hot.

Butternut Squash Lasagna

Angela Logan Keifer

Ingredients

- 1 box oven-ready lasagna
- 2 cups cooked and mashed butternut squash
- 1 large log goat cheese (8 oz)
- 1 oz. block feta cheese
- 2 cups fresh spinach
- 67 oz. bottle spaghetti sauce
- 4 cups shredded mozzarella cheese

1. Preheat oven to 375°F

2. Blend the spaghetti sauce with ½ cup water to give the noodles the extra liquid they need to cook. Put a layer of sauce in the bottom of a 9"x13" baking dish. Put a layer of noodles over the sauce. Add a layer of all the squash over the noodles. Crumble the goat cheese and the feta over this and then sprinkle 1 cup of the mozzarella cheese over that.

3. Add another layer of sauce to completely over the cheese. Place another layer of noodles, then the spinach and another cup of mozzarella. Pour remaining sauce on top and smooth over so it's all covered.

4. Bake approximately 30 minutes and check for noodle doneness with a fork. If noodles feel soft, sprinkle the remaining mozzarella over the top and return to the oven until the cheese is bubbly.

5. Let the lasagna rest about 15 minutes before serving.

Cauliflower and Potato Sukké
(fresh fruits optional)

Rita Mathew

Ingredients

• 3 cups cauliflower (wash and cut into 1-inch florets)
• 1 cup potato (peeled and cubed into 1-inch pieces)
• ½ cup cut fresh fruit optional (grapes, pomegranate seeds, mango)
• 1 tsp salt
• 4 Tbsp water
• Kari leaf seasoning (see page 36)

For the Masala:
• 1 cup fresh grated coconut, blended to a fine consistency
• 1 tsp red chilli power
• 1 Tbsp coriander powder
• ¼ tsp fenugreek powder
• ½ tsp tamarind paste
• ¼ cup water

1. In a blender, use enough water to grind the coconut to a coarse paste, so that the consistency of the masala is thicker than a cooked cereal.

2. Separately, dry roast the chilli, coriander, fenugreek, and add them to the coconut masala along with the tamarind.

3. To the hot pan in which Kari Leaf seasoning has been prepared add the masala and stir for a minute.

4. Add cauliflower, potatoes, salt and water. Stir well to coat the vegetables with the masala.

5. Cover and cook on moderate heat for 10 minutes (depending on the cooking range and pan).

6. Cut fresh fruit may be mixed in before serving.

Cream of Peanut Soup
Margaret Agner

Ingredients

- 1 med. onion, chopped
- 2 ribs celery, chopped
- ¼ cup butter
- 1 Tbsp all-purpose flour
- 2 quarts chicken stock
- 1 cup smooth peanut butter
- 2 cups light cream
- Peanuts, chopped

1. Sauté onion and celery in butter until soft but not brown. Stir in flour until well blended.

2. Add chicken stock, stirring constantly, bring to a boil.

3. Remove from heat and rub through a sieve.

4. Add peanut butter and cream, stirring to blend thoroughly. Return to low heat, but do not boil, and serve garnished with peanuts.

Note: this soup is also good served ice cold. Serves 10 – 12.

Creamy Cucumber Soup
Nancy Welch

Ingredients

- 1 (10 ¾ oz) can cream of celery soup
- 1 cup milk
- 1 cucumber, peeled
- 1 small green pepper, seeded
- ¼ cup green pimiento stuffed olives
- 1 cup sour cream
- 1 Tbsp lemon juice
- Dash of hot sauce (like Frank's)
- Cucumber slices, optional

1. Combine soup, milk, cucumber, green pepper, olives, and hot sauce in bowl of food processor and puree.

2. Add sour cream and lemon juice and blend until mixed.

3. Refrigerate at least 4 hours. Garnish with cucumber slices.

I love starting with a can of soup. When my cucumbers were ripe in my garden a few years ago, this was a perfect summertime, cold soup.

Curried Sweet Potato Salad
Juanita Broom

Ingredients

- 4 medium sweet potatoes
- ½ cup mayonnaise
- ¼ cup plain yogurt
- 2-3 teaspoon curry powder
- 1 tablespoon brown sugar
- 1 teaspoon coarse ground mustard
- ½ cup craisins
- ½ cup toasted pecan pieces
- ½ cup chopped celery or apple
- salt and pepper

1. Peel potatoes and chop into 1-2 inch cubes. Roast at 400 degrees until tender but firm (20-30 mins).

2. Whisk together mayonnaise, yogurt, curry powder, brown sugar, mustard, and a sprinkle of salt and pepper. Chop celery or apple into small pieces and add to dressing. Add raisins and pecan pieces. Fold potatoes in gently so it is well mixed but not mashed.

3. Chill for an hour before serving.

Gingered Mincemeat Pie
Suzanne Keifer

Ingredients

For the crust:
- 2 cups regular flour
- ½ cup gingersnap crumbs
- ½ tsp salt
- ⅔ cup shortening
- 5-6 Tbsp water

For the pie:
- 1 28-oz jar prepared mincemeat
- 1 cup chopped pecans (or walnuts)
- ¼ cup crystallized ginger
- ¼ cup Amaretto or brandy
- 2 Tbsp flour
- 1 egg
- 1 Tbsp milk

1. Combine the first 3 ingredients in a medium bowl, cut in the shortening. Sprinkle water evenly over the surface; stir with fork until moistened. Roll in a ball and chill for 1 hour.

2. While you're waiting for the crust to chill, combine mincemeat, nuts, ginger, liquor and flour; stir until well-blended and set aside.

3. Roll out half of the dough to fit a 9" pie pan. Pour mincemeat over crust in pie pan. Roll out the other half of the dough and place on top – seal and flute. Cut 4-5 slits into top crust. Combine egg and milk and brush to coat the top of the pie.

4. Bake at 425°F for 15 minutes; drop temperature to 350°F and bake another 35 minutes. You can cover the edges with aluminum foil so they don't burn.

Grilled Sweet Potato and Scallions

Pam Tidwell

Ingredients

- 4 large sweet potatoes, partially cooked, peeled, and cut into ½" slices
- 8 scallions
- ¾ cup good olive oil, divided
- 2 Tbsp Dijon mustard
- ½ cup apple cider vinegar
- ¼ cup balsamic vinegar
- 2 tsp honey
- ¼ cup coarsely chopped Italian parsley
- Salt and fresh ground black pepper to taste

1. Pre-heat grill to high.

2. Brush the potatoes and scallions with ¼ cup of the oil and arrange on the grill. Grill the potatoes for 3-4 minutes on each side, or until tender.

3. Grill the scallions until softened and grill-marked. Remove scallions from the grill and cut into thin slices.

4. In a large bowl, whisk the remaining oil, mustard, vinegars, and honey. Season with salt and pepper.

5. Add the potatoes, scallions, and the parsley. Gently toss until the potatoes are well-coated.

Kélae Phodi (Roasted Plantain Fritters)

Rita Mathew

Ingredients

- 1 raw plantain
- ⅓ cup rice flour
- Dash of asafoetida (If you don't have asafoetida powder you can substitute; per ¼ teaspoon needed: ¼ teaspoon onion powder plus ¼ teaspoon garlic powder. ... OR - Substitute ½ teaspoon garlic or onion powder)
- Dash chili powder
- ¼ tsp oil
- Salt, to taste

1. Cut the plantain into 3 equal pieces. Cut 4-5 length-wise slices from each of the cut pieces.

2. Apply salt, asafoetida, and chili powder and set aside for about 5 minutes.

3. Roll the slices in the rice flour and make sure they are uniformly coated.

4. Medium heat a flat pan and add oil. Place the coated slices gently in the pan. Cover and cook for 4-5 minutes. Flip over and cook for a few more minutes. Do not shake the pan since the coating may come off.

Substitute Sweet Potato or Taro Root (See Picture of Thalli 1 on page 73)

Lamb Curry

Suzanne Keifer

Ingredients

- 1 ½ tsp flour
- 1 tsp salt
- ½ tsp garlic salt
- 1 ½ lb cooked lamb, cut into 1" cubes
- ¾ cup water
- 2 Tbsp butter
- 1 ½ Tbsp curry powder
- 1 ½ Tbsp sugar
- 2 medium onions
- 2 Granny Smith (or similar) apples

1. In a zippered bag, combine the first 4 ingredients and shake to coat the lamb.

2. Melt the butter in a large pan, adding curry, sugar, apples and onions and cook approximately 10 minutes on medium heat.

3. Remove this from the pan, add the lamb and brown in juices from the onion/apple mixture. Put the saved ingredient back in the pan, add the water, cover, and simmer for about 1 hour.

4. Serve over rice. You can garnish with some flaked coconut, chutney, or golden raisins.

Lizzy's Apple Crisp

Liz Conroy

Ingredients

- 1 cup plus ¼ cup whole wheat pastry flour (don't use regular flour!)
- ¼ tsp each of salt, baking soda, baking powder
- 1 tsp ground cinnamon
- 2 cups quick-cooking oatmeal
- ½ cup safflower (or other gold, mild vegetable oil)
- ½ cup honey
- 6-8 firm apples (such as Granny Smith), cored, and chopped into small pieces

1. Pre-heat oven to 350°F. Butter a 9 x 9 x 2" baking dish.

2. Sift the flour, salt, baking soda, baking powder and cinnamon into a mixing bowl. Then mix in the oatmeal. In another mixing bowl, pour the oil and use the same measuring cup for the honey (the remaining bit of oil helps the honey slide out easily).

3. Place the apples in the buttered baking dish. Pour the dry ingredients into the bowl of wet ingredients and combine well. Then scatter the mixture over the apples.

4. Bake 30 to 35 minutes until golden brown.

5. Serve warm (best) or cold.

My apple crisp includes honey, oats, and fresh apples. It works well for breakfast when topped with plain yogurt or for dessert when topped with vanilla ice cream. It became a traditional favorite for my two daughters for their birthdays. These days, my older daughter asks me to bring it to her for comfort food while she cares for her newborn daughter (my first grandchild). She says it's good food for busy, breastfeeding mothers because it also serves as a quick, nourishing, and satisfying snack.

From the center, clockwise: Green mung beans, Masoor, Chana Dal, Kala Chana, Tuvar Dal, pigeon peas, bush beans, dried green peas.

Legumes *(Pulses, Dal)*   *Rita Mathew*

Legumes, also known as pulses, are the edible seeds of plants in the legume family. Compared to cereals, which are harvested from grasses, legumes have less carbohydrates and more protein. They include beans, lentils, and peas. Some examples are as follows
(Indian names are included to make it easier to shop):

Beans: Mung beans (green when whole, or yellow when hulled and split), black gram bean (black when whole, or ivory when hulled and split - Urad Dal), small black chick peas (Kala Chana - dark brown when whole, and yellow when hulled and split), Turkish or Math beans (Matki), pink bean, black kidney bean, red kidney bean (Rajma).

Lentils: Pink or salmon lentils (hulled Masoor Dal), yellow lentils (Mung Dal), black lentils (whole Masoor Dal).

Peas: Pigeon peas (whole brown, or yellow split peas - Tuvar Dal), whole chick-peas (Brown or Black Chana Dal), black-eyed peas (Chowli).

Legumes may be cooked as a whole grain; or in its hulled and split form; or sprouted before cooking as in the case of Mung bean, Matki, and Kala Chana. Whereas the hulled beans have only to be rinsed before cooking, the WHOLE GRAIN HAS TO BE SOAKED OVERNIGHT AND TAKES SLIGHTLY LONGER TO COOK. All the beans can be soaked in water until they sprout. Sprouts contain essential vitamins such as Vitamin A, B1, B6, C and K; and mineral elements such as iron, phosphorus, potassium, calcium, magnesium and manganese.

Directions for Sprouting Mung Bean Grains:
To sprout Green Mung Beans (200g makes 3 cups sprouted beans):
Rinse mung beans thoroughly and drain the water. Place in a deep bowl and fill with enough water to soak the beans completely. Cover and leave it overnight. Next day, drain the water and rinse again, but do not put any water. Cover and leave overnight. Repeat the process till the beans start to spout. May be used uncooked in salad or cooked as a side dish.

Directions to Cook Mung Bean Sprouts:
Place the sprouts in a pan and add 1 cup water. Cover with a transparent lid. Cook on medium heat for 10 minutes. Half way through you will see the skin rise to the top. Scoop it up and discard. The skin can be removed two or three times during the process of cooking. When done, sprouts should be softened but not mushy. Drain the water and let it cool.

Lentil (Dal)

Rita Mathew

Ingredients

- 1 cup Yellow Split peas (Tuvar Dal)
- 3 cups water
- 1 green chilli (slit and seeds removed)
- ½ tsp turmeric
- 1 tsp Salt

For the Seasoning:
- ½ tsp mustard seeds
- 10-12 Kari leaves
- ⅛ tsp Asafoetida (hing)
- 2 tsp Oil

1. Rinse the split peas thoroughly. Cover and cook it in water on medium high heat for 15 minutes or till done. Mash dal and add the chilli and salt. Cook for a few minutes till it comes to a boil. Remove from the fire.

2. Separately, heat the oil and put the mustard seeds in the pan till they pop. Remove from the fire and add the Kari leaves and Asafoetida. Season dal.

Dal is a favorite with children, and a source of protein. See Thalli 2 picture on page 222.

Optional - For a sweet and sour variation add ½ tsp tamarind paste and 2 tsp brown sugar along with the chilli and salt.

Mung Bean and Brown Sugar Dessert (Sweet Khichdi)

Rita Mathew

Ingredients

- ½ pound mung dal
- 4 oz rice
- 6 oz grated jaggery (unrefined cane sugar)
- 6 oz grated coconut
- 2 Tbsp ghee (clarified butter)
- 1 Tbsp raisins
- 1 Tbsp chopped cashew

1. Sauté mung dal until it becomes slightly brown and allow to cool.

2. Wash the rice and the dal and boil together in enough water to cover until half-cooked, about 15 minutes.

3. Add jaggery and cook over low heat. Once jaggery melts, add grated coconut and mix well. Allow to cook until the rice and dal are soft and remove from heat. Add the ghee, cashews and raisins.

4. Serve hot.

Mung Bean in Coconut Milk Gravy
(Ghashi)

Rita Mathew

Ingredients

- 2 cups sprouted cooked Mung beans
- Kari Leaf Seasoning
- 1 13.5 oz can of Coconut milk
- 1 tsp red chilli powder
- ½ tsp turmeric powder
- 1 tsp tamarind paste
- ½ cup chestnut
- 1 tsp salt

1. Sprout mung beans (directions on page 137).

2. Prepare the Kari Leaf Seasoning as directed on page 36.

3. To the hot oil add the chilli and turmeric powder and give it a stir. Pour the coconut milk and heat for a minute. Add the mung beans and tamarind and cook on a medium fire for 5 minutes.

4. Serve hot with rice.

Mung Bean Stir Fry (Usal)

Rita Mathew

Ingredients

- 2 cups cooked sprouted green mung bean (Optional Matki beans)
- Kari Leaf Seasoning
- ½ tsp turmeric
- 2 – 3 Tbsp fresh grated coconut
- 1 tsp salt

An upakari made with sprouted beans is called an Usal. Matki beans (Turkish beans or Vigna aconitifolia), and Black Chana Dal are popularly used for Usal.

1. Sprout mung beans (directions on page 137).

2. Prepare the Kari Leaf Seasoning per directions on page 36.

3. Add cooked mung bean, grated coconut, salt and cook for a couple of minutes. Garnish with cilantro before serving.

Nutmeg Cauliflower

Greg and Laura Killmaster

Ingredients

- Head of Cauliflower
- Fresh ground nutmeg
- Salt
- Pepper (optional)
- Butter or Olive Oil (optional)

1. Separate the florets from the cauliflower. Preserve the fleshy part of the main stem and any tender intact leaves. If the stem is too pithy, use a peeler to remove fibrous parts.

2. In a 12" skillet, add water to just barely cover the inside, salt lightly. Bring to a boil, add cauliflower, then reduce heat and cover. Adjust heat to maintain a nice simmer. Cook 8-9 minutes. (Cauliflower should be tender enough for a fork to pass through the center of the floret without too much resistance). Water should also be cooked away at this point.

3. An option is to let it cook a little more with the lid off and brown the underside.

4. Serve with salt and pepperand sprinkle with nutmeg by grating it directly onto the cauliflower with a fine spice/cheese grater. Drizzle with olive oil or high quality butter like Brittany from Trader Joe's or organic grass fed (I usually have it plain without).

Pecan Pie

Beverly Simpson

Ingredients

- 4 eggs
- 1 ½ cups sugar
- ⅓ cup maple syrup
- ⅓ cup melted butter
- 1 teaspoon vanilla
- 1 ¼ cups pecans
- 1 9-inch unbaked pie shell

1. Preheat oven to 400°F.

2. Use a whisk to mix eggs and sugar together. Add maple syrup, melted butter and vanilla and mix well with whisk. Add nuts and pour into a 9-inch unbaked pie shell.

3. Bake for 20 minutes. Turn heat down to 350 degrees and bake 25 minutes or until done. If crust edge is getting too brown, lay a piece of tinfoil lightly across pie toward end of baking.

Poires Belle Hélène

Suzanne Keifer

1. Combine the cinnamon sticks, sugar, and ½ cup of water in a medium saucepan.

2. Bring the mixture to a boil, and then reduce the heat and simmer for 2 to 5 minutes, until it becomes a thick-like syrup and turns golden brown.

3. Turn the heat to the lowest setting and gently whisk in the remaining 2 cups water, until the syrup is completely incorporated into the water.

4. Add the prepared pears to the sugar syrup mixture and bring to a gentle simmer for 15 minutes. Test the doneness with a knife by pricking in the thickest part of the fruit; the pears are poached when they are just cooked through, but not completely soft. Be careful not to overcook or the pears will collapse, Bosc pears are renowned for doing dissolving too quickly.

5. Allow the pears to cool in the syrup until they are at room temperature. Lift the pears carefully from the pan with a slotted spoon.

6. Serve with two small scoops of vanilla ice cream and a drizzle of chocolate sauce.

Pictured on Back Cover

Ingredients

- 2 whole cinnamon sticks
- ¾ cup granulated sugar
- 2 ½ cups water (divided)
- 4 firm Bosc pears (peeled, cored and with stem intact) – see following directions
- 8 small scoops vanilla ice cream
- ½ cup chocolate sauce (for drizzling) – See following recipe

How to Core a Pear

1. Lay the pear on its side. Using a sharp knife, take a thin slice from the base of the pear; this will expose the core and create a flat surface on the base, so much easier for serving the pear.

2. Take a paring or vegetable knife and very carefully cut tight in and around the core (keep as close as you can to the core so as not to spoil the fruit or risk breaking through). The core should come away easily, if not use a teaspoon to scoop it out.

Chocolate Sauce

- 1 cup semisweet chocolate chips
- 3/4 cup whipping cream
- 1 teaspoon vanilla

1. In a small saucepan over low heat, heat the chocolate chips and whipping cream, stirring constantly.

2. Continue to cook while stirring constantly, until the chocolate chips have melted and the sauce is smooth.

3. Remove the sauce from the heat and add the vanilla extract. Stir to blend.

Pumpkin Flower Savory Cake *Rita Mathew*

Ingredients

- 2 cups Pumpkin Flowers (washed and finely chopped)
- ½ cup Rice flour
- ½ cup Gram Flour
- ½ cup grated fresh coconut (optional)
- ¼ cup yogurt
- ½ tsp fresh grated ginger*
- 1 tsp roasted red chilli powder
- 1 tsp tamarind
- ⅛ tsp asafoetida (See Glossary for substitutes.)
- ½ tsp eno fruit salt or baking soda
- 1 tsp salt
- ½ cup water
- Kari Leaf Seasoning (optional)

1. Mix all the ingredients in a bowl, except the eno fruit salt, and add enough water to make a batter thicker than that used for a cake.

2. Separately prepare the Kari Leaf seasoning (see directions on page 36) and mix in to the batter. Add the eno fruit salt and stir gently.

3. Immediately, transfer to a shallow greased pan and press down with the back of a spatula.

4. Steam for 30 – 35 minutes or until a toothpick comes out clean. Cool and serve as bars, squares or slices.

* Pumpkin flowers are available in Asian Markets. They may be substituted with:
- 2 cups chopped spinach
- 2 cups grated bottle gourd
- 2 cups grated pumpkin/winter squash

---

* Mathew, R. "Value your Herb Garden, Gingerly!" UGA Extension Shades of Green newsletter - July 2021

Roasted Butternut Squash and Apple Soup

Suzanne Keifer

1. Preheat oven to 375°F.

2. Brush the olive oil over the cut side of the squash and on the shallots. Place the squash (cut side down) on a baking sheet with sides. Tuck the garlic cloves INSIDE the hollowed-out portion of the squash and place the shallots on the sheet.

3. Bake for 30 minutes or until the squash feels soft.

4. When the squash is cool enough to handle, scoop out the flesh and place it, the shallots, and the garlic in a large stockpot. Add the apples, thyme, bay leaf, salt, pepper, broth and wine. Stir, bring to a boil, reduce heat and let simmer for about 15 minutes.

5. Remove from the heat, remove bay leaf and thyme sprigs. Puree the soup with an immersion blender, or you can use a food processor or blender. Add the half-and-half, nutmeg and stir these into the soup. Top with chives.

Delicious with a crusty baguette and whatever wine you used in the soup. Serves 6.

Ingredients

- 1 Tbsp good olive oil
- 4 pounds butternut squash, halved lengthwise, seeded
- 4 shallots, peeled
5 cloves garlic
- 2 tart apples (like Granny Smith), cored, peeled, and roughly chopped
- 6 sprigs fresh thyme (or 1 tsp dried)
- 1 bay leaf
- 2 tsp kosher salt
- ½ tsp black pepper
- 2 (14-oz) cans chicken broth (I use low sodium)
- ½ cup dry white wine (Chardonnay or Viognier)
- ¼ cup half-and-half
- ¼ tsp grated nutmeg (or a pinch of dried)
- 1 Tbsp minced chives (optional)

Roasted Kabocha Squash Soup

Christine Guilloton

Ingredients

- One half of a large Kabocha squash or 1 small one
- 1 Tbsp olive oil
- Salt
- 1 ½ Tbsp olive oil
- 2 cups chopped onions
- 2 ribs celery
- 3 cloves chopped garlic
- 1 ½" fresh ginger*, peeled and grated
- 1 ¼ tsp ground cumin
- ½ tsp ground coriander
- 4 cups chicken stock
- ¼ tsp ground black pepper
- Parsley for garnish

1. Cut the squash into large chunks (it's not easy so be careful!). Scoop out the seeds and stringy bits. Coat with the 1 Tbsp olive oil and salt. With the skin side up, roast in a 400°F oven for 45 minutes – 1 hour. Remove and let sit.

2. Sauté onions, garlic in the remaining olive oil for 8-10 minutes. Add spices and sauté an additional 2 minutes.

3. Remove skin from squash and add it to the onion mixture. In a large pot, place all the mixed ingredients along with the stock, salt, pepper. Increase the heat to high, then reduce to simmer/low and cook about 8-10 minutes.

4. Off the heat, using an immersion blender, purée the soup. Garnish with parsley.

* Ginger, Zingiber officinale, was an important export item from India to the Roman Empire, where it was valued for its medicinal properties including as an antioxidant and anti-inflammatory agent.

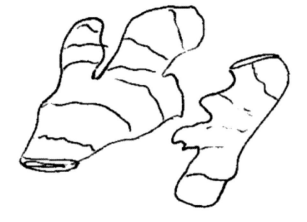

Roast Savory Cornish Hens
Rita Mathew

Ingredients

- 2 Cornish hens
- 2 ½ tsp Ginger garlic paste
- 2 Tbsp Oil

Spices
- 2 tsp chilli powder
- ½ tsp Cumin powder
- ½ tsp Coriander powder
- ½ tsp Black pepper powder
- ½ tsp Fennel powder
- ¼ tsp Cinnamon powder
- ¼ tsp Clove powder
- ¼ tsp Turmeric powder

- ½ tsp salt
- Lemon juice- a few drops
- Lemon wedges-3-4 slices
- 2 garlic cloves

1. Clean the cornish hens, pat dry the outside and the cavities. Remove the skin and make a few gashes.

2. Dry roast the spices on a medium flame for 4-5 minutes except for the turmeric powder. Mix all the spices with the ginger garlic paste, oil and salt. Mix well and marinate the hens inside and outside with this paste. Cover and refrigerate overnight or at least for two hours.

3. Layer the roasting pan with aluminum foil. Place the Cornish hens on the rack of the roasting pan. Squeeze lemon juice and oil over the hen and loosely stuff the cavities with lemon wedges, a slice of onion and two garlic cloves.

4. Pre heat oven to 375-degree F. Bake for 25 minutes. Baste the hens with the juice in the bottom of the pan. Reduce the heat to 300-degree F heat and bake for another 25 minutes. The meat is cooked when the internal temperature at the thickest part of the meat 165-degree F (use a meat thermometer). If you want to roast it crispy on the outside turn oven setting to broil for 4-5 minutes. Take it out of the oven and loosely cover it with aluminum foil for 10-15 minutes to keep warm.

5. Pouring any cavity juices in the roasting pan into a medium saucepan and boil until liquids reduce to a sauce consistency, about 6 minutes. Cut hens in half lengthwise and arrange on plates. Spoon sauce around hens.

Pictured on page 180.

Shrimp Complement Soup

Claire Hopkens,
Charleston, SC Master Gardener

Ingredients

- 1 lb small shrimp, peeled and de-veined (cut larger shrimp into pieces)
- 3 cups chopped raw broccoli
- 2 medium carrots, grated
- 1 medium onion – chopped
- 1 (15-oz) can whole kernel corn (do not drain)
- ½ stick margarine
- 2 cups sharp cheddar cheese, grated
- 1 cup provolone cheese, grated
- 2 cans cream of potato soup
- 2 cups milk

1. In a large pot on medium-high heat, combine broccoli, carrots and onions with margarine and cook until tender, then add shrimp and cook until shrimp turn pink.

2. Add corn, reduce heat to medium.

3. Add both cheeses and potato soup, stirring constantly until melted.

4. Stir in milk and heat, but do not boil.

5. Remove from heat and serve it while hot as an appetizer or main dish. It is a great complement to a seafood entrée.

In the early 2000's I was invited to speak to a group of South Carolina Master Gardeners in the Charleston area. I can't remember the topic I spoke on, but I remember the outstanding food they served at their luncheon. A lady by the name of Claire Hopkens made a soup called Shrimp Complement. Much like chowder, it was one of the best soups I had ever eaten. I asked if she would share the recipe with me. Several days later she emailed it to me. I serve it at Christmas, at dinner parties and other special occasions. People rave about it and always want more. I hope you enjoy it as much as my family and I have. -Gary Wade, MG 2007

Squash Casserole

Ingredients

- 2 cups cooked yellow squash
- 2 medium onions, sautéed
- 1 cup mayonnaise
- 1 dozen saltine or Ritz crackers, crumbled
- 3 eggs, well beaten
- 1 cup grated cheese (may choose variety)
- ½ package Ranch dressing mix

1. Mix, mash, and drain the squash and onion completely.

2. Mix all ingredients well. Pour in a casserole dish, top with cornbread stuffing mix (or fine breadcrumbs).

3. Bake for 30 minutes at 350° or until it does not shake.

Sweet Potato Apple Casserole
Kie Johnson

Ingredients

- 4 medium sweet potatoes (parboil and remove skins)
- 2 tart apples (skin, core and slice)
- 3 Tbsp honey
- ½ teas salt
- ¼ cup butter

1. Layer slices of sweet potatoes and apples.

2. Drizzle with honey to taste.

3. Salt to taste. Dot with butter.

4. Repeat with a second layer of the same

5. Use a deep-dish casserole. Bake covered at 350 for 45 minutes.

Sweet Potato Pie

Allan Cobb

Ingredients

- 4 oz butter - softened
- 2 cups sugar
- 5 oz can evaporated milk
- 1 teaspoon vanilla
- 1 ½ teaspoon cinnamon
- ⅛ teaspoon allspice
- ½ teaspoon nutmeg
- 3 eggs beaten
- 2 cups cooked mashed sweet potatoes

A great way to use your abundant harvest of sweet potatoes!

1. Preheat your oven to 350. Mix butter, sugar, potatoes, and milk until well blended.

2. Add vanilla, eggs, spices, and blend until smooth.

3. Pour into 2 9" pie crusts. Bake for about an hour, or until set. (Use a water bath for a consistent bake.)

Sweet Potato Soufflé

Donna Yates

Ingredients

- 2 cups mashed sweet potatoes
- 2 eggs
- 1 cup milk
- ½ tsp cinnamon
- 1 cup sugar
- ¾ stick of butter
- ½ tsp of nutmeg
- 1 tsp of vanilla

For the Topping:
- 1 cup light brown sugar
- ¾ self-rising flour
- 1 cup chopped pecans
- ½ stick margarine, melted

1. Mix all souffle ingredients and pour in casserole dish and bake at 375-400 degrees for 20 minutes.

2. Mix the topping ingredients together.

3. Remove souffle from oven and spread topping evenly over top of potato mixture return to oven and cook 15 more minutes.

Taco Soup

Rosemary Stancil

Ingredients

- 2 pounds boneless skinless chicken breasts or thighs*
- 1 onion, chopped
- 2 cloves garlic, minced
- 3 tablespoons olive oil
- 1 (15-ounce) can white hominy, undrained
- 1 (15-ounce) can yellow corn, undrained
- 1 (15-ounce) can pinto beans, undrained
- 1 (15-ounce) can kidney beans, undrained
- 1 (10-ounce) can Rotel tomatoes, mild or hot, undrained
- 1 (28-ounnce) can diced tomatoes, undrained
- 32 ounces chicken broth
- ½ teaspoon sugar
- 1 (1-ounce) package dry Taco seasoning or 1 ½ tablespoons
- 1 (1-ounce) package dry Ranch seasoning and salad dressing mix or 1 ½ tablespoons

- For serving: Top with sour cream, chopped cilantro, and/or grated Cheddar cheese and serve with corn chips.

1. In a 6-8 quart soup pot, sauté chicken, onion and garlic in oil.

2. Add hominy, corn, pinto beans, kidney beans, Rotel tomatoes, diced tomatoes, broth, sugar, taco seasoning, and Ranch seasoning and dressing mix.

3. Stir together and let simmer for 1 hour.

4. Serve with a dollop of sour cream, minced cilantro, and/or grated Cheddar cheese and corn chips on the side.

*Two pounds of ground beef may be substituted for chicken. When using ground beef, substitute beef broth for chicken broth.

Yield: 10-12 servings

Taro Leaves with Coconut Gravy (Aalwathi)

Rita Mathew

Ingredients

- 10 Taro leaves
- 3 roasted whole red chillis
- ¼ cup coconut gratings
- ¼ tsp Tamarind paste
- ½ inch fresh ginger, sliced
- 2 Thai green chillis, seeded and slit in ½
- 1 tsp lime juice
- 2 tsp oil
- Salt to taste

1. Cut the stalk of the Taro leaves. Wash leaves thoroughly and cut into small strips. Add salt and boil in water that is just sufficient to cover the leaves. Add ginger and green chilis.

2. Grind the coconut gratings, red chilis, and tamarind to a fine paste consistency. Add the paste to the cooked leaves and mix well. Allow the mixture to boil and then turn off heat.

3. Add the oil and lime juice and mix well. Serve hot.

The heart-shaped leaves of the taro plant (Colocasia esculenta), commonly grown in subtropical and tropical regions, are a staple food in South Asian cuisines. See Glossary for details.

Texas Caviar

Candi Hoard

Ingredients

- 1 green pepper, small dice
- 1 med red onion, small dice
- 3 tsp Garlic (finely diced)
- ¼ to ½ cup chopped Jalapeño (small can) (**** Less heat – use small can green chilies)
- 2 limes – juiced
- 2 (14.5 oz) cans diced tomatoes
- 2 (15 oz) cans black-eyed peas – drained
- 2 cans black beans – drained
- 4 Tbsp olive oil
- ¾ cup red wine vinegar
- Salt and Pepper
- Fresh cilantro to taste (about ½ cup)

1 Mix above ingredients in a large mixing bowl.

2. Serve as a side salad or with tortilla chips or Fritos.

Theek Sana Polo *(Savory Mini Pancakes)*

Rita Mathew

Ingredients

- ½ cup Rice flour
- ½ cup Gram Flour
- ¾ cup water
- ¼ cup finely chopped Onion
- 1 cup chopped Cabbage
- ⅛ tsp red chili powder
- ⅛ tsp asafoetida (See Glossary for substitutes.)
- ¼ tsp lemon juice
- 1 tsp Salt
- Oil

This side dish may also be served as an appetizer with a yogurt dip. It could easily pass for a vegetarian omelet.

1. Mix the Rice and Gram flour with water to make a thick batter. Set aside for 10 minutes.

2. Just before cooking, stir in the onions, cabbage, and spices into the batter. On a moderately hot, heavy frying pan, apply a little oil. Pour 2 Tbsp batter gently spread using circular motion to make a 4-inch pancake.

3. Cover for 2-3 min (time may vary depending on how hot the pan is). Flip and cook the other side for about 2 minutes or until golden brown. Remove when both sides have cooked sufficiently. Serve hot.

Gram Flour is made from ground chick peas. It is readily available in Asian Markets.

Notes

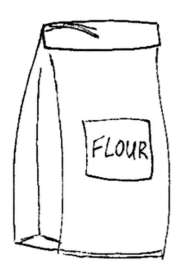

Vimalji's Kala Chana Usal

Vimal Sinha

This is a simple North Indian dish, and does not use any coconut!

1. Soak the Kala Chana overnight in 3 cups water. Drain and set aside. In a heavy bottom pan heat the oil. Add all the spices and stir for a minute. Add the onion and garlic till onion is tender. Add the drained Kala Chana and salt.

2. Cook with remaining water for 45 min on medium fire till chana is cooked. Add more water if needed.

Optional: When chana is cooked, add 1 cup peeled and cubed zucchini, or ivy gourd and cook for additional five minutes.

Vimalji's Cumin Squash

• 1 lb yellow winter squash (peel, remove seeds and fiber, cube in ½ in pieces)
• 1 Tbsp Oil
• 1 tsp cumin seeds
• 1 whole red chilli
• 1 tsp salt
• ½ cup water

This is an easy preparation without coconut or onions.

1. In pan heat add 1 tablespoon oil. Add cumin and let it crackle. Add the whole red chilli and stir for 30 seconds. Add cubed squash, salt and water.

2. Cook on medium heat till it is tender. Serve with rice or naan.

Ingredients

• 1 cup Black Chana (whole, with skin; See page 137 for details.)
• 2 Tbsp oil
• ½ tsp cumin powder
• 1 tsp coriander powder
• ¼ tsp red chilli powder
• ¼ tsp asafoetida (See Glossary for substitutes.)
• 1 cup chopped onions
• 2-3 cloves garlic (finely chopped)
• 1 tsp salt
• 5 cups water

World's Best Split Pea Soup   *Claire Clements*

Full of fiber, antioxidants, vitamins and minerals!

1. Cut carrots, celery, and onions into large enough chunks so as to be recognizable after cooking for about 8 hours. Place them in a crockpot or slow cooker. Sort, wash and put peas into crock pot/slow cooker.

2. Add water to within 1 ½ inches of the top of the pot. (So it will not spill over when cooking) Cook on low temperature in the slow cooker for 6, 7, or 8 hours, or on stove top for much less time, until you cannot tell what the peas are! Soft with little or no graininess.

3. Stir, save, and don't smash the big chunky veggies. Blend in blender to a smooth consistency and add the veggies back! Reheat and enjoy!

4. Serve piping hot, with any of the following: cornbread, on top we sometimes put ground flax seeds and/or cheese, a dollop of plain, non-fat yogurt or sour cream. Experiment! We like it plain too.

Ingredients

• 4 large carrots
• 1 bunch of celery – use it all leaves, joints, heart, etc.
• 4 onions quartered
• 1 16 oz package of dried split peas
• 2 cans of beef, chicken, or vegetable broth (unsalted or low salt).
**Especially if you use a ham hock, or smoked meat of any kind. Might not need the canned broth if ham hock is used. That might give enough flavor by itself. As you like it!

Spices:
• 4 big garlic cloves - crush each one and add whole
• 6 bay leaves
• Basil, dried or fresh, 1/8 cup more if fresh, less if dried, to taste.
• Milled or ground pepper to taste

"A Radish Bunch"

©2021 *Bob Clements*

Of Yams and Sweet Potatoes[1]

Chris A. Joseph Ph.D.

Chris Joseph is a cultural anthropologist who is also an avid gardener, and foodie. These interests are the source of inspiration for her travels which have taken her across foodscapes, like the rice fields of Bali, olive groves of Morocco, and community gardens of Innsbruck. She loves visiting farmers markets wherever she travels and her treasured souvenirs include salt from the ancient Peruvian salt pans in the Sacred Valley, juniper berries from the Austrian alps, and piri-piri pepper from Portugal. Her next adventure will take her to the bergamot marmalade factories in Calabria, Italy.

As an anthropologist, there were many reasons to have Papua New Guinea (PNG) on my bucket list. After all, fieldwork became enshrined as the methodology of our discipline in the 1910s thanks to Bronisław Malinowski's seminal research in the Trobriand archipelago. Other riveting accounts of anthropologists venturing deep into the isolated Highland areas that bisect the mainland, further fueled my imagination and curiosity about the people of PNG. In 2017, a study-abroad program in Australia and New Zealand put me a short hop away from PNG, and my dream became reality.

I arrived on Kiriwina Island (part of the Trobriand archipelago), just after the yam harvest in June. A tour of the gardens, with their neat piles of enormous teytu, or lesser yams, and the decorative kuvi variety that were over 3-4 feet long, transported me back to Malinowski's accounts. I was told that the harvest would be followed by the yam festival where the Paramount Chief would receive the largest yams in tribute, and his log yam house would be meticulously stacked to the rafters. In the Trobriands, yams are a unit of exchange, and anthropologist Annette Weiner found that "if a man has yams, he can find anything else he needs" (1988). So, besides being exceedingly nutritious and a good source of fiber, vitamins B6 and C, and protein, yams play an important role in kinship and social relationships.

From the Trobriands, my journey took me to the Highlands, which produce 75% of the sweet potatoes in PNG. Near Mount Hagen, I visited the beautiful horticultural garden patches where women were planting sweet potatoes, or kaukau, in neat mounds of rich, black soil. Other mounds were ready to be harvested, and my local guide casually reached into one and pulled out a ripe sweet potato. Later the village head, arrayed in the distinctive clay face paint of his tribe, and a chief's headdress, welcomed me to a sing-sing (a gathering with dance and music) complete with a delicious array of sweet potatoes baked in a mumu (an underground earth-oven lined with heated rocks and wet banana leaves). Each variety had a distinct taste and texture, some as creamy as butter, others sweet and caramelized as candy.

---

1 While yams and sweet potatoes are botanically distinct, the terms are used interchangeably in the US. When I use the term "sweet potatoes," I refer specifically to Ipomoea batatas. It is what we commonly find in our grocery stores. Yams are usually found in Asian grocery stores.

Today sweet potatoes, baked somewhat more mundanely in our oven, are a weekly staple for our household, but mainly for our pit bull, Milka, who is on a hypoallergenic diet. They are also a great source of beta-carotene or vitamin A. For our own consumption, my default recipe is still this simple childhood one used by my mother, Jean Joseph.

PHOTO 1: The Paramount Chief of Kiriwina Island has the largest bwema (yam house) in the village. A full yam house is a sign of prestige and power. Sadly, years of drought in the Trobriands have reduced recent harvests.

PHOTO 2: Andrew, driver extraordinaire (who skillfully navigated the most potholed roads I've ever traveled) and the mumu specialist in his village near the city of Mount Hagen, places heated rocks in the pit for radiant heat to bake the sweet potatoes.

PHOTO 3: Inspired by the Mt. Hagen sweet potato gardens, I decided to grow sweet potatoes in my improvised coronavirus raised-beds garden consisting of Chewy.com shipping boxes that brought Milka's hypoallergenic dog food. Original watercolor by my sister Wendy J. Joseph.

PHOTO 4: I quickly learned that I had to first grow slips (shoots). Seeing these shoots emerge from the sweet potatoes immersed in water has perhaps been the most exciting part of my "yam" journey. Original watercolor by my sister Wendy J. Joseph.

Ingredients

- 1 large sweet potato
- Salt, turmeric powder, cayenne pepper mixed to personal taste
- Olive Oil
- Cilantro

1. Slice the sweet potato (with the peel) about ½ an inch thick across.

2. Adjust and mix the spices to taste and rub well onto both sides of sweet potato slices.

3. In a shallow pan, heat just enough olive oil to keep the yam slices from sticking to the surface. Cook both sides till done. Sweet potatoes absorb quite a bit of oil. Add more as needed. For a lower fat version, brush on olive oil and bake on a cookie sheet in the oven at 350° F till done.

4. Garnish with chopped cilantro and serve hot. Enjoy!

NOTE: On cold winter days, street vendors in Delhi also serve sweet potatoes hot from charcoal stoves with boiled chickpeas, chopped cilantro, a dash of lime juice, and a sprinkle of chaat masala (a spicy mix available in Indian grocery stores).

GROWING TIPS IN GEORGIA:

Start slips from sweet potatoes (see Photo 4) indoors in the winter; they take a few weeks to emerge and root. Sweet potatoes require warm soils, so wait at least two weeks after the last frost when the soil temperatures are consistently in the upper 60's, or higher, before planting. Once established, sweet potatoes will tolerate dry soil. Keep it evenly moist with an inch of WATER once a week. Don't water during the final three to four weeks prior to harvest in order to keep the mature tubers from splitting. They take nearly four months from setting plants to harvest. Harvest sweet potatoes when the ends of the vines start to yellow. Before cooking, let unwashed sweet potatoes cure in a warm, well-ventilated area for 10 days. Sweet potato vines – green and purple – can also be used as ornamentals in pots. My sister found a surprise sweet potato in her pot when she dug up her ornamental!

Raised Garden Beds and Soil Mixes

David Berle

David has held many professional horticulture positions, and has been planting, and watching plants grow, for over 40 years. He is currently professor of horticulture at UGA, and director or UGArden, a student-run community farm. He is interested in gardening practices that do not waste resources or cost too much, and which, hopefully, leave the world a better place for everyone, especially those who are not able to garden themselves, or may not be able to afford to do so.

A raised garden bed can mean many things. Raising the soil to form a bed is a common practice among vegetable growers. Raising the soil warms it in spring and improves drainage. On a farm scale, raised soil beds are shaped with a bed-shaping tool. They are often covered with plastic to further warm the soil, reduce weeds, keep vegetables free of dirt, and maintain soil moisture. On a garden scale, raised beds typically mean some type of structure built to contain the soil above the soil level, sometimes on top of a hard surface. The structure is often built of wood, especially if home-made. Nowadays, it's common to see garden beds made of corrugated metal and composite lumber, or rocks and cement blocks. No matter how the raised bed is constructed, the need to fill it with some type of soil brings up many questions and issues.

Soil for raised beds is often an afterthought, with little scientific basis for selecting materials, and little consideration for long-term effects. True topsoil takes thousands of years to form and is not readily available anywhere in the southeast. The most important physical properties of any soil, native or artificial, are good aeration, drainage, and water-holding capacity. Decomposition and settling are important issues, as are cost and availability. We can adjust the pH, and add nutrients based on a soil sample, so nutrition is not a consideration in picking a soil mix. A study conducted several years ago at UGarden revealed some interesting facts about the materials a gardener might use to fill a raised bed. Here is an overview of what we learned.

POTTING MIX

This is the same mix you might use for potting houseplants or starting seed. They are in bags which are light, and easy to find at most stores. Potting mixes typically have peat as a base, to which are added many things: vermiculite and perlite, to improve drainage; wetting agents to help water penetrate the peat; a starter fertilizer; and sometimes, even bark and sand. Our study found that a good potting mix provided a high yield the first season, but quickly dropped in yield in the next two seasons. This was mostly due to the high rate of decomposition which caused settling and compaction. Potting mixes do best when they are fresh and fluffy, and provide no nutrition; so, keep an eye on fertilization. It should be noted that due to the source of fertilizer, and the type of wetting agent added, most potting mixes do NOT meet the requirements for organic certification.

PINE BARK

Ground pine bark is cheaper than potting mixes, and light, just like potting mix. We found that unless you adjust the pH with lime, and add more fertilizer than your plants usually need, pine bark results in lower yield than potting mix and decomposes even faster than potting mix. In which case, the pine bark was probably still decomposing, and that process used up all the nitrogen.

WOOD CHIPS

Wood chips come from trees growing locally. They are reasonably priced (often free) and widely available. However, because wood chips are very high in carbon, it takes time and nitrogen to make wood chips suitable for growing vegetables. Wood chips are best used for mulching walkways and possibly as a carbon source in a nitrogen-rich compost pile.

COMPOST

Compost is the easiest, and fastest way for a gardener to build organic matter in the soil. There are numerous other benefits to the use of compost. It provides nutrients; introduces beneficial microbes; increases water retention; improves drainage. No wonder it is considered the holy grail of garden amendments. In our study, we added compost to all the other materials evaluated. We even grew vegetables in pure compost. The addition of 50% compost improved the performance of all the other materials we evaluated, even the wood chips. In a later study, we found that 25% compost was enough for all other materials except the wood chips. Because compost does decompose over time, we found that adding one to two inches between each crop helped maintain soil organic matter (SOM) and keep the boxes sufficiently full. One of the biggest problems with compost is availability and cost - another reason to make your own.

NATIVE SOIL

For Georgia gardeners, native soil means red clay. That is because our topsoil is long gone, and the red clay is what's left. Clay soil gets a bad rap, but clay does have positive attributes, like a higher nutrient and water-holding capacity, and maybe even a little SOM. Furthermore, clay is certainly readily available, and cheap. For our study, we used what would be classified as fill dirt - soil excavated from the UGA campus. We tested this fill dirt by itself, and with a 50% mix of compost. We found that the fill dirt alone grew a pretty decent crop, and the fill dirt with compost grew almost as good a crop as the mix of compost and potting mix. In later studies, we found 25% compost did just as well as 50%, and still better than fill dirt alone.

Environmental Footprint

Most people assume that growing vegetables in a box is the perfect solution for the environment. This is probably true, but the materials you use and where they come from do have some impact. For example, there are now concerns about sourcing of peat. The energy to package and ship products has come under scrutiny. In our study, we chose to look at the carbon footprint, since this is a popular subject these days. We determined the amount of CO_2 each of the soil mixes released after three crop seasons. The native soil and the 50/50 mix of native soil plus compost released the least amounts of CO_2. The highest was the wood chips plus compost, followed closely by peat, wood chips, pine bark and even compost alone.

And the winner is...

It should be no surprise after reading this article that our winner and suggested soil mix for filling a raised garden bed is plain old clay soil with 25% compost. If the bed is held up by legs or attached to a structure, then clay soil would likely be too heavy, but otherwise, it's the best all-around choice when looking at availability, price, carbon footprint, settling, and crop growth.

Soil Mix	Availability	Cost	Yield	Weight	CO₂ Release
Compost	Medium	Low	High	Heavy	High
Native Soil	High	Medium	Med-High	Heavy	Low
Native Soil + 25% Compost	Med-High	Low	High	Heavy	Low
Pine Bark (Fine)	High	High	Low	Medium	Medium
Pine Bark + Compost	Med-High	Medium	Medium	Medium	Medium
Potting Mix	High	High	High	Light	High
Potting Mix + Compost	Med-High	High	High	Medium	High
Wood Chips	High	Low	Low	Medium	V. High
Wood Chips +Compost	Med-High	Low	Low	Heavy	High

Jessica Cudnick conducted much of the research for this article while a graduate student at UGA. This article is a revision of an early draft of a fact sheet she wrote based on her work.

Grow Your Own Transplants

Robert Westerfield

Robert Westerfield is a University of Georgia horticulturist at the Griffin Campus. He has been with the University for over 30 years, and specializes in fruit and vegetable production. His responsibilities include developing agent consumer resources, conducting agent trainings, and teaching master gardener classes.

When it comes to the summer garden, most folks purchase their tomatoes, peppers, and other vegetables, as transplants from a garden center. While it is relatively easy to start some vegetables by direct seeding into the garden soil, others are more temperamental and are normally started as finished transplants. Undoubtedly, if you have purchased any transplants in the southeast, they have likely come from Bonnie Plant Farm. Bonnie basically has a monopoly on the market and keeps most garden centers and nurseries stocked with healthy transplants in the southeast, as well as other parts of the United States. This is for good reason. Bonnie does an excellent job of growing healthy, stocky, vegetable transplants that are ready to be planted in the home garden. If your goal is to only plant a couple of tomatoes, peppers or other items, it certainly makes sense just to buy your transplants from a local distributor. On the other hand, if your goal is to plant several rows of tomatoes, broccoli, or Brussel sprouts, you should consider growing your own. Transplants are not tough to grow, and you can save money when planting large amounts of them. In addition, by growing your own transplants, you can select the varieties you prefer and will not be reliant on what the garden centers offer. By following a few basic steps, you can have transplants ready for this fall garden or next year's spring crop.

Perhaps the first item of discussion should be the growing medium. In most cases, it is best to select a soilless medium that is intended as a germination mix. These mixes are normally light and airy, allowing seeds to germinate and root out easily, while providing superior drainage. Garden centers, as well as greenhouse supply companies, sell different germinating mixes that you can purchase to use. I buy my growing mixes from a place called Griffin Greenhouse that is located up in North Georgia. Do not make the mistake of using potting soil, or worse yet, raw garden soil to germinate your seeds. Most potting soils are too heavy, and garden soil can be full of diseases that can hamper germination and growth.

You will also need to obtain some type of containers from which to germinate your seeds. These will also be available from greenhouse supply companies, but you should be able to find them in the back of most vegetable seed catalogs. There are many different styles and sizes of growing containers out there. Some folks like to start their seeds in one big tray and transplant them to a larger container after they germinate and develop. I prefer to direct seed into three- or four-inch pots that are approximately three inches deep, so that I do not have to take the additional step of shifting them up to a larger container. These little pots fit into a slotted tray that holds anywhere between fifteen and twenty containers at a time. When we seed our vegetables, we fill the pots up just shy of the top of the container. We then carefully sprinkle two to three seeds per cell to ensure that at least one germinates. We take a small handful of soil and put a quarter-inch or so layer over the top of the seeds. The final step is that we use the back of an empty container to lightly tap the soil on top to firm up the seedbed, making sure there is good soil-seed contact.

The next major considerations are temperature and light. Most seeds require a tremendous amount of light to germinate and grow healthy transplants. When it comes to light, there is no good substitute for actual sunlight. A small-frame hobby green house or south-facing sunroom might be the best locations for growing your transplants. If those areas do not exist, you can successfully grow them under artificial light. The best artificial light comes from growers' lights that can be found in the back of seed catalogs. These lights emit a broad spectrum of light waves that are beneficial to good plant growth. In the absence of a true grow light, you can use an adjustable hanging shop lamp that utilizes three- or four-foot-long soft fluorescent bulbs. When using any type of artificial light, you must adjust it to within an inch of the soil prior to germination. After germination, when true leaves are formed, begin to slowly raise your light a few inches above your plants. The trick is to keep it close enough without burning the foliage. Plants will benefit from twelve to fourteen hours of artificial light per day in the absence of sunlight. Germinating seeds also need room temperatures between 65 to 75 degrees Fahrenheit. If you are growing outdoors in a cold frame, you may have to run some type of heating lamp or use a germinating heating pad that goes underneath your containers.

The other requirement for growing successful transplants will be to provide them with ample water and fertilizer. Soluble liquid fertilizers are usually the easiest way to provide nutrition to your developing transplants. A balanced formulation of a 20-20-20 liquid fertilizer should carry your transplants all the way to completion. Fertilize at planting time and then approximately one time a week throughout the life of the transplant. Transplants typically take five to seven weeks to develop, depending on the type of vegetable. While you only fertilize on occasion, you need to irrigate the transplants on a daily basis. Depending on the soil and temperature, you may need to lightly irrigate once or twice a day. Take care to water gently so that you do not disturb the seeds prior to germination. Some type of fine-misting head would be the best tool to use when watering your transplants. If you suddenly begin to see your transplants wilting or a green, crusty soil appears in the top of the container, you may be keeping the soil too wet. Make adjustments to improve the situation.

While growing transplants is not difficult, you do need to keep your eye on them for any invading greenhouse pests or diseases. If it appears that your transplants are too tall and spindly, it is most likely from your light not being intense enough or your plants being too crowded. A trick to try if your transplants seem spindly is to gently agitate them by taking a piece of cardboard or magazine and slowly brushing them back and forth, to where you are causing the stems to move, but not dislodge. By doing this for about thirty seconds once or twice a day, you will actually cause a beneficial stress on the plants that will trigger them to thicken up their stems.

With the rising costs of transplants at the garden centers and sometimes limited availability of the cultivars you wish to grow, growing your own transplants makes great sense. It does not take a lot of sophisticated equipment to get the job done. I have even seen transplants grown in something as simple as egg cartons or small drink cups. By paying attention to a few details, you will soon be producing your own transplants and adding a new level of enjoyment to your gardening.

Winter

A Time to Reap

Beets
Brussels Sprouts
Cabbage
Carrots
Celery
Collards
Kale
Leeks
Onions
Parsnips
Potatoes
Rutabegas
Turnips
Winter Squash

Beets
Broccoli
Collards
Carrots
Lettuce
Mustard
Onions
Spinach

A Time to Sow

| | | | Produce (1 Cup, raw. Unless otherwise stated) | | | | | | | | | | | | | | Cereals and Grains (1 cup cooked) | | | | | |
			Beets	Brussels Sprouts	Cabbage	Collard Greens	Green Papaya	Parsnips	Plantains	Rutabagas	Turnips	Winter Squash, Acorn	Dates (100 gm)	Kiwi (California)	Persimmons (100 gm)	Ripe Papaya	Millet	Oatmeal	Quinoa	Rice (white, long grain, regular)	Soy (flour, full-fat, raw)	Wheat Flour (white, all purpose, unenriched)
Nutrition		Calories	58.5	37.8	22.2	10.8	54.6	99.7	181	50	36.4	56	277	108	127	54.6	207	166	222	205	366	455
	Grams	Carbohydrates	13	7.9	5.2	2	13.7	23.9	47	11.4	8.4	14.6	75	25.9	33.5	13.7	41.2	31.8	39.4	44.5	29.6	95.4
		Protein	2.2	3	1.1	0.7	0.9	1.6	1.9	1.7	1.2	1.1	1.8	2	0.8	0.9	6.1	5.9	16	4.2	29	12.9
		Fat	0.2	0.3	0.1	0.2	0.2	0.4	0.5	0.2	0.1	0.1	0.2	0.9	0.4	0.2	1.7	0.7	3.6	0.4	17.3	1.2
		Fiber	3.8	3.3	2.2	1.3	2.5	6.5	3.5	3.5	2.3	2.1	6.7	5.3	-	2.5	2.3	4	5.2	0.6	8.1	3.4
Vitamins	%DV	Vitamin A	1	13	2	48	31	0	33	0	0	10	3	3	0	31	0	0	0	0	2	0
		Vitamin C	11	125	54	21	144	38	45	58	46	26	0	273	110	144	0	0	0	0	0	0
		Vitamin K	0	195	85	230	5	37	1	1	0	-	3	89	3	5	1	1	0	0	73	0
		Folate	37	13	10	15	13	22	8	7	5	6	4	11	2	13	8	4	19	23	72	8
Minerals		Iron	6	7	2	0	1	4	5	4	2	5	5	3	14	1	6	12	15	11	30	8
		Calcium	2	4	4	5	3	5	0	7	4	5	6	6	2	3	1	2	3	2	17	2
		Potassium	13	10	4	2	10	14	21	13	7	14	20	16	7	10	3	5	9	2	60	4
		Sodium	4	1	1	0	0	1	0	1	4	0	0	0	0	0	0	0	1	0	0	0

Aji de Huacatay – Green Rocoto Chilli and Huacatay Sauce

Allan Cobb

1. Heat the oil in a pan over medium heat, add the chilis, onion, garlic and sauté for 8-10 minutes until the onion is golden and translucent. Remove from heat and drain the oil without discarding it.

2. Put the sautéed chili mixture in a blender with the roasted peanuts, chopped huacatay, queso fresco, crackers, vinegar, and parsley. Blend together, gradually drizzling in the oil from the sautéed chilis, until you have a smooth emulsion.

3. Keep refrigerated.

Huacatay has a spicy, minty flavor, like basil. It may be substituted with 2/3 basil and 1/3 mint. Rocoto chilis are like jalapenos in flavor and spiciness.

Classic Peruvian condiment best served with sandwiches, empanadas, potatoes, or corn on the cob.

Ingredients

- 1 cup (8 fl oz) vegetable oil
- 1 lb 8oz green rocoto chillis -- seeded, white insides removed and cut into small pieces
- 1 small red onion - chopped
- 3 cloves garlic -- chopped
- 8 oz roasted peanuts
- ½ tablespoon chopped huacatay leaves
- 3 ¼ oz queso fresco
- 4 saltine crackers -- or similar brand
- 1 tablespoon white wine vinegar
- ½ tablespoon chopped parsley

Amazing Cinnamon Apple Pie *Candi Hoard*

Ingredients

For the Filling:
- 2 heaping cups of sliced green granny smith apples
- 1 Tbsp cinnamon
- ½ cup sugar
- 1 9-inch unbaked pie shell

For the Topping:
- ½ cup sugar
- ½ cup flour
- ½ of a stick of SOFT butter

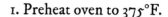

1. Preheat oven to 375°F.

2. Combine the filling ingredients and place in an unbaked pie shell (can use frozen).

3. Mix topping ingredients butter with fork or fingers.

4. Crumble topping over the apple pie filling. It does not have to be uniform.

5. Bake for 1 hour.

Apple-Orange Cranberry Sauce

Suzanne Keifer

Ingredients

- ½ orange
- 2 cups water
- 1 Granny Smith, peeled, cored, chopped into ½" cubes.
- 3 cups fresh cranberries
- 1 ¼ cup sugar
- ½ tsp cinnamon
- ¼ tsp ground cloves

1. Squeeze orange for juice and set juice aside. Remove and discard membrane from inside orange rind.

2. Cut rind into ¼" diced pieces.

3. In a medium saucepan, over high heat, combine the rind and water and boil for 10 minutes. Drain and set the rind aside.

4. Sort the cranberries, throwing away any soft ones.

5. In the same medium saucepan, place the diced apples, the cranberries, the orange rind, the reserved orange juice, sugar, cinnamon, and cloves. Bring this to a boil, reduce to low/simmer. Simmer gently until the sauce thickens and the cranberries burst, about 10-15 minutes. Stir occasionally to prevent from sauce sticking to the pan.

6. Transfer the sauce to a heat-proof bowl and let it cool. You can cover and refrigerate but bring to room temperature before serving.

Makes 3-4 cups.

Ayam Masak Merah

Tinu Ann Thomas

Marinate (A)
- 1kg chicken (cut into 2 inch pieces, roughly 10- 15 pieces)
- 1tsp turmeric powder
- 2 tsp salt

Blend(B)
- 8-10 shallots
- ¾ inch ginger
- 5-8 red chillis
- 6 cloves garlic

Others(C)
- 1 big tomato
- 3 tsp palm sugar or jaggery
- Salt to taste
- 4 Tbsps Vegetable oil

1. Marinate the chicken for half hour.

2. Fry the marinated chicken until it is nearly cooked or turns slightly brown, drain and set aside.

3. Add some oil into a pan and sauté the onions.

4. Next add in the blended ingredients(B) and sauté till fragrant.

5. Add the fried chicken and stew over low heat until the chicken is fully cooked.

6. Next step is to add the ingredients (C) and reduce the heat to barely boil. At this point you may add some water but not too much. When the chicken is cooked, they will release their juice and dilute the gravy.

7. Simmer over low heat, that is when it is barely boiled, for about 30 minutes.

8. When the chicken is done garnish it with some spring onions.

Ayam masak merah is a Malaysian traditional dish. This literally means "Chicken cooked-red".

Ayam = Chicken.   Masak = Cooked.   Merah = Red.

Tinu Ann, Rita's niece, who lives in Malaysia, shared this anecdote about a Chicken dish. "I want to share with you couple of recipes that we often cook at home. These recipes are simple and very easy to make. So here is the take of the recipe by Amma (my husband, Deepak's mum). The recipe I am about to share is not the actual recipe. Amma has changed few things from the original recipe to suit our taste buds. Ayam masak merah is a home-cooked dish. So many variations of this recipe exist."

Baked Apple

Suzanne Keifer

Ingredients

- Ingredients for 1 Apple – Gala work best
- 1 rounded tbsp brown sugar
- 1 Tbsp unsalted butter
- ½ tsp cinnamon
- Raisins and chopped pecans, optional

1. Grease an apple baker (or a small oven-proof bowl).

2. Core the apple and place in the baker. Fill the cored center with a mixture of the brown sugar, butter and cinnamon. Sprinkle the raisins and nuts over this, if desired.

3. Place the baker in a COLD oven. Turn the oven on to 350°F and bake for 30-40 minutes. You could microwave this as well for approximately 8 minutes.

4. For a truly decadent dessert, the apple could be topped with vanilla ice cream, frozen yogurt, or whipped cream.

Beetroot Kochumbir *(Side Dish/Appetizer)*

Rita Mathew

Ingredients

- 4 medium Beetroots
- ½ cup roasted peanuts
- 1 small green chilli (optional)
- 1 tsp lemon juice
- 1 tsp salt
- Kari Leaf Seasoning (See page 36)
- 1 Tbsp fresh chopped cilantro leaves

1. Prepare the Kari Leaf Seasoning per directions on page 36.

2. Boil the Beetroots first, since it is easier to peel the skin. Grate or dice.

3. Coarsely crush the peanuts. Trim the ends of the chilli and slice in half.

4. Although the spicy chilli adds a touch of flavor to the sweet beetroot it can be omitted; remove the seeds if you want a less spicy dish, and then finely chop the chilli.

5. Mix all the ingredients and add to the hot pan with Kari Leaf seasoning. Cook for two minutes and scoop into a serving bowl. Garnish with Cilantro. Serve hot or cold.

Kochumbir usually has raw vegetables. In this version the beetroot is cooked. This is a sweet, hot and sour dish that could be served on toasted bruschetta as a starter, or as a side dish with naan or rice.

Best Chicken Pot Pie

Beverly Simpson

1. Place butter in a deep saucepan, as it melts, stir in vegetables. Allow to simmer until vegetables are tender-crisp—about 6-8 minutes. Add flour and stir in until smooth. Add broth and stir until smooth.

2. Add spices, taste, and adjust if needed. Allow mixture to thicken to pot pie consistency. Add chicken and peas and heat through. Pour mixture into a 9 x 13-inch pan. Cover with puff pastry. Cut slits in pastry to allow steam to escape.

3. Cook on 400 degrees for about 30 minutes or until pastry puffs and turns golden.

So good it will only serve 4 adults!!

Ingredients

- 2 ½ cups chicken breasts or tenders, simmered until done and chopped
- ¼ cup butter
- ⅛ cup flour
- 1 cup carrots, chopped
- ¼ cup red bell pepper, chopped
- ¼ cup celery, chopped
- 1 cup fresh mushrooms, chopped or canned and drained
- ½ cup onion, chopped
- 1 ½ - 2 cups chicken broth
- 1 ½ cup frozen green peas
- Salt and pepper to taste
- 1 Tbsp dried parsley
- 1 Tbsp dried thyme
- 1 package of puff pastry or pie crust

Best Macaroni and Cheese

Jean Colquett

1. Cook macaroni and drain. Place half the macaroni in a rectangular dish and top with half the cheese.

2. Layer the remainder of the macaroni and cheese. Beat milk, eggs, salt and pepper, and mustard. Pour over the macaroni and cheese.

3. Bake at 350° for 40 minutes

Ingredients

- 1 8oz box macaroni
- 6 cups sharp cheddar cheese, grated
- 3 eggs, beaten well
- 3 cups milk
- ½ tsp dry mustard
- salt and pepper to taste
- 1 stick butter, melted and poured over the top

Brussels Sprouts

Suzanne Keifer

Ingredients

- 1 ½ lbs Brussel sprouts
- ¼ lb bacon, crisp and coarsely crumbled
- 10 chestnuts, roasted, peeled, quartered
- 1 ¾ cup chicken broth
- 1 Tbsp unsalted butter
- 1 ½ tsp fresh thyme
- Salt and pepper to taste

This is a delicious way to get Brussel Sprout haters to like them. I have found the chestnuts in jars, already peeled at good local markets.

1. Blanch sprouts in boiling salted water for 4-5 minutes. Drain and dunk in ice water. Once cooled, slice them in ½ and set aside.

2. Cook bacon approximately 8-10 minutes, remove them with tongs, leaving the fat in the pan. Coarsely crumble the bacon once cool enough to handle. Add the chestnuts and cook for 2 minutes, add the crumbled bacon and the sprouts, and bring up to high heat.

3. Pour in the broth and cover the pan with a lid. When the mixture boils, reduce the heat to simmer, mix in the butter, salt, pepper, and thyme. Serve warm. Serves 6.

California Salad

Rosemary Stancil

Ingredients

For the Salad:
- 8 cups Romaine or leaf lettuce, washed, spun dry and torn in bite size pieces
- 1 large grapefruit or 3 oranges, peeled and sectioned
- 12 large dates, pitted and halved
- 1 small purple onion, thinly sliced vertically
- 18 pecan or walnut halves, toasted
- 2 tablespoons toasted sesame seeds

For the Dressing:
- ¼ cup olive oil
- 2 tablespoons fresh lemon juice
- 1 teaspoon salt
- ¼ teaspoon freshly ground black pepper
- 1 teaspoon Worcestershire sauce
- 1 teaspoon dark sesame oil
- 1 avocado, peeled and sliced

To make dressing:
1. In a small bowl, whisk together olive oil, lemon juice, salt, pepper, Worcestershire and sesame oil. Place the avocado slices in the dressing to coat each slice.

To assemble salad:
1. Place lettuce on individual salad plates or one large plate. Arrange grapefruit sections, dates, onion slices, nuts, and avocado slices over the lettuce. Sprinkle with sesame seeds.

2. Drizzle with the dressing.

Yield: 6 Servings

Carrot Soufflé

Linda Tedrow

Ingredients

For the Topping:
- ½ crushed corn flakes or walnuts
- 3 Tbsp brown sugar
- 2 tsp butter, room temperature

For the Souffle:
- 2 pounds carrots, peeled and cooked until tender
- 3 eggs
- ⅔ cup sugar
- 4 Tbsp all-purpose flour
- 1 tsp vanilla
- ½ cup melted butter
- Dash nutmeg
- 1 tsp baking powder
- Pinch of salt (optional)

1. Preheat oven to 350°F.

2. Mix topping ingredients and set aside.

3. Purée carrots and eggs in a blender. Add remaining ingredients and blend until well mixed. Pour into a 1 ½ quart baking dish and bake for 40 minutes.

4. Sprinkle the topping over the souffle and bake 5-10 minutes longer, until the topping is lightly browned.

Cashew-Cranberry Energy Balls

Pam Tidwell

Ingredients

- 1 cup old-fashioned oats
- 3 Tbsp roasted, salted cashews, roughly chopped
- 3 Tbsp dried cranberries
- ½ tsp ground ginger
- ⅛ tsp salt
- ½ cup creamy peanut butter
- ¼ cup honey

1. In a medium bowl, combine the oats, cashews, cranberries, ginger, and salt and stir to mix well.

2. Add the peanut butter and honey, mix and combine thoroughly.

3. Cover and refrigerate 20 – 30 minutes or until the mixture is easy to handle.

4. Shape into small balls (1" or slightly larger). Store in airtight container in the refrigerator.

5. They can be frozen for up to 1 month.

Clam Chowder

Ingredients

- 2 slices bacon or 2 tbsp olive oil
- 2 potatoes
- 1 medium onion
- 1 green or red bell pepper
- 2 stalks celery
- 1 quart water
- 1 large can tomatoes--whole or diced, if whole, you must chop
- 2 Tbsp tomato paste
- 2 cans (10 oz Bumble Bee) diced clams, drain and save juice
- 1 tsp thyme
- Salt and pepper, to taste

1. If you are using the bacon, brown it and save the grease for sautéing the potatoes and onions.

2. Sauté the chopped potatoes and onion in grease or oil.

3. Add the water, tomatoes, tomato paste, celery, green pepper, clam juice and thyme.

4. Boil lightly for 20 minutes or until potatoes are tender.

5. Add clams and salt and pepper to taste.

6. Heat but avoid boiling.

Cooked Carrot Raita

Rita Mathew

Ingredients

- 3 cups Carrot (peeled and grated)
- 1 medium onion (thin sliced)
- 1 tsp toasted whole cumin seeds
- 1 small green chilli
- 1-inch fresh ginger (peeled and finely grated)
- 1 tsp salt
- 1 Tbsp oil
- 2 cups Yogurt
- 1 Tbsp fresh Coriander leaves.

1. Stir fry the sliced onions on a medium hot pan till translucent. Add the grated carrots, cover, and cook for 2 – 3 minutes.

2. When carrots are cooked, place the onion and carrot mixture in a serving bowl and allow to cool.

3. Take the top off the chilli, remove seeds, and finely dice it. Add the chilli, grated ginger and salt to the onion and carrot mixture and stir in the yogurt. Garnish with Cilantro.

> Substitute:
> - 1 lb pumpkin (To prepare - trim ends, peel, remove seeds and fibrous pulp, grate, and cook)
> - 1 lb butternut squash (Prepare the same as pumpkin)

Copper Pennies

Pam Tidwell

Ingredients

- 2 pounds carrots, peeled and thinly sliced
- 1 can tomato soup
- ½ cup oil
- 1 tsp salt
- 1 bell pepper, chopped
- 2 small onions, chopped
- ¼ tsp mustard
- 1 tsp black pepper
- ¼ cup plain white vinegar
- ¾ cup sugar

1. In a medium saucepan, cook carrots until tender and drain.

2. Add the remaining ingredients to the carrots and mix well.

3. Store in an airtight container and refrigerate.

Dark Chocolate Brownies

Caroline D'Souza

Ingredients

- 3 eggs
- 230 gms dark chocolate (8.2 oz)
- 260 gms butter (9.3 oz or just a little more than a stick)
- 200 gms sugar (7.1 oz)
- 120 g all-purpose flour (4 1/4 oz - just a little over 1/4 cup)
- Few drops vanilla essence

1. Melt butter and dark chocolate over a double boiler.

2. Beat separately the eggs and sugar. When the butter mixture cools, add beaten eggs and sugar to it. Add flour.

3. Optional: You can mix finely chopped walnuts into batter (after rolling in flour) and also sprinkle on top.

4. Bake in well greased trays at 350 degrees F for about 35 to 40 minutes. The crust is crisp and lighter in texture. The inside is darker and moist.

Dark Fruitcake

Margaret Slevin (Suzanne Keifer's aunt)

Ingredients

- 6 cups sifted plain flour
- 1 teaspoon cinnamon
- 1 teaspoon nutmeg
- ¼ teaspoon cloves
- ⅔ teaspoon allspice
- 1 teaspoon salt
- 2 pounds citron
- 2 pounds dates
- 2 pounds raisins
- 2 pounds currants
- 1 pound butter
- 1 pound sugar
- 12 eggs, slightly beaten
- 1 teaspoon soda
- 1 cup molasses
- ⅔ cup bourbon whiskey

1. Divide the flour into 2 equal parts. Ad the spices and salt to one part. Dice the fruit and mix with remaining flour.

2. Cream butter and sugar and add the eggs.

3. Dissolve soda in one tablespoon of warm water and add to molasses.

4. Add the spiced flour and molasses alternately to the egg and butter mixture. Stir in the whiskey and then add the fruit. Mix thoroughly.

5. Batter should be divided into two greased and paper-lined 8 x 4" pans. Bake at 250 degrees for approximately 4 ½ hours. DO NOT open the oven door for the first 1 ½ hours. A straw will come out clean when the cakes are done. Leave them in the pans until cold.

6. Remove pans and wrap in foil (or douse with more bourbon like Aunt Marge did...). Store in a covered tin. This cake will keep several months. It is best when at least two to four weeks old.

My aunt would start making her fruit cakes in October, wrap them in old sheets and weekly, add a tablespoon or two of bourbon until Christmas. This fruit cake is full, rich, and incredibly moist (not just from all the bourbon). It's not a cheap cake to make and don't substitute more raisins for currants.

Dulce de Leche Bundt Cake *Suzanne Keifer*

1. Preheat oven to 350°F and position oven rack to the middle.

2. Generously butter a 10-inch Bundt pan and sprinkle with flour or use Baker & Joy™ cooking spray.

3. Tip the pan and tap out excess flour. Warm the dulce de leche a little bit to soften it and pour it over the bottom of pan to coat evenly.

For the cake:
1. In a large bowl, beat the butter and sugar with an electric mixer at medium-high speed until light in color. Scrape the bowl. Beat in the egg. Sift together the flour, cake flour, baking powder, baking soda, cinnamon, and cocoa. With the mixer on medium-low, beat in about 1/2 of flour mixture, followed by 1/2 of buttermilk. Repeat. Scrape bowl, then raise the speed to medium-high and beat for 1 minute. Pour batter into the Bundt pan and spread evenly.

For the flan:
1. In a blender combine the sweetened condensed milk and evaporated milk, the eggs, and both extracts. Blend until smooth. Slowly pour the flan mixture over cake batter.

2. Pull out the oven rack, set the cake into larger pan, then set both pans on rack. Pour 6 cups of hot water around the cake. Carefully slide the pans into the oven and bake for about 50 to 55 minutes or until a toothpick comes out clean. Remove from the water bath and cool at room temperature for 1 hour.

3. Refrigerate cake for several hours or overnight. Carefully run a thin bladed knife around the edge of the cake to free the edges. Invert a rimmed serving platter or large plate over the cake pan, grasp the two tightly together, then turn them upside down. Gently jiggle the pan back and forth and let the cake release and drop.

4. Drizzle the reserved cup of dulce de leche over the cake and sprinkle with pecans. Slice and serve.

Ingredients

For the cake:
- 1 cup dulce de leche
- ¾ cup butter, softened
- 1 cup sugar
- 1 whole egg
- ¾ cup regular flour
- 1 cup cake flour
- ¾ tsp baking powder
- ¾ tsp baking soda
- ⅓ cup plus 2 tablespoons cocoa powder
- 1 tsp ground cinnamon
- 1 cup plus 2 tbsp buttermilk

For the flan:
- 1 can (14 oz) sweetened condensed milk
- 1 can (12 oz) evaporated milk
- 4 whole eggs
- 1 tsp vanilla extract
- 1 tsp coconut extract

Cake toppings:
- 1 cup dulce de leche
- ½ cup finely chopped pecans

See picture on Back Cover.

Eggplant (Bujji) Dip or Raita *Rita Mathew*

1. Wash the eggplant and pat dry. Brush the Eggplant with oil and prick holes about 5 to 6 times with the tines of a fork.

2. To cook in a microwave: Microwave for 10 minutes turning frequently. To cook in an oven: Preheat oven to 400° F. and bake for 30-35 minutes until soft.

3. When cooked, peel the skin. Mash the flesh to a coarse texture with a fork.

4. Mix the puree with all the other ingredients. Serve chilled.

VARIATIONS
Eggplant may be substituted with following:
• 1 lb Pumpkin (2 cups. To prepare trim ends, peel, remove seeds and fibrous pulp. Cut in cubes, cook and mash)
• 1 lb Bottle Gourd (2 cups. Prepare same as pumpkin)
• 1 lb Sweet Potato (2 cups. Boil, remove skin and mash)
• 1 large slightly ripe plantain (peeled, cooked, mashed)

Vegan Option: Omit yogurt.

Ingredients

• 1 large Eggplant
• ½ cup finely diced onions
• 1 cup yogurt
• ½ tsp crushed garlic
• 1 Tbsp fresh chopped Coriander leaves
• ¼ tsp salt

Bujji means to mash or puree. Traditionally, the Eggplant is roasted over a charcoal fire, which gives it a distinctive, smoky aroma. Alternately, it can be cooked in an oven or the microwave. A simple preparation of Eggplant Bujji is a good option for vegan diets. With the addition of yogurt, it may be served as an appetizer dip.

Spicy Eggplant Side Dish

Rita Mathew

1. To cook the eggplant, follow the instructions on page 179.

2. Heat the oil in a pan, and add mustard seeds. Cover for about a minute till the seeds have popped. Add the dry spices and fry for a minute. Stir in the scallions and garlic, cover and cook for 2 minutes. Add tomatoes and simmer for 5 minutes. Add the pureed eggplant, mushrooms and peas.

3. Cover and cook till peas are done. Serve garnished with fresh Cilantro.

See top right of picture below.

Ingredients

- 1 large Eggplant
- 3 Tbsp Oil
- ¼ tsp mustard seeds
- ½ tsp chilli powder
- ½ tsp ground cumin
- 1 tsp ground coriander
- ¼ tsp turmeric powder
- 1 bunch scallions (trim ends, chop)
- 1 tsp garlic crushed
- 3 – 4 fresh tomatoes
- 1 cup button mushrooms
- ½ cup English peas
- 2 Tbsp fresh chopped Coriander leaves

Gingersnaps

Suzanne Keifer's Mom

Ingredients

- 1 firmly packed cup dark brown sugar
- ¼ cup good applesauce
- ⅓ cup molasses
- 2 ¼ cup all purpose unbleached flour
- 1 tsp baking soda
- 2 ½ tsp ground cinnamon
- 1 ½ tsp ground ginger
- ¼ tsp ground cloves
- ¼ tsp ground black pepper
- ¼ tsp salt
- 2 egg whites
- ~ ½ cup sugar with a pinch of cinnamon for rolling the cookies in

1. Preheat oven to 350°F.

2. In a stand mixer, beat sugar, applesauce, and molasses for 5 minutes.

3. In a separate bowl, sift together the flour, baking soda, spices, and salt.

4. After 5 minutes of mixing the sugar, applesauce and molasses, scrape sides of bowl and add the egg whites; mix at medium speed for 1 minute. After the 1 minute, turn mixer to slowest speed and add the dry ingredients. Once incorporated, turn mixer back up to medium and mix for 1 minute.

5. Chill the dough completely. Line 2 cookie sheets with parchment paper. Mix up the sugar/cinnamon in a shallow bowl. Scoop dough with a 1" melon baller and roll in the sugar/cinnamon mixture. Place cookies 3" apart. Bake 13 minutes or until they feel just barely set in the center. Cool on wire racks. Makes about 50 cookies.

Green Chicken

Alice Roshin Jacob

Ingredients

- 2 ½ lb chicken
- 4 medium onions
- 6 shallots
- 8 cloves garlic
- ½ inch ginger
- 8 to 10 green chillies
- 1 tsp garam masala
- 2 cups coconut milk (optional canned coconut milk)
- 1 ½ Tbsps of coriander powder
- 4 Tbsps oil
- Salt to taste

1. To marinate chicken: Add salt, a little turmeric powder and soya sauce, can add a little tomato sauce, optional. Keep for an hour or two.

2. Slice 2 medium onions thinly, and 2 others into big cubes. Blend the cubed onions and keep aside.

3. Slice the shallots, ginger, garlic and green chillies and add to the sliced onions.

4. Add oil to a large pan.

5. Sauté the sliced ingredients till slightly brown.

6. Add the blended onion and sauté, adding more oil if necessary. Sauté till nicely browned.

7. Now add the garam masala, the coriander powder, and salt. Stir for five minutes.

8. Add the chicken and mix well. Now pour in 1 cup of hot water. Close the wok and cook till chicken is tender.

9. When chicken is cooked and gravy reduced, add the coconut milk. Let it boil for a minute.

10. Can garnish with potato slices or toothpick thin fried potatoes.

Note from Tinu Ann: The following recipe is from my dearest Amma, she wanted me to send this recipe to you. Amma says that this recipe belonged to Kozencherry Mummy (Mrs. K. M. Mathew - my grandmother)!

Harvest Kale Salad

SNAP Ed

Ingredients

- 6 cups kale, chopped and stems removed (1 bunch)
- 4 cups red cabbage, chopped (⅓ – ½ head)
- 2 green apples, diced
- 8 strips turkey bacon
- ¼ cup olive oil
- 1 Tbsp apple cider vinegar
- 1 tsp honey
- 1 Tbsp mustard

1. Remove stems from kale. Rinse and dry kale leaves, outside of cabbage, and apples.

2. Chop kale and cabbage. Dice green apple.

3. In a jar with a tight-fitting lid, combine olive oil, vinegar, honey and mustard. Shake well. Pour over salad and toss to coat all ingredients.

4. Cook turkey bacon and roughly chop. Sprinkle bacon over top of salad and serve.

Hashbrown Casserole

Pam Tidwell

Ingredients

- 2 cans cream of chicken soup
- 8 oz sour cream
- ½ tsp pepper
- 1 package (30-32 oz) frozen hashbrowns
- ¾ cup sliced green onions (or to taste)
- ¾ cup shredded sharp Cheddar cheese
- ¾ cup shredded Swiss cheese
- ¾ cup Parmesan cheese

1. Preheat oven to 375°F.

2. Combine soup, sour cream, and pepper in a large bowl.

3. Stir in the potatoes, onions, the Cheddar and Swiss cheeses.

4. Spoon into an 8x8" dish. Sprinkle with the Parmesan.

5. Bake, uncovered, for 60-75 minutes.

Hobo Stew

Kathie Eastman

Ingredients

- 1 lb Ground beef
- 1 qt water
- Salt and Pepper to taste
- 1 cup coarsely chopped cabbage
- 1 can crushed tomatoes
- ⅛ tsp garlic powder
- 1 small onion chopped
- ¼ tsp dried rosemary
- ¼ tsp dried marjoram
- ½ tsp dried oregano
- ¼ tsp dried basil
- ½ tsp dried thyme
- 1 bay leaf
- 2 cups cubed potatoes
- 2 cups sliced carrots
- 1 med package mixed veggies or soup veggies

1. Brown Ground beef in Dutch oven and drain.

2. Add water, seasonings, herbs, onion, tomatoes, and cabbage, cover and simmer for 30 minutes. Adjust seasonings to taste, yours, and then add carrots, potatoes, and frozen veggies and add water as needed to cover veggies.

3. Simmer another 30 minutes or until veggies are tender. This should be almost soup like. Thicken if you like.

Note: I adjust the herbs to my taste and cook the carrots with the tomatoes and onion. I also add chopped celery if available. If you wish you may thicken the broth a little. Serve with crusty bread. This is a satisfying meal. It freezes well too.

Individual Chicken Pot Pies   *Linda Tedrow*

1. Preheat oven to 375°F. In a large saucepan, heat the broth/stock and bouillon cube over medium heat until the cube is melted and the mixture is hot.

2. In a Dutch oven, melt butter over medium heat. Add the onions, carrots, celery, chives, and garlic and sauté. Season with salt and pepper. Add the flour and stir together until it becomes pasty and no lumps, about 2 minutes. Stir the hot broth/stock mixture, heavy cream, sherry, chicken, frozen onions and peas. Bring to a boil then reduce to simmer.

3. With a ladle, fill 6 oven-proof ramekins or bowls with the filling and place on a lipped baking sheet.

4. Sprinkle flour on flat surface and roll out pie dough 1" larger. Cut the dough to cover the ramekin/bowl with about ½" hanging over. Crimp the dough over the edge of the ramekin. Brush with the egg wash and make 4 small slits on the top.

5. Bake for 35 minutes. Let cool 5 minutes before serving.

Ingredients

- 4 cup chicken broth (or stock for a richer taste)
- 1 bouillon cube
- ½ cup butter (1 stick)
- 1 onion, finely chopped
- 2 large carrots, peeled and sliced in ½" slices
- 1 rib celery, sliced
- 3 Tbsp chopped fresh chives
- 2 cloves garlic, minced
- ½ cup all-purpose flour
- ¼ cup heavy cream
- 3 Tbsp dry sherry
- 1 store-bought 2-pound rotisserie chicken, shredded.
- 1 (7-oz) bag frozen pearl onions
- 1 (9-oz) bag/box frozen peas
- 2 (9-oz) packages pie dough
- 1 egg, beaten with 1 tbsp water
- Salt and Pepper to taste

Lime Caesar Dressing

Greg and Laura Killmaster

1. Mince garlic and set aside for about 10 minutes (this allows it to develop the most allicin - https://en.wikipedia.org/wiki/Allicin)

2. Combine all ingredients into a 16 oz. ball jar and whisk to combine.

Ingredients

- 1 cup olive oil
- ¼ cup tahini
- Juice of 1 lime or lemon (or more to taste) - prefer lime
- 2 Tbsp apple cider vinegar
- 1 tsp honey
- 2 clove minced garlic
- 2 Tbsp Tamari, soy sauce or Shoyu
- ⅛ tsp ground black pepper
- ¼ cup finely grated hard parmesan (optional)

Mulligatawny Soup

Christi Heston

1. In a medium to large size skillet, melt the butter.

2. Sauté all the vegetables, apples, cloves, sugar, spices for about 5 minutes.

3. Put this mixture in a large stock pot.

4. Add the raisins, sour cream, chicken stock, rice, and parsley and simmer approximately 45 minutes or until vegetables are tender.

Ingredients

- 4 tbsp butter
- 3 chicken breasts, cooked and shredded
- 3-4 tsp curry powder
- 1 Tbsp red pepper, less or more according to your taste
- 2 quarts chicken stock
- 1 Tbsp salt
- Black pepper to taste
- 4 long carrots, peeled and chopped
- 3 stalks celery, chopped
- 2-3 Granny Smith apples, peeled, cored, and chopped
- 3 whole cloves
- ½ cup sour cream
- ½ cup chopped fresh parsley
- 2 Tbsp sugar
- 2-3 cups cooked rice
- 1 cup Golden raisins

Nasi Lemak

Tinu Ann Thomas

- ¼ tsp salt
- 1 lemongrass stalk
- 2 pandan leaves
- 75 ml coconut milk
- 1 ½ cups water
- 1 cup rice

1. Wash rice and put into a pot. Add coconut milk, water, a pinch of salt, pandan leaves (knotted) and lemon grass.

2. Bring to boil, then lower heat to minimum. Cover the pot with lid and allow the rice to cook for 15-20 minutes until it dries up and holes appear on the surface.

3. Turn off the stove. Leave the lid on for another 10 minutes before serving.

Nasi lemak is a Malay cuisine dish consisting of fragrant rice cooked in coconut milk and pandan leaf. It is considered a national dish in Malaysia. Pandan leaves (Pandanus amaryllifolius) have a sweet aromatic flavor and may also be used to flavor desserts. Thai Basil, Kaffir Lime or Pandan extract are good substitutes.

To the right is a picture of Ayam Masak Merah with Nasi Lemak. Served with cucumbers, boiled eggs, fried anchovies and peanuts.

Salsa Chicken Chowder

Rosemary Stancil

1. Cut chicken into ½ to ¾ inch pieces.

2. Melt butter in a large stock pot. Add chicken, onion and garlic; sauté, stirring, until the chicken is brown and no longer pink inside.

3. Add salsa and corn; stir. Add chicken stock and cook until hot. Stir in cheese until melted; slowly add half and half. Stir to combine all ingredients and simmer until thoroughly heated.

*Vary spiciness by using a mild or hot salsa, as desired. For less spicy soup, substitute Monterey Jack cheese for Pepper Jack cheese.

Yield: 6 servings

Ingredients

- 1 ¼ pounds boneless skinless chicken breasts
- 4 tablespoons butter
- 1 small onion, chopped
- 1 large clove garlic, minced
- 1 (16-ounce) jar chunky Salsa, medium heat*
- 1 (15-ounce) can creamed corn
- 2 cups chicken stock
- 1 pound Pepper Jack cheese
- 2 cups half and half or milk

Notes

Schnitzel with Mayo

Mariam Jacob

Ingredients

For the chicken:
• Two chicken breasts
• Salt as required
• 1 Tbsp dried mixed herbs
• 1 tsp dried parsley
• 1 cup shredded Parmesan cheese
• 1 ½ cups plain Panko bread-crumbs
• 2 eggs
• 2 cups all-purpose flour
• Oil for frying

For the mayo:
• ½ cup classic mayonnaise
• ¼ cup ketchup

1. Take the chicken breasts and halve them horizontally so that you get four thin pieces from two.

2. Lay them over a table and cover them with a baking sheet. Using your rolling pin, beat the slices, especially where they are thicker to get even slices of the chicken breasts.

3. Dry brine them with salt and let them rest for about 20 min(do not miss this part).

4. Mix the breadcrumbs, herbs, parsley, and cheese.

5. After a minimum of 20 minutes, pat dry the chicken breasts.

6. Arrange in three flat dishes the flour, eggs (slightly beaten) and the breadcrumb mix.

7. Take one of the slices of the chicken breasts, first, coat them in flour, then dip them in the egg and last coat them completely with the bread crumb mix.

8. Heat oil in a pan, at least ½" in height so that the chicken piece is completely immersed. Once the oil is hot, put in the chicken pieces one by one and cook both sides until they are golden brown.

9. For the mayo, mix the classic mayonnaise and the ketchup in a small bowl and we are ready to go.

10. Serve hot.

Shrimp and Grits

Harry Keifer

1. Bring water, grits, and salt to a boil in a heavy saucepan with a lid. Stir in half-and-half and simmer until grits are thickened and tender, 15 to 20 minutes. Set aside and keep warm.

2. Sprinkle shrimp with some salt and cayenne pepper and set aside in a bowl.

3. Place the sausage slices in a large skillet over medium heat and fry until browned, about 5-8 minutes.

4. Remove skillet from heat. Cook bacon or Tasso in a large skillet over medium-high heat, turning occasionally, until evenly brown, about 10 minutes. Keep the drippings in the pan and transfer the slices to paper towels.

5. Cook and stir the peppers, onion, and garlic in the bacon drippings until the onion is translucent and remove to a plate. In the same skillet, deglaze with white wine and cook shrimp 2-3 minutes until they become pink. Remove to another plate.

6. Melt the butter in the same skillet over medium heat, adding the flour slowly to make a roux. Turn heat to low and cook until light brown. Watch carefully as it can easily burn.

7. Pour in the chicken broth, Hot Sauce, Worcestershire sauce, cooking and stirring until mixture thickens. If you feel it's too thick, you can add a little milk or cream.

8. Just before serving, mix the Cheddar cheese into the grits and stir gently until the cheese is melted and the grits are nice and creamy.

9. Plate the grits on the bottom, then the sausage and veggies over that with the gravy and shrimp topping it all. Garnish with the green onions.

Ingredients

• 1 cup coarsely ground grits (NOT instant)
• 3 cups water
• 2 cups Half and Half
• 2 tsp salt
• 2 pounds uncooked shrimp, peeled and deveined
• 1 pinch cayenne pepper
• 1 pound andouille sausage, cut into ¼" slices (if you don't like andouille, you can use kielbasa or other similar sausage)
• 5 slices bacon, or ¼ pound Cajun Tasso ham, cut into ¼" slices
• 1 red bell pepper, chopped
• 1 yellow, or orange, or green bell pepper, chopped.
• 1 cup chopped onion
• 1 tsp minced garlic
• 3 Tbsp white wine (to deglaze pan)
• ¼ cup butter
• ¼ cup flour
• 1 cup chicken broth
• 1 Tbsp Worcestershire sauce
• 2 Tbsp Louisiana Hot sauce (you can omit if you don't want this spicy)
• 1 cup shredded sharp Cheddar cheese
• Green onions for garnish

Uncle Carl's Dip

Donna Yates

Ingredients

- 1 lb. -hamburger
- 1 sleeve of Jimmy Dean Sausage (hot or mild)
- 1 98 oz. block of Velveeta cheese
- 1 can of Rotel tomatoes

1. Cook hamburger meat and sausage together until done and then drain the grease.

2. Cut the Velveeta into small cubes and add to the hamburger and sausage slowly letting the cheese melt into the meat.

3. When you are done combining the cheese and meat into the pan then you will add the can of Rotel tomatoes. Stir together until everything is mixed and serve.

This dip is great with Tostitos chips.

Notes

Venison Meatballs with Cranberry Port Wine Sauce

Christi Heston

1. Mix all meatball ingredients together and roll into 1 ½" balls. Sauté the meatballs in a large skillet in a small amount of olive oil and brown on all sides.

2. Combine all sauce ingredients together into a medium saucepan and cook over medium heat until sugar melts and cranberry sauce has been reduced, about 10 minutes.

3. Combine meatball and sauce into a bowl and mix. Best served warmed in a chafing dish or slow cooker set to low. This makes a great appetizer during holiday seasons.

Anecdote by Suzanne Keifer:
I had never been a fan of venison as I had not had it prepared well. This dish was being served at a Christmas party I attended and I really chowed down on the meatballs. Only after I had eaten quite a few, I was asked how I like them and I readily responded, "Best meatballs I've ever had!". Only after that I was told they were venison; I've been a convert ever since.

Ingredients

For the Meatballs:
- 2 lbs ground venison (if you're unable to find venison, you can substitute with bison)
- ⅓ cup chopped fresh parsley
- ½ cup finely chopped onion
- 2 tbsp soy sauce
- ½ tsp garlic powder
- 1 cup dried Italian breadcrumbs
- 2 eggs
- ¼ tsp pepper
- ¼ tsp seasoned salt

For the Sauce:
- ½ cup catsup
- 1 (16oz) can whole cranberry sauce
- 1 (12oz) bottle chili sauce
- 2 Tbsp brown sugar
- 1 Tbsp lemon juice
- ¼ tsp pepper
- ½ cup ruby port
- ½ tsp crushed red pepper, optional if you don't like spicy sauce
- ⅛ tsp cayenne, optional if you don't like spicy sauce

Venison Pie

Harry Keifer

Ingredients

- 2 Tbsp olive oil
- 2 leeks, washed, trimmed, and chopped
- 2 ½ pounds ground venison (you can use beef, lamb, or pork if no venison available)
- 2 Tbsp fresh chopped parsley
- 1 ¼ cup beef consommé (or stock if consommé not available)
- Salt and fresh ground pepper, to taste
- 3 ½ pounds mixed root vegetables, such as sweet potato, rutabaga, parsnips, peeled and coarsely chopped
- 1 to 1 ½ Tbsp horseradish sauce
- 2 - 3 Tbsp butter

1. Heat the oil in a large skillet over medium heat. Add leeks and cook for about 8-10 minutes. Add the ground meat and cook for about 10 minutes, or until the meat is browned. Stir frequently.

2. Add the chopped parsley, stir in thoroughly. Add the consommé, salt, and pepper.

3. Bring the mixture to a boil, then reduce heat and allow to simmer for about 20 minutes, stirring occasionally.

4. Turn oven on to 400°F.

5. In a stock pot, cook the chopped root vegetables in boiling salted water. Put lid on and cook for about 15 minutes. Test firmness with a fork; they should not feel "mushy".

6. Drain the vegetable, put in a bowl, and mash with a potato masher, adding the horseradish sauce and butter to the mixture.

7. Place the meat mixture in a large baking dish and top with the root vegetable mixture.

8. Bake in the preheated oven for 20 minutes, or until topping begins to brown.

9. Serve immediately.

Wild Rice and Vegetable Soup

Sharon Keifer

Ingredients

- 6 cups either vegetable or chicken stock
- 1 cup uncooked wild rice
- 8 oz. sliced baby bella mushrooms
- 2 medium carrots, diced
- 2 ribs celery, diced
- 4 cloves garlic, minced
- 1 lb. sweet potato, peeled and diced
- 1 bay leaf
- 2 large handfuls kale, chopped
- 1 ½ Tbsp Old Bay© seasoning

For the roux:
- 3 Tbsp butter
- ¼ cup flour
- 1 ½ cup milk

1. This is a Crock Pot recipe but a Dutch oven could be used, as well. You can also add cooked chicken for added protein, if desired.

2. Combine stock, rice, mushrooms, garlic, carrots, celery, sweet potato, onion, bay leaf, and seasoning in the Crock Pot. Stir briefly to mix. Cook on HIGH 4 hours, or LOW 8 hours.

3. During the last 10 minutes of cook time, prepare the roux. Cook butter on medium, whisk in flour and whisk for 1 minute.

4. Add the milk slowly and whisk until thickened.

5. Add the roux and kale to the soup and stir gently. Season to taste with salt and pepper.

Going clockwise:
• Master Gardeners harvesting Potatoes (June 2021)
• Gary W. with Sweet Potatoes (September 2020)
• Rita M. with Potatoes (June 2021)
• Squash (2020)
• Turnips (2020)
• Bell Peppers (2020)
©Dave Giordano

"Farmer's Market"
©2021 **Susie Burch**

Year–Round

Athens Area Master Gardeners Help Feed the Hungry

Gary Wade, Ph.D. - Coordinator of the Oconee Garden

Gary Wade is a retired UGA Professor, Extension Program Coordinator for the Department of Horticulture, and AAMGA member. He was the first statewide coordinator of the Georgia Master Gardener program. He edited the first training manual, developed training resources and helped initiate new Master Gardener training programs in over 50 counties across Georgia. In 1987 he helped form the Georgia Master Gardener Association, one of the first statewide organizations in the U.S.

For twelve years, the Athens Area Master Gardener Extension Volunteers have planted and managed a half-acre vegetable garden at Thomas Orchards on Hwy. 441, just south of Watkinsville. The garden has twenty-five rows of irrigated crops from March to October, including tomatoes, cucumbers, summer squash, okra, southern peas, green beans, pole beans, Irish potatoes, sweet potatoes and herbs. A production schedule is followed so that when one crop stops producing, another crop takes its place. Thus, no rows are left fallow for long. For example, in the fall season, lettuce, turnips and collards are planted to replace some of the summer crops. (See pictures on page 196)

The produce is delivered weekly to the program in Bishop, GA, Supporting our Seniors (SOS), which provides assistance to low-income seniors in Oconee County. The recipients of the produce from the Oconee garden must meet certain criteria: some can no longer garden due to physical disabilities; or, may not have space to garden; but all have low incomes, and many are food insecure.

The SOS program provides clients other services, such as monthly grocery bags filled with staples like soap, laundry detergent and canned goods. Monthly educational programs are conducted by local county Extension professionals and social service agencies on such topics as preparing nutritional meals, canning and freezing vegetables, budgeting, financing and preparing tax forms.

In 2019, the Oconee garden provided 3,500 lbs. of produce to the SOS program. The 2020 program is well on its way to matching that volume. Approximately twenty Master Gardener Volunteers plant, manage the garden and harvest the crops. It is a team effort. Although the 2020 pandemic changed the way we all live our lives, Master Gardeners have adapted by working individually on weekly tasks required to keep the garden thriving.

Providing healthy, nutritious choices for others in the community fits well with the mission of the Athens Area Master Gardeners, a unit of the University of Georgia's Outreach/Service program.

Warm Season Vegetable Cheat Sheet

Robert Westerfield

Robert Westerfield is a University of Georgia horticulturist at the Griffin Campus. He has been with the University for over 30 years, and specializes in fruit and vegetable production. His responsibilities include developing agent consumer resources, conducting agent trainings, and teaching master gardener classes.

February in Georgia marks a time when days begin to get longer and temperatures creep up ever so slowly. Experienced vegetable gardeners, as well as first timers, begin to get eager to jump out into their planting beds and get started. However, we must be patient in February to wait for the magical soil temperature of 65 degrees or higher to be reached. February can also be a wet month, so gardeners must take care not to work their soil while it is still soupy. Regardless of whether you can actually get into the garden, or are just at the point of ordering seeds and developing a plan, there is a myriad of vegetable possibilities for your warm-season planting. This fast cheat sheet below should help you to get started for your best warm-season garden ever.

TOMATOES

Tomatoes are probably at the top of the list when it comes to summer vegetables. Perhaps the biggest question on tomatoes is which one should the home gardener plant. Cherry tomatoes are always a great selection, as they are the most productive and easiest to grow. Being prolific producers, only one or two plants per family will support your evening salad craving. If you have an interest in canning tomatoes, or making sauce, choose a determinate variety that produces the majority of its harvest at one time. The paste varieties, as well as the other determinate tomatoes, have a stockier, bush-growing habit and can sometimes be grown without cages. For a continuous supply of medium to large tomatoes, throw a few indeterminate varieties into your garden mix as well. Indeterminate types grow in a more vining manner and will definitely need some type of cage or other structure to grow on. Regardless of what type of tomato you grow, always plant them as transplants in the garden, and give them a good head start by planting them deep. Nip off all of the foliage below the halfway mark of your tomato plants, and plant this entire section underground. Tomato stems are full of dormant roots that will create a strong root system.

PEPPERS

Just like its cousin the tomato, there is an endless selection of peppers that can be chosen. You can find virtually any size, shape, and color that appeals to you while looking through the catalogs. In general, peppers are divided into three groups based on their relative hotness. The traditional sweet bell peppers are a favorite among gardeners and are relatively easy to grow. There are also sweet, non-bell varieties such as the horn and banana shape peppers that produce an abundant crop. Some of these non-bell varieties can be described as having a flavor that is between mild to spicy. Hot peppers include everything from the cayenne types to the jalapenos. There is even a category of ornamental, edible peppers that make a great addition to the home landscape. Just like tomatoes, peppers should be planted as transplants in the garden as soon as soil temperatures are warm enough.

SUMMER SQUASH

Summer squash is a traditional favorite, and includes both the yellow types as well as green zucchini. Summer squash can be seeded directly into the garden and is best planted in hills with three-foot spacing on all sides of the plants. As long as pollinators are flying around the garden, these plants develop quickly and start producing early. While easy to grow, summer squash in Georgia is frequently plagued by insects. Squash bug and squash vine borer are the two primary pests that can make growing squash challenging. Plant fresh squash seeds every two weeks to help combat these pests, and maintain a fresh harvest throughout the season.

WINTER SQUASH

You would think with the name winter squash, this vegetable would be grown during cool temperatures. However, this is definitely a warm-season plant that gets its name from the harvested vegetable's ability to stay fresh into the winter months. There are numerous shapes and sizes of winter squash available, but they all require ample room to spread out. Unlike summer squash, winter squash are left on the vine until they become fully, mature and hard to the touch.

CUCUMBERS

Cucumbers are an annual favorite that need plenty of space for good growth. Grow cucumbers vertically, when possible, to increase space and air circulation. While cucumbers are normally divided into two types, fresh slicing, or pickling, they could be used for both intentions. Cucumbers require a substantial amount of water as they begin to develop fruit, and can turn bitter if they go dry during the late stages of development.

OKRA

Okra should be planted when soil temperatures reach at least 70 degrees, as this plant thrives in hot, humid conditions. Once the okra plant begins producing, it needs to be harvested about every other day to prevent the pods from getting too long. Pods over five inches will become woody and nonedible. Keep an eye on your okra in the later season for damaging pests such as stinkbugs and leaf-footed bugs.

EGGPLANT

Eggplant is in the same family as peppers and tomatoes and should always be planted as a transplant. Perhaps the biggest pests on eggplants are flea beetles. They are a common problem on eggplant and will put small holes all over the leaves if left unchecked. Harvest eggplants with a sharp knife or clippers when the fruits are firm and shiny in appearance.

GREEN BEANS

Green beans are another warm season vegetable that will do well until we hit the hottest part of the summer. Seeds can be purchased as either bush beans, pole beans, or half-runners. Pole beans will need some type of a trellis, or support to grow on and climb. Bush beans stay more compact, while half-runners spread out along the ground. Regardless of type, harvest all beans continuously at the immature stage. Allowing beans to grow to their full, mature potential will signal the plant to stop producing and will also make the beans too stringy to eat.

SWEET CORN

Perhaps nothing says summer like fresh corn on the cob that was cooked and harvested only hours earlier. Corn varieties are categorized into genetic types. At the lower end are sugary varieties like the ubiquitous "Silver Queen." From there, we move into the sugar-enhanced varieties that retain a little bit more of their sweetness when stored. Moving up the ladder, you may also want to try the super sweet varieties, or the multi-gene varieties that have superior sweetness and storability. Within these genetic types, there are numerous selections whether you prefer white, yellow, or bicolor varieties. Corn should always be planted in several rows, as it is primarily wind-pollinated. Corn requires a substantial amount of water and fertilizer to produce a good ear. It is a heavy nitrogen feeder.

ASPARAGUS

Asparagus is the only perennial vegetable that we grow in the Georgia garden. Established asparagus beds can last for decades. Asparagus will not tolerate poor drainage and should be planted in either raised beds or heavily amended soils. Establish asparagus by purchasing healthy crowns and planting after danger of frost in the spring. Asparagus needs to be planted deep, six to eight inches in the soil, for best success. The first year is considered an establishment period, and none of the asparagus spears should be harvested. Prune the fern-like foliage that develops late in the season after it has gone dormant. Harvest can begin the following season for a couple of weeks and can be extended each year as the plants become more established.

Growing Medicinal Herbs

David Berle

David has held many professional horticulture positions, and has been planting, and watching plants grow, for over 40 years. He is currently professor of horticulture at UGA, and director or UGArden, a student-run community farm. He is interested in gardening practices that do not waste resources or cost too much, and which, hopefully, leave the world a better place for everyone, especially those who are not able to garden themselves, or may not be able to afford to do so.

There is a lot of interest these days in medicinal herbs. At UGArden, over twenty different medicinal and culinary herbs have been grown, as well as elderberry, rose and reishi mushrooms have been processed that are put into our herbal teas. The term "medicinal herb" typically refers to a plant grown for its medicinal or healing properties. The term "herb" means a plant is either an annual or perennial that dies down to the ground with cold weather, though many medical plants are shrubs, like elderberry and rose. In Georgia, many herbaceous perennials do not die to the ground, and some continue to grow throughout a mild winter.

The use of medicinal herbs dates back to early humans, and is often associated with culture, religion and early medicine. In modern times, the use of medicinal herbs is often seen as a gentle way to help the body respond to infection or stress. There is a current trend, even in conventional medicine, to make use of plant products to help with certain medical conditions. This article specifically avoids the recommendation of any specific herb or plant product for medical use, as it is always best to consult with people more knowledgeable than this author.

Most medicinal plants are grown for their phytochemicals. These can be broken down into different categories, each providing different responses in the human body. While herbalists are of the opinion that it is typically a combination of plant compounds that provides the benefit, those in the pharmacy trade maintain that just one isolated chemical is sufficient. This is what often separates the medicinal herb industry from the pharmacy trade.

The concentration and quality of plant phytochemicals is highly dependent on cultural practices. Stress to the plant appears to increase phytochemicals in many instances. It is thought that these phytochemicals are manufactured in the plant as a defense mechanism.

There are some basic cultural practices that a horticulturist can recommend for growing medicinal plants. First of all, most medicinal herb plants are not native to the US. While there are many native plants with medicinal properties, of the medicinal herbs we grow at UGArden, only anise hyssop, stinging nettle, blue vervain, elderberry, and purple coneflower are native. The rest come from the Mediterranean region (rosemary, thyme, lavender, sage, and oregano) or eastern India and/or China (hibiscus, lemongrass, holy basil) or Europe (calendula, chamomile, dandelion, motherwort, plantain). Lemon verbena is from South America. Knowing the country of origin provides valuable information about the use of medicinal plants, and also informs us of preferred soil and climate conditions.

While it may be counterintuitive, less water is usually better for medicinal plants than too much water. This does not mean you should ignore mulching or watering medicinal plants, but it does mean that you should probably water medicinal herbs a little less than most vegetables. Some herbs prefer drier soils due to their origin. For example, Mediterranean plants prefer drier soils due to their natural habitat. So it's also important to consider where a plant comes from when managing water.

Fertilization is another practice that master gardeners learn is important to healthy plant growth. From our experience at UGArden and research, most medicinal plants produce higher levers of essential oils and other phytochemicals with little to no nitrogen fertilization at all. Our research has shown that the rate of nitrogen should be about half of the rate of nitrogen applied to moderate-feeding vegetables. This works out to about 1-1.5 pounds of nitrogen per 1,000 square feet. There are some exceptions, such as lemongrass, that require a higher rate of nitrogen, much like corn. In general, if you can't find a knowledgeable reference guide, it's better to apply no nitrogen to a medicinal plant than too much. Most medical plants seem to have little response to the other two important nutrients, phosphorus and potassium.

At UGArden, we follow all organic practices. In preparing a plot for medicinal herbs, we start with a soil test, and look for a pH between 5.5 and 6.5, which seems to work for most medicinal herbs. We strive to get the phosphorus and potassium levels up to a moderate level in the beginning. Nitrogen is applied using feather meal mixed into the soil before planting at a low rate. For crops like holy basil and anise hyssop that are harvested multiple times, we apply a small amount (half the original rate) after we harvest the leaves two times. This seems to be a good balance between growing a healthy plant that produces a lot of material and a good phytochemical content. The lemon grass gets a high rate at planting (4.5 pounds of nitrogen per 1,000 square feet) and sometimes a side dressing if we harvest more than twice and there has been a lot of rain).

We have also learned there are better times for planting and harvesting medicinal herbs. Chamomile and calendula, for example, are best planted in early fall and can be harvested in late fall (in a mild season) and again in the spring. They both suffer under the heat of the summer. Stinging nettle can be planted almost anytime, but the best crop, with highest phytochemicals, comes in early spring and fall. The tender annuals, those from India or China, are planted in the spring, after danger of frost is past.

One common misconception is about light requirements. Of all the medicinal plants we grow at UGArden, only stinging nettle prefers shade (less than six hours of direct sun). We still grow it in full sun, but it does better with some shade. Essentially, all common culinary herbs prefer full sun as well. You can grow all of these herbs in a shady location, but they will not do nearly as well in the shade. There are, however, many medicinal plants, both native and non-native, that grow very well in the shade. These include plants like goldenseal, ginseng, black cohosh, boneset, and Solomon's seal.

It is funny to think that across the road from UGArden is a turf-research facility that is focusing on weeds in turf. At UGArden, we grow two weeds of turf: dandelion and plantain. It's even more curious that we often have to weed out the bermuda grass growing in our dandelion row. Plants are only a weed to some people, but to others, a course of healing.

A very important lesson we have learned from years of growing medicinal plants is that there are a lot of misconceptions about growing these plants. For example, stinging nettle (*Urtica dioicais*) is not the same plant many call horse nettle. Another example is that many seed companies do not properly label their holy basil (*Ocimum tenuiflorum*). As it turns out, there are at least four different types of holy basil and many different cultivars, and even two different species floating around the industry. As it turns out, there are several species of plants that go by the name lemon grass. All produce similar compounds, so it's probably not an issue, but the point here is that you need to be sure you are getting what you thought you were purchasing and learn to identify medicinal herbs by their scientific names when researching or ordering seed. You learn about scientific names as master gardeners for a reason, and the field of medicinal plants requires this knowledge be put to use.

Dancing to the Music

Viviane Van Giesen

Viviane Van Giesen is from Porto Alegre, Brazil. After receiving her BA in Fine Arts at UFRGS in 1986, she moved to Georgia in 1989 where she married Edward Van Giesen. Together they raised their children, Cedric, Ian and Isabella and were partners at a design and construction company for over 15 years. Viviane is passionate about watercolor and is president of the Georgia Watercolor Society. She believes strongly in giving back to the art community and collaborating to make local art groups stronger and long-lasting.

"Tell me who you walk with and I'll tell you who you are" is a well-known saying that could very well be changed to "Tell me what you eat and I'll tell who you are." Food is powerful; it stirs up all kinds of emotions and responses. It triggers not only feelings of pleasure, health, community, and a sense of place and love, but it also activates sentiments of manipulation, stress and addiction. Human history is plagued by a troubled relationship involving food and power. While some have always been starving and fighting for left-overs, others - very few of them - overindulge and gorge on abundance.

Food production in the mid-20th Century presents us with the irony of two opposite trends as we witness both a rise in the manufacturing of processed food as well as the growth of the organic farming movement. On one hand, the planting of commercial crops became disconnected from natural processes, and on the other, there was increasing awareness of the damage being done by pesticides and synthetic fertilizers to the environment and to our bodies. Convenient instant powders that are transformed into food in minutes became the main staple in American kitchens. The lavish production of starchy snacks was seen as a blessing. Processed food has taken over the whole world. We see rampant obesity coupled with all of its collateral damage - heart disease, diabetes, kidney failure, depression, and anxiety. How could we have done this to ourselves?

Here we are now in 2020, living through a pandemic and another irony of history. While the novel coronavirus wreaks havoc on our bodies, here in Georgia we are living through one of the most wonderful springs. During the last three months as I walked outside in the heavenly spring weather, I thought how dissonant it was with the current dreadful events. If this were a Hollywood movie, the set designer would have been fired! Yet, even in these conflicting times, there is a lesson to be learned.

We all have more time on our hands. We pay more attention to our meals. At the grocery store, the produce section is buzzing with people, kindling my memories of shopping with my kids and teaching them.

"When you buy food, choose the ones with the least number of letters on the ingredients list. APPLE, one word - okay, this is a good one!"

People are baking, chopping, grilling, and sharing recipes like never before. Is there anything more peaceful and satisfying than preparing a nice meal and choosing the textures, seasonings, and colors that go into a dish made for the people you love?

The garden centers are crowded with people buying vegetable seedlings. Avid customers are also allured by the beauty, the perfume, and the colors of the flowers, acting as willing participants in nature's conspiracy to attract pollinators. Oh! The joy of a vegetable garden in all its glory! In our home, all our scraps from over 21 years have slowly built a beautiful compost pile; a little hill about 18 feet long and four feet high. What used to be soil so poor and hard that felt like broken ceramic, is now rich, dark, and nutrient rich soil. Do not lose hope. You can save your soil too. All your food can feed your compost, which in turn will feed your garden, and ultimately will come back to feed you again. All you need is food scraps, time, and patience.

Spring continues in its splendor as trees, shrubs, flowers, and grasses sprout, and green things abound all around me like a loving mother's embrace. This exuberance is a testimony of hope, a promise that everything will be fine. We are like misbehaved kids with mother nature showing us unconditional love. Maybe, just maybe, we may squeeze this lemon and make some lemonade. May this spring and the unexpected quarantine have the power to change some minds and hearts, may more people learn the satisfaction of growing their own food, may they continue to bake and eat at home with their families, and may the feeling of eating natural food be so potent and energetic that they will leave behind their diet of processed food.

As I look around the green, humid, and luxurious landscape, I feel grateful for living here in this part of the universe, with a green patch of earth under my feet and a peaceful sky above my head. Like the poet said, "Why shouldn't I dance, if I can hear the music?"

30 Minute Mozzarella

Isaac Swier

Ingredients

• 1 gallon whole milk (not ultra-pasteurized)*
• 1 ½ tsp citric acid
• ¼ tsp liquid rennet – or a rennet tablet, crushed (if using a tablet, refer to manufacturers recommendation on amount used)
• 1 Tbsp kosher salt – or 'cheese salt'
• lukewarm water

*If possible, find raw or farm fresh milk.

Equipment:
• Accurate thermometer, preferable digital quick-read
• Knife to cut curds
• Spoon or ladle to stir curds
• Large colander or strainer
• Large bowl
• Food safe gloves

Because cheese is so susceptible to both bacterial and mold growth, it is important to prepare your work area in a way that lowers the chances of contamination while working. I recommend removing dirty dish towels, sponges, etc. away from your work area and sanitizing with an antibacterial cleaner before beginning.

1. If using a rennet tablet, prepare it according to instructions or mix ¼ tsp of rennet liquid into ¼ cup tepid water and set aside.

2. Mix 1 ½ tsp citric acid with one cup of lukewarm water, stir until dissolved, and set aside.

3. Pour 1 gallon of whole milk into a stock pot and add the citric acid and water mixture, stirring regularly over medium-low heat until the milk reaches 90 degrees F. Remove the pot of milk from the heat.

4. Add in the rennet mixture and stir gently for 30 seconds. Cover the milk and allow it to process for 5 minutes. After five minutes, curd should have formed at the top of the pot. If it is still liquid without curd, cover and allow it to stand for an additional 5 minutes.

5. Once curd is set, slice the curd through to the bottom of the pot in a cross-hatch pattern (approximately 1 inch squares).

6. Place the pot back on the stove, set to low, and bring the curds and whey to 105 degrees F.

7. Gently stir occasionally – trying not to break up the curds.

8. Once 105 degrees is reached, remove the pot from the heat and let stand for 5-10 minutes

9. Place colander or strainer over a large bowl and carefully scoop the curds into the strainer, gently pressing the curds to squeeze out excess whey. Allow to drain for up to 10 minutes. The curds should form one large mass.

10. While it's draining, add 1 tbsp of salt to the whey, pour some off into a bowl to cool, and return the rest to the stove until it reaches 180 degrees F.

11. Separate cheese into 2 similar sized masses. In a bowl, pour hot salted whey, and add one of the curd masses. When the mass reaches an internal temperature of 135 degrees F, put on your gloves and gently start pulling the cheese. Let gravity do the work for you, aim for smooth, silky, and elastic stretched cheese. If it starts to become too stiff, return it to the hot whey to bring it back up to temperature.

12. Once the curd is well stretched and is no longer 'chunky', wrap the cheese curd on itself to form a ball.

13. You can tuck the edges under, and with some pressure should be able to get it to stick. To set the cheese, place it back in the bowl of whey you set aside earlier. If you're in a hurry, you can set it in ice water, but the whey is best for flavor. If you're not using it immediately, you should store it in the left-over whey as well.

Apricot and Currant Chicken *Marilyn Fuller*

Ingredients

- 2 whole chickens, quartered, or 2 ¼ to 3 pounds thighs and breasts
- Salt and freshly ground black pepper, to taste
- 1 tsp ground ginger
- 1 ½ cup bitter orange marmalade (like Dundee)
- ⅓ cup apple juice
- ⅓ cup fresh orange juice
- 8 oz dried apricots
- 8 oz dried currants
- ¼ brown sugar

1. Preheat the oven to 375°F. Place the chicken pieces, skin side up, in a shallow roasting pan and sprinkle generously with salt and pepper and the ginger. Spread the marmalade over the chicken and pour the two juices into the pan. Bake for 20-25 minutes.

2. Remove from the oven and add the apricots and currants to the pan, making sure they're evenly mixed.

3. Sprinkle the fruit with the brown sugar and return to the oven. Bake, basting fairly frequently, until the chicken is golden brown and shiny on top, about 40 – 45 minutes.

4. Remove the chicken, apricots, and currants to a warmed serving platter. Pour some of the pan juices over the top; the rest can be poured into a sauceboat, if desired.

5. Serve immediately. (6-8 servings)

Best-Ever Baked Beans *Pam Tidwell*

Ingredients

- 1 pound ground beef
- ½ tsp salt
- ¼ tsp pepper
- 2 Tbsp vinegar
- 2 Tbsp sugar
- 1 (16-oz) can pork and beans
- ½ cup onion, chopped
- ½ cup ketchup
- ¼ tsp Tabasco sauce (optional)

1. Cook beef and onions slowly (in a small amount of fat, if necessary) until beef is no longer pink. Drain.

2. Mix remaining ingredients with meat mixture.

3. Heat oven to 350°F. Bake in a 2-quart casserole dish for approximately 30 minutes. As another option, cooked bacon slices can be added on the top.

Bride's Punch *(Serves 50)*

Jean Colquett

Ingredients

- 2 12 oz cans frozen lemonade
- 4 4.6 oz cans frozen orange juice
- 1 4.6oz can pineapple juice
- 6 cups sugar
- 10 cups water
- 1 6.4 oz bottle ginger ale

1. Bring water and sugar to a boil until sugar dissolves completely. Cool. Add lemonade and orange juice plus water to dilute as directed on cans; add pineapple juice.

2. Add 1 64-oz bottle ginger ale into a punch bowl. Add the above ingredients and gently stir to mix.

Carolina Cole Slaw

Robert Clements

Ingredients

- 1 large cabbage (finely chopped)
- 1 bell pepper (diced)
- 1 onion (diced)
- 1 tsp salt
- 1 tsp dry mustard
- 1 tsp celery seed
- 1 cup cider vinegar
- ½ cup vegetable oil

1. Mix all above ingredients together in a large bowl.

Bob Clements loves this vinegary coleslaw. He says that it is fine to let it set in the refrigerator for hours or days so the flavors blend.

Chocolate Chip Pie

Pam Tidwell

Ingredients

- ¼ cup plus 2 tbsp butter or margarine, softened
- 1 cup sugar
- 1 tsp vanilla
- 2 eggs
- ½ cup all-purpose flour
- 1 (6 oz) package semi-sweet chocolate chips
- ¾ cup chopped pecans
- ½ cup flaked coconut
- 1 unbaked 9" pie/pastry shell

1. Preheat the oven to 350°F.

2. Combine butter, sugar, and vanilla in a medium mixing bowl; beat well. Add the eggs and beat well. Stir in flour.

3. Gradually stir in chocolate morsels, pecans, and coconut. Pour mixture into pie shell.

4. Bake for 35 – 40 minutes.

Crème Brûlée

Suzanne Keifer

1. Preheat oven to 356°F. (I translated this recipe from French and converted metric to Imperial, hence the strange temperature setting. If your oven can't do this, set it at 350°). Place 4 ramekins in an 8" or 9" cake pan.

2. Pour cream and milk into a medium-size saucepan. Cut the vanilla pod in ½ lengthwise and scrape out the beans and put them in the milk/cream mixture. Set this aside.

3. Put egg yolks and sugar in a mixing bowl and whisk until mixture becomes pale and fluffy (about 6-7 minutes).

4. Place the milk/cream mixture on a burrner and bring to ALMOST a boil. As soon as you see bubbles on the edge, remove from heat. Pour the hot cream mixture into the eggs, stirring with a whisk all the time, making sure you're incorporating the vanilla beans. Pour this mixture through a fine sieve into another mixing bowl, discarding any foam. Stir the final mixture one more time.

5. Pour enough hot water into the cake tin so that it reaches about ½ way up the ramekins. Pour the hot cream into the ramekins, covering them with a baking sheet. The baking sheet should cover the ramekins but allow a small gap for air circulation.

6. Bake 30-35 minutes, until softly set. They should still wobble when the cake pan is moved. Lift the ramekins out of the pan and set on a wire rack to cool. Once cooled, place in the refrigerator to cool completely.

7. Now the fun part! Sprinkle 1 ½ tsp of sugar over each ramekin, making sure it's level. Spray a little water over the sugar. Hold a torch just above the sugar and keep it moving until it's beautifully brown and caramelized. If you don't have a torch, you can use a long lighter; it'll just take longer.

Ingredients

- 14 oz heavy cream
- 3 ½ oz whole milk
- 1 vanilla pod
- 5 large egg yolks
- 4 Tbsp superfine sugar – about ½ cup
- 6 tsp superfine sugar for topping

See picture on Back Cover.

Jalapeño Cornbread 1

Allan Cobb

Ingredients

- 1 ½ cups cornmeal
- 1 heaping tablespoon flour
- 1 tsp salt
- ½ tsp baking soda
- 1 teaspoon baking powder
- 1 cup buttermilk
- 2 large eggs -- well beaten
- 16 oz corn -- removed from cob and smashed
- ½ cup finely chopped bell pepper
- 1 finely chopped jalapeno pepper
- 4 spring onions -- chopped
- 1 ½ cups shredded sharp cheddar cheese

Always at the table every Thanksgiving in my family.

1. Preheat the oven to 375 degrees F.

2. Sift together the cornmeal, flour, salt, baking soda and powder. Add the remaining ingredients, but reserve ½ cup of cheese.

3. Pour mixture into a 9 x 13 baking pan, lightly greased. Sprinkle the rest of the cheese on top and bake for 45 minutes.

Jalapeño Cornbread 2

Pam Tidwell

Ingredients

- 1 ½ cup cornmeal mix
- 1 cup buttermilk
- ½ tsp baking soda
- 2 eggs
- 1 medium onion, diced
- ⅓ cup oil
- 1 small can creamed corn
- 1 cup grated cheese
- 2 – 4 jalapeños, seeded and sliced

1. Mix all ingredients in a medium mixing bowl.

2. Pour the mixture into a hot, greased cast iron pan.

3. Bake at 425°F for 25 minutes until toothpick inserted comes out clean.

Lime Layer Cake

Rosemary Stancil

Preheat oven to 350F degrees. Line 2 (9-inch) cake pans or 1 (9X13 inch pan) with parchment or brown paper.

Cake: In a mixer bowl, place cake mix, lime gelatin, orange juice, eggs, flavoring, and oil and beat several minutes to mix well. Pour equal amounts into the prepared layer cake pans, or pour all the batter in a 9X13 inch pan. Bake 20-25 minutes or until a toothpick inserted in the center comes out clean.

Drizzle: While the cake is cooking, in a 4-cup glass measuring cup mix together lime zest, 1/3 cup lime juice, powdered sugar, and butter. Microwave on high for about 1 minute or until butter is melted and the mixture is hot. Stir to combine ingredients. When the cake is done, remove it from the oven and make holes over the cake with a skewer. Immediately drizzle each layer of hot cake with the hot lime juice mixture. Allow to cool a few minutes; remove from pans and allow to completely cool on baking racks.

Whipped Cream Frosting: Chill the mixing bowl and wire whip. Add cold heavy whipping cream and beat until it thickens. Add pudding mix, sugar, flavoring, lime juice and cream cheese. Beat until smooth, and stiff peaks form.

When the cake is completely cool, frost it with the Whipped Cream Frosting. Sprinkle blueberries over the top of the cake and add additional berries when serving. Store in the refrigerator.

*The pudding mix helps stabilize the whipped cream so it keeps its structure longer.

Ingredients

Yield: 10-12 servings
Cake:
• 1 (15-16 ounce) box lemon supreme cake mix
• 1 (3-ounce) package lime gelatin
• ¾ cup orange juice
• 5 eggs
• 1 teaspoon vanilla flavoring
• 1 cup vegetable oil

Drizzle:
• 1 tablespoon finely grated lime zest
• ⅓ cup lime juice
• ¼ cup powdered sugar, sifted
• ½ sticks (1/4 cup) unsalted butter

Whipped Cream Frosting:
• 1 pint (2 cups) cold heavy whipping cream
• 1 (3-ounce) package White Chocolate or Vanilla Instant Pudding Mix *
• ⅓ cup powdered sugar
• 1 teaspoon vanilla or almond flavoring
• ¼ cup lime juice
• 4 ounces cream cheese, softened
Fresh blueberries

Lizzy's BOP (Banana, Oatmeal, Pecan) Muffins

Liz Conroy

Ingredients

- ⅓ cup quick rolled oats
- ¼ cup plain yogurt
- 2 eggs
- 2 Tbsp vegetable oil
- 3 Tbsp maple syrup
- 3 medium ripe, mashed bananas (about 1 cup)
- 1 cup whole wheat pastry flour (found at most specialty groceries)
- ½ tsp baking powder
- ½ tsp baking soda
- 2 tsp cinnamon
- ½ cup chopped pecans

1. Have muffin tin for 12 muffins greased or lined with baking cups. Preheat the oven to 375°F.

2. In a small bowl, stir yogurt and oatmeal together and set aside.

3. In a medium bowl, mix eggs, oil, maple syrup, mashed bananas, and add the oatmeal/yogurt mixture.

4. In another medium bowl, sift together the pastry flour, baking powder, baking soda, cinnamon. Add the dry ingredients and the pecans to the banana mixture and stir just until no pastry flour is visible.

5. Spoon batter into muffin cups and bake for 20 minutes until tinged with light brown appearance.

Note: No time for breakfast? Grab this muffin and you've got oatmeal, fruit, pecans, and yogurt in hand!

Magnificent Mixing Seven

Harry Keifer

The quantities below are according to my taste. Feel free to alter them – be creative! This mix is great on chicken, pork, beef and does well for months in a well-sealed container.

1. Mix all ingredients in a container with a tight-fitting lid. Stores well in or out of the refrigerator.

Ingredients

- 1 cup raw sugar
- 2 Tbsp granulated garlic
- 3 Tbsp chili powder
- 3 Tbsp kosher salt
- 2 tsp ground cumin
- 3 tsp ground ginger
- 2 tsp cayenne pepper

Mango Ginger Jam

Allan Cobb

1. Mix ingredients together in a large saucepan.

2. Stir over low heat until sugar dissolves, then increase heat and bring to a rolling boil.

3. Stir often and boil until mixture reaches 220 degrees F.

4. Transfer to hot, sterile jars, leaving ½ - ¼ inch air space at the top. Process in a water bath to make shelf stable or refrigerate.

Ingredients

- 2 pounds mango pulp
- 4 cups white sugar
- 2 oz lemon juice
- 1 Tbsp fresh grated ginger root
- 1 tsp apple cider vinegar

Marinated Cheese

Linda Tedrow

- ½ cup olive oil
- ½ cup white wine vinegar
- 1 (2-oz) bottle diced pimentos, drained
- 3 Tbsp fresh parsley, chopped
- 3 Tbsp scallion, minced
- 3 cloves garlic, minced
- 1 tsp sugar
- ¾ tsp dried basil
- ½ tsp salt
- ½ tsp black pepper
- 1 (8-oz) package sharp cheddar cheese
- 1 (8-oz) package cream cheese, cold

1. In a jar with a tight-fitting lid, combine the olive oil, vinegar, pimentos, parsley, green onion, garlic, sugar, basil, salt, and pepper. Shake vigorously. Set aside.

2. Cut the cheddar cheese in half lengthwise. Cut crosswise into ¼ inch slices to form squares. Repeat with the cream cheese. Arrange cheese squares alternately in a shallow baking dish with the slices standing on edge. You can arrange in a single long row or 2 parallel rows, depending on the size of your dish.

3. Pour the marinade from the jar over the cheese slices, cover, and refrigerate for at least 6 hours or overnight.

4. Serve with crackers. To serve, remove the slices to a serving platter so that they are still arranged in an alternating pattern. You can spoon some of the extra marinade over the top, if desired.

Mexican Fudge

John Aitkens

Ingredients

- 4-cup package of shredded cheese blend (such as Fiesta Blend)
- 7 eggs
- 1 (12-oz) jar jalapeños

1. Pre-heat oven to 400°F

2. Grease a 9'x13" glass baking dish. Spread the package of shredded cheese blend to cover the bottom of the dish. Beat the eggs by hand until well blended and pour over the cheese mixture. Drain the jar of jalapeños and spread evenly over the eggs and cheese.

3. Bake approximately 30 minutes, until the top begins to brown. Cool for approximately 30 minutes. Loosen the edges and bottom with a spatula and slide onto a cutting board.

4. Cut into 2" squares. Enjoy!

Pineapple Crumble

Jean Colquett

Ingredients

- 2 8 oz cans pineapple tidbits (use juice of only 1 can)
- 1 cup sugar
- 5 Tbsp flour
- 1 ½ cup cheese
- ¾ cup Ritz crackers, crumbled
- 1 stick butter or margarine

1. Pour pineapple into a square, 8-inch Pyrex dish. Mix flour and sugar together and pour over pineapple.

2. Sprinkle cheese over that mixture. Spread cracker crumbs over the top; melt butter and pour over all.

3. Bake at 350 degrees for 45 minutes.

4. Serve with turkey or ham.

Pumpkin Skin Chutney

Rita Mathew

Ingredients

- 1 cup skin of pumpkin (finely chopped)
- ½ cup fresh grated coconut
- ¼ cup roasted ground peanuts
- 1 tsp roasted red chilli
- 1 Tbsp oil
- 1 Tbsp water
- 1 tsp salt
- ½ tsp lime juice (to taste)

1. Fry the pumpkin skin in oil on medium-low heat.

2. Let it cool and then grind all the ingredients to a paste.

3. Use as a spread on toast. Serve as dip or as a side dish.

Substitute:
- Skin of Ridge Gourd

Ridge Gourd Chutney

Rita Mathew

Ingredients

- ½ cup skin of ridge gourd (if you can't find this, you can substitute with zucchini or summer squash)
- ½ cup coconut grating
- 2 green chilis
- 1 tsp cumin
- Tamarind, peanut size
- ⅛ tsp mustard seed
- Curry leaves, optional
- Dash asofoetida (If you don't have asafetida powder you can substitute; per ¼ teaspoon needed: ¼ teaspoon onion powder plus ¼ teaspoon garlic powder. ... OR - Substitute ½ teaspoon garlic or onion powder)
- Salt, to taste

1. Sauté the gourd skin in a small amount of oil until lightly browned. Add cumin and continue to sauté for another minute.

2. Grind together the coconut gratings, green chilis, roasted gourd skin, tamarind, salt to a smooth paste.

3. If needed, a small amount of water can be added.

4. Mix oil, mustard seed, and curry leaves. Add the asafoetida to this seasoning before adding to the ground paste.

Salsa Criolla

Allan Cobb

Ingredients

- 1 small red onion -- thinly sliced
- Ice cubes
- 1 limo chili -- seeded, white inside removed, and thinly sliced
- 1 tablespoon chopped cilantro
- Juice of 3 small limes
- Salt

An essential accompaniment to Peruvian dishes tacu tacu, chicharrones and jalea.

1. Soak the sliced onions in ice water for about 5 minutes to crisp. Remove from water, drain, and place in a bowl.

2. Add the sliced chili, cilantro, and lemon juice to the onions. Add salt to taste and mix thoroughly. Best served immediately.

3. Limo chilli is very hot. Substitute with Habanero and a squeeze of Lemon juice.

Simple Chocolate Mousse

Sona Mariam Jacob

Ingredients

- 8 oz dark cooking chocolate finely chopped (semi-sweet recommended; do not use chocolate chips)
- 1 ½ cups fresh cream (heavy cream or heavy whipping cream; do not use milk)

1. Make chocolate ganache* by heating ½ cup of the fresh cream on a very low flame for 2 – 3 minutes just enough to melt the chocolate pieces; pour it into the previously chopped dark chocolate pieces. Let it rest for 1 minute and then mix them gently together.
Your Ganache is ready.

2. Next whip the remaining 1 cup of cream to medium peaks.

3. Once the ganache has cooled down, fold the whipped cream into the ganache with a spatula.

4. Scoop it into shot glasses, or a small pudding dish and chill overnight. Enjoy!

* Ganache, a filling made from chocolate and cream, is versatile! It can be served as a dip, spread, frosting, topping, or a layer in a cake.

Tomato Chutney

Rita Mathew

Ingredients

- 2 medium tomatoes
- ¼ cup coconut gratings
- Pinch asafoetida (If you don't have asafoetida powder you can substitute; per ¼ tsp needed: ¼ tsp onion powder plus ¼ tsp garlic powder. ... OR - Substitute ½ tsp garlic or onion powder)
- 1 tsp red chilli powder
- Salt, to taste

1. Dry roast coconut gratings until light brown.

2. Cut tomatoes into chunks, remove seeds. Puree and roast coconut gratings.

3. In a small pan, heat two taplespoons oil. Add the asafoetida and chilli powder. Stir for a minute. Add the tomotoes and coconut mixture to the pan.

4. Cover and cook for a few minutes. Serve hot or cold with rice, naan, or chapati. May be used as a spread on sandwiches.

See centre of Thalli 2 picture below.

Thalli 2 Clockwise from top – Savory Cake (Dhokla), Okra upkari, Sago kheer, Chapati, Cucumber raita, Dal, Chana upkari, Rice. Tomato chutney in centre.

Glossary

A

ASH GOURD - white pumpkin. Can be purchased in most Asian/International markets.

ASAFOETIDA – Also known as Hing, or Kayam, the spice is used as a condiment and in pickling. It has a pungent aroma reminiscent of leeks or other onion relatives. An oleoresin from the rhizome of perennial herbs belonging to the celery family, Umbelliferae, it can be purchased in most Asian/International markets and on-line. Substitute ½ tsp onion powder and ½ tsp garlic powder.

B

BROWN CHANA - brown or black chickpeas. Can be purchased at some local markets and on-line. Substitute with white chickpeas. See article on page 137 for description on preparation.

BECHAMEL SAUCE – an important base for soufflés. Béchamel, a French sauce made from butter, flour, scalded milk and seasoning such as pepper or nutmeg.

BOTTLE GOURD – calabash squash. Can be purchased at Asian/International markets. Can substitute with zucchini.

BROWN CHANA – brown chickpeas. See Black chana above.

BRULÉE – Process of caramelizing sugar on the surface of (a dessert).

C

CASSEROLE – A casserole (French: diminutive of casse, from Provençal cassa 'pan') is a variety of a large, deep pan or bowl used for cooking a variety of dishes in the oven; it is also a category of foods cooked in such a utensil.

CHAAT MASALA – could substitute with garam masala. Can be purchased on-line and international markets.

CORIANDER LEAVES – Also known as cilantro leaves (and stems). Substitute with equal parts parsley, tarragon, and dill.

CURRY LEAVES – Also referred to as Kari leaves, or Kaddi patta. Although it is a tropical plant, in North America, it may be grown outdoors in zones 8 through 12, bearing in mind it is sensitive to temperatures below 40°F. See article, "Naming Rites" on page 11 for history and use in cooking. Substitute with lime/lemon zest, lime leaves, lemon balm leaves, lemon basil.

D

DAL - It may refer to a dish or to dried, split pulses. See article on page 137 for the various types of Dals, how to sprout and prepare them for cooking.

E

ENO FRUIT SALT - Eno is 60% baking soda and 40% citric acid. Use this proportion to substitute in a recipe if not easily available. It can be purchased on-line.

F

FENUGREEK POWDER - Fenugreek, family Fabaceae, is an annual herb similar to clover. It has a sweet, nutty flavor. The leaves are edible and the seeds are used as a spice. Can be purchased at local health food stores, international markets, and on-line.

G

GRAM FLOUR - Ground dried chickpeas. Substitute with buckwheat or quinoa flour. Can be purchased on-line.

GRIND – Puree in a blender.

I

IVY GOURD - Ivy gourd (Coccinia grandis), Kovakka, Tindora, Tendli, belongs to the Cucurbitaceae family and is also known as a little gourd or p erennial cucumber. A fast grower, the seeds can be purchased on-line.

J

JAGGERY - Jaggery is a traditional raw sugar obtained by evaporating water from sugarcane juice. The color can vary from golden brown to dark brown. Also called NCS or non-centrifugal cane sugar.

JEERA – Cumin seeds.

JULIENNE - Julienne, allu-mette, or French cut, in which the food item is cut into long thin strips, similar to matchsticks. Common items to be julienned are carrots for carrots julienne, celery for céléris remoulade, or potatoes for Julienne Fries.

K

KALA CHANA – Black garbanzo beans or chickpeas. They can be substituted with white chickpeas. Can Be purchased on-line and in some local grocery markets. See page 137 for details on preparation.

KARI LEAVES – or Kaddi patta. See Curry leaves above.

M

MANDOLINE – A vegetable slicer, it is a cooking utensil used to cut firm vegetables or fruits into different shapes: disks, slices, juliennes. It is made of a plate of wood, metal or plastic, with a blade fitted horizontally into it. Available at stores selling kitchen gadgets.

MASALA – The term may refer to a combination of spices, or to the gravy prepared with pureed fresh coconut and spices. Some dishes may use finely chopped onions as the base for the masala. See page 11 for more details.

MUNG BEANS VS. MOONG BEANS - Mung beans are also referred to as moong. See article on page 137 for a description and how to sprout and prepare for cooking. Can be purchased at local and international food markets.

P

PANDAN LEAVES – aromatic tropical plant, with long, narrow, dark leaves, belonging to the Pandanus family (Pandanus amaryllifollius). It is also known as screwpine. Vanilla bean extract has a similar aroma. It may be purchased fresh, frozen, or dried at many International/ Asian food markets.

PUMPKIN FLOWERS - flowers from the pumpkin. Substitute with zucchini flowers if pumpkin unavailable.

S

SAGLÉ –Saglé means whole and thus whole vegetables are used in the preparation. For example, okra and baby eggplant. In contrast, vegetables are cubed or julienned for Upkaris.

SNAKE GOURD – similar to summer squash. It can reach up to 5' in length! Can be purchased on-line or in some local Asian markets.

T

TAMARIND PASTE - Prepared from the pulp of tamarind fruit pods by stripping the outer husk and removing the seeds. The tamarind tree (Tamarindus indica) is a tropical tree but prospers in plant hardiness zones 10 and 11. Tamarind paste has a sweet and sour, or tangy taste and often used for balancing spicy and salty flavors in a dish. Tamarind drink is popular in Mexico. There are two common substitutes for tamarind paste - one is Balsamic vinegar with sugar; and the other is pureed dates with fresh lime juice. It can be purchased on-line and in some local grocery markets.

TARO LEAVES – Arvi, Chama, Venti, Chembu are heart shaped leaves of the herbaceous perennial plant Colocasia esculenta, better known for its roots which are marketed as gourmet chips. It is not to be confused with Elephant Ears. Taro leaves are rich in several important micronutrients, such as vitamin C, vitamin A, potassium, folate, and calcium, as well as disease-fighting antioxidants. Can be substituted with Swiss chard, beet greens, or collard greens. For more information see: https://plants.ifas. ufl.edu/plant-directory/colocasia-esculenta/

TINDORI – see Ivy Gourd.

U

UPKARI – Dry preparation made with vegetables which have been cut, julienned, or chopped and added to a Kari leaf s easoning and steam cooked.

Index

Categorical:

Appetizers/Soups:

Entrees:

Vegetables/Sides: